# Living Stones

A Historical Survey of the Churches of the Dioceses of Derry and Raphoe

**First published in 2001**
**by Canon David W. T. Crooks**



This book has been supported financially by the
Rt. Rev. J. Mehaffey, Bishop of Derry and Raphoe.

*Cover illustration – Mosaic depicting St. Columba in the Sanctuary of St. Columb's Cathedral, Londonderry*
Front cover photograph by Fred McClelland.

ISBN 0-9541540-0-2

Typeset in Garamond 10 pt
Designed and Printed by
Styletype Printing Limited

# Living Stones

A Historical Survey of the Churches of the Dioceses of Derry and Raphoe

Canon David W. T. Crooks

# Contents

**Diocese of Raphoe:**

DIOCESE
OF
DERRY
MAP OF PARISHES
AND LOCATION OF CHURCHES
1 Aghadowey
2 Aghanloo
3 Ardstraw
4 Badoney Lower and 5 Greenan
6 Badoney Upper
7 Ballynascreen
8 Ballyscullion
9 Balteagh
10 Banagher
11 Baronscourt
12 Bovevagh
13 Camus-juxta-Bann
14 Camus-juxta-Mourne
15 Cappagh
16 Carrick
17 Castledawson
18 Castlerock
19 Christ Church
20 Clanabogan
21 Clooney and 22 Strathfoyle
23 Culmore
24 Cumber Lower
25 Cumber Upper
26 Derg
27 Desertmartin
28 Desertoghill
29 Donagheady
30 Drumachose
31 Drumclamph and 32 Clare
33 Drumragh
34 Dunboe
35 Dungiven
36 Dunnalong
37 Edenderry
38 Errigal
39 Faughanvale
40 Fermoyle
41 Glendermott and 42 New Buildings
43 Kilcronaghan
44 Killelagh
45 Killowen
46 Kilrea
47 Langfield Lower
48 Langfield Upper
49 Learmount
50 Leckpatrick
51 Lislimnaghan
52 Maghera
53 Mountfield
54 Muff
55 St Augustine's
56 St Peter's
57 Six Towns
58 Tamlaghtard
59 Tamlaghtfinlagan and 60 Myroe
61 Tamlaght O'Crilly Lower
62 Tamlaght O'Crilly Upper
63 Templemore
64 Termonamongan
65 Termoneeny
66 Urney and 67 Sion Mills
LOUGH
FOYLE

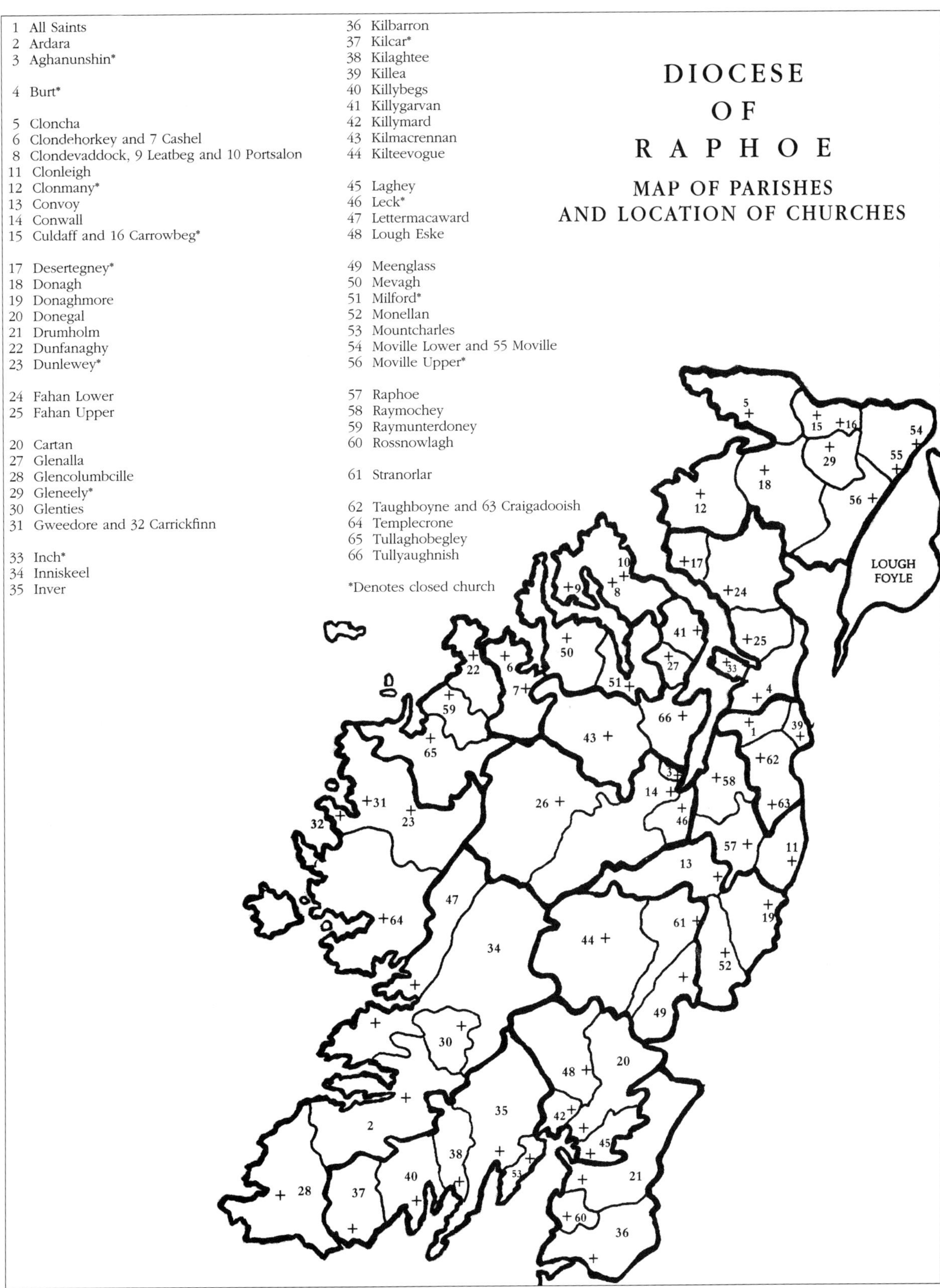
DIOCESE
OF
RAPHOE
MAP OF PARISHES
AND LOCATION OF CHURCHES
1 All Saints
2 Ardara
3 Aghanunshin*
4 Burt*
5 Cloncha
6 Clondehorkey and 7 Cashel
8 Clondevaddock, 9 Leatbeg and 10 Portsalon
11 Clonleigh
12 Clonmany*
13 Convoy
14 Conwall
15 Culdaff and 16 Carrowbeg*
17 Desertegney*
18 Donagh
19 Donaghmore
20 Donegal
21 Drumholm
22 Dunfanaghy
23 Dunlewey*
24 Fahan Lower
25 Fahan Upper
20 Cartan
27 Glenalla
28 Glencolumbcille
29 Gleneely*
30 Glenties
31 Gweedore and 32 Carrickfinn
33 Inch*
34 Inniskeel
35 Inver
36 Kilbarron
37 Kilcar*
38 Kilaghtee
39 Killea
40 Killybegs
41 Killygarvan
42 Killymard
43 Kilmacrennan
44 Kilteevogue
45 Laghey
46 Leck*
47 Lettermacaward
48 Lough Eske
49 Meenglass
50 Mevagh
51 Milford*
52 Monellan
53 Mountcharles
54 Moville Lower and 55 Moville
56 Moville Upper*
57 Raphoe
58 Raymochey
59 Raymunterdoney
60 Rossnowlagh
61 Stranorlar
62 Taughboyne and 63 Craigadooish
64 Templecrone
65 Tullaghobegley
66 Tullyaughnish
*Denotes closed church
LOUGH FOYLE

# Foreword

## Living Stones: A Historical Survey of the Churches of the Dioceses of Derry and Raphoe

CHURCH BUILDINGS are an essential part of our history and tradition in the Diocese of Derry and Raphoe. For many Church of Ireland parishioners they are intimately bound up with their sense of identity and their understanding of the Christian faith. The devoted care expended on them and the considerable costs involved are indicative of the regard in which they are held.

A collection of essays on the history, furnishings and stained glass of all the churches of the Dioceses together with their photographic representation is an invaluable resource. We are deeply indebted to the Reverend Canon David Crooks for the tremendous work he has put into it and his boundless enthusiasm for the project. It was an exceptional solo effort but for him it was also a labour of love.

I warmly commend "Living Stones" and I know that it will be greatly appreciated by the people of the Dioceses.

+James Derry and Raphoe

RIGHT REVEREND JAMES MEHAFFEY, MA, BD, PHD., D.LITT.

# Introduction

TO CELEBRATE the Centenary of the Disestablishment of the Church of Ireland in 1970, a little book, *In His Hand,* was produced by a Committee under the chairmanship of Canon J. H. Gebbie, Rector of Ardstraw. *In His Hand* was a survey of the parishes of the United Dioceses of Derry and Raphoe. Each group of parishes, with each church in the group, was described briefly by Rural Deanery. The illustrations were provided by the artist, Canon G. J. A. Carson.

In this survey, I have described each church in alphabetical order on its own, rather than by group and Rural Deanery. I did not consider it necessary to say much about the groupings of parishes, and when they were effected, as such things can and do change from time to time. My aim has been to say something of the history of each church from earliest times, describing briefly any older churches which pre-date the present one. I have kept to the mimimum, technical architectural terminology, as I would like the description of the churches to be simple and clear. More detail of a technical kind can be found in Professor Alistair Rowan's excellent survey of North West Ulster in the *Buildings of Ireland* series.

In this volume, the church exterior is described. Inside, I describe the windows, furnishings and monuments. I realised at the beginning that in describing the stained glass windows and monuments of each church, I would really need to be as inclusive as possible, at the risk of such descriptions becoming top-heavy, there being so many monuments. However, monuments and stained glass windows tell us a great deal about the people who have lived in the community and worshipped in the churches over many centuries, and so, our perspective at the beginning of the 21st century is broadened. The one exception in which I could not describe every monument, was St. Columb's Cathedral, Londonderry, which has more monuments than any other church in Ulster! They are catalogued in the Cathedral Office for anybody who wishes to find out more there. Also, I realise, that, whilst giving a certain amount of detail about names on monuments may not make for the easiest of reading, it will provide useful information for people doing family and genealogical research.

With 121 churches in use and twelve closed churches, it is inevitable that, despite taking the greatest care, something or somebody will have been left out. If anybody is offended, I can only apologise sincerely. I have not made the greatest possible effort to be totally consistent in describing churches. For example, I may have included a hymn board or a prayer desk in one that I have omitted in another. However, believe me when I say that to achieve total consistency over such a wide range would have been impossible, and things can easily be missed. Some may feel that I have included things that are trivial, others may feel that I have left out things that are important, but if you recognise your church from its description in this book, then I will be satisfied. There is, incidentally, a small number of chapels, such as the chapel of the See House in Derry, and a few hospital chapels which are shared with other denominations. I have not included these in this survey.

A great source of help whilst doing this survey, were the Parish Histories. Over the years, many clergy and some lay folk have put pen to paper to write about their church, and so, have produced a mine of information which, while of great interest to the local people, is also of great help to a wider range of people. I have included those which I came across in the Bibliography.

Quite a number of the churches have recently been renovated after very costly repairs. All of them have been well maintained over the years, and each church possesses items of furniture and other aids to worship that have been lovingly given by people to the Glory of God in memory of loved ones. As I went round, I could not help being struck by the memorial monuments to those from each parish who served and who fell in the two World Wars of the 20th century, and to those who lost their lives through terrorism over the years of the conflict in Northern Ireland. They are, as they are meant to be, reminders of the strengths and weaknesses of human nature, just as the churches are testimonies to the love of their people for God. Every church gave the impression of being a holy place where Almighty God is worshipped by a community of committed people. In these days of agnosticism and carelessness about holy things, that is a tremendous sign of hope in the new century.

# Acknowledgements

THE PRODUCTION OF a book of this nature is dependent upon the co-operation of a great number of people. My sincerest thanks are due first and foremost to the Bishop of Derry and Raphoe, the Right Reverend Dr. James Mehaffey, for all his encouragement, interest in and support of this project. Nobody knows better that he, the people and parishes of these United Dioceses, of which he has been Bishop for over twenty years. I greatly appreciate the kindness and co-operation of the Staff of the Diocesan Office in Londonderry, Mr Geoffrey Kelly and Miss Sandra Wallace, whom I pestered a great deal, but who were at all times most courteous and helpful. I sincerely appreciate the tremendous expertise, professionalism and friendliness and co-operation of the firm of Styletype Printing Limited, Glengormley, who have produced this book. In particular, I thank Mr. Derek Johnston and his staff for all their help and advice. I also appreciate the expert guidance of my good friend of many years, the Rev. Iain Knox, who read through the manuscripts, and corrected some historical inaccuracies, and made many valuable suggestions. I am also very grateful to Mr and Mrs George and Ruth Johnston, my brother-in-law and sister, for their painstaking reading of the proofs. Any errors that have survived are my own responsibility.

Above all, I wish to thank very sincerely my fellow clergy of Derry and Raphoe, and hundreds of their good parishioners who met me, gave me kind hospitality, opened up their churches to me, lent or gave me documents and papers, and gave me many little pieces of information which I would otherwise have missed. Many people went to great trouble to take me round, and to facilitate me, and without them, this book could not have been attempted, let alone completed. I wish that I could acknowledge them all by name.

The photographs of the foundation stone and of the nave and chancel on page 2, and of the nave of St. Columb's Cathedral, Londonderry, on page 3, and the photograph of the portrait of Governor Walker on page 8, and the photograph of the portrait of Bishop Hervey on page 35, are taken from the Cathedral Guide Book, 1987 edition, by kind permission of the Dean. The photograph of the portraits of Primate and Mrs Alexander on page 27 are taken from, "Primate Alexander, Archbishop of Armagh, A Memoir", edited by Eleanor Alexander, London, 1913. I thank Mr William West for the photograph of the new organ in Christ Church, Londonderry on page 37, the Rev. Derek Creighton for the photograph of the old church at Clare on page 50, and Mr D. Hutchinson for the photograph of the old church at Omagh on page 51. The drawing of Raphoe Cathedral before 1893 on page 97 came from the Cathedral Guide Book, and the drawing of Raphoe Castle on page 99 was kindly given by the Raphoe Development Office. I thank Mr David Biggar for the photograph of the old church at Milford on page 151. The picture of Bishop Inglis on page 131 came from Raphoe Diocesan Magazine, March 1963, Church of Ireland Monthly inset. I also thank Mr. Billy Kennedy for compiling the index.

# Abbreviations

Abbreviations are minimal, and most are on monuments in churches. A few could not be understood, and so are not included, though they appear in the text.

**B**

| | |
|---|---|
| Bt or Bart | Baronet |

**C**

| | |
|---|---|
| CBE | Commander of the Order of the British Empire |
| CVO | Commander of the Royal Victorian Order |

**D**

| | |
|---|---|
| DD | Doctor of Divinity |
| DFC | Distinguished Flying Cross |
| DL | Deputy Lieutenant |
| DSC | Distinguished Service Cross |
| DSO | Distinguished Service Order |

**F**

| | |
|---|---|
| FRCSI | Fellow of the Royal College of Surgeons of Ireland |
| FTCD | Fellow of Trinity College, Dublin |

**G**

| | |
|---|---|
| GCB | Grand Commander of the Bath |

**H**

| | |
|---|---|
| HML | His/Her Majesty's Lieutenant |

**J**

| | |
|---|---|
| JP | Justice of the Peace |

**K**

| | |
|---|---|
| KBE | Knight Commander of the Order of the British Empire |
| KCB | Knight Commander of the Bath |

**L**

| | |
|---|---|
| LL.D. | Doctor of Laws |

**M**

| | |
|---|---|
| MBE | Member of the Order of the British Empire |
| MC | Military Cross |
| MD | Doctor of Medicine |
| MRCS | Member of the Royal College of Surgeons |
| MRCVS | Member of the Royal College of Veterinary Surgeons |

**O**

| | |
|---|---|
| OBE | (Officer of the) Order of the British Empire |

**P**

| | |
|---|---|
| PC | Perpetual Curate |

**R**

| | |
|---|---|
| RAF | Royal Air Force |
| RAMC | Royal Army Medical Corps |
| RIC | Royal Irish Constabulary |
| RN | Royal Navy |
| RNR | Royal Naval Reserve |
| RNVR | Royal Naval Volunteer Reserve |
| RUC | Royal Ulster Constabulary |

**U**

| | |
|---|---|
| UDR | Ulster Defence Regiment |

# Bibliography and Sources


Alexander, Eleanor, ed., *Primate Alexander, Archbishop of Armagh,* Edward Arnold, London, 1923

Banister, Judith, ed., *English Silver Hall-Marks,* W. Foulsham & Co., Ltd., London, 1995

Colby, *Ordnance Survey of the County of Londonderry,* Vol I, Hodges and Smith, Dublin, 1837

*Convention of Drumceatt, 575, XIVth Centenary, 1975,* Booklet of essays by various authors, 1975

Crockford's *Clerical Directories*

de Breffny, Brian and Mott, George, *The Churches and Abbeys of Ireland,* Thames and Hudson, London, 1976

dePaor, Máire and Liam, *Early Christian Ireland,* Thames and Hudson, London 1958, 1st paperback ed., 1978

*Dictionary of National Biography,* 22 volumes, London 1908-1909

Fawcett, F.W., *Columba, Pilgrim for Christ,* 1963

Fawcett, F.W. and Crooks, D.W.T., *Clergy of Derry and Raphoe,* Updating of Canon Leslie's Succession Lists, Ulster Historical Foundation, 1999

Ferguson, W.S., Rowan, A.J., Tracey, J.J., *Historic Buildings, Groups of Buildings, Areas of Architectural Importance in and near the City of Derry,* Ulster Architectural Heritage Society, 1970.

Fothergill, Brian, *The Mitred Earl, An Eighteenth Century Eccentric,* Century Hutchinson, London, 1988

Galloway, Peter, *The Cathedrals of Ireland,* The Institute of Irish Studies, Queen's University, Belfast, 1992

Girvan, W.D., *Buildings of North Derry,* Ulster Architectural Heritage Society, 1975

*In His Hand,* A Survey of the Parishes of Derry and Raphoe, published to celebrate the Centenary of Disestablishment.

*Irish Church Directory*

James, Dermot, *John Hamilton of Donegal (1800-1884), This Recklessly Generous Landlord,* Woodfield Press, Dublin, 1998

Kingsmill Moore, H., *Ireland and her Church,* W. Tempest, Dundalgan Press, Dundalk, 1941

Leslie, J.B., *Succession Lists of the Clergy of Derry,* 1937

Leslie, J.B., *Succession Lists of the Clergy of Raphoe,* 1940

Lewis, Samuel, *The Topographical Dictionary of Ireland,* 2nd Edition, London, 1847

Lovell, E.W.O'M, *A Green Hill Far Away,* a Life of Mrs C. F. Alexander, 2nd Edition, Published by the Friends of St. Columb's Cathedral, Londonderry, 1994

MacArthur, C.W.P., *Francis Robertson, Founder of the Robertson Schools,* Article in *Donegal Annual,* 1999

McFarlan, Diana, *The Mothers' Union in Ireland Centenary History, 1887-1987,* published by the Mothers' Union, 1987
Nolan, William; Ronayne, Liam; Dunlevy, Mairéad; ed., *Donegal History and Society,* Geography Publications, Dublin, 1995.
Ó'Bróin, Art, *Beyond the Black Pig's Dyke, A Short History of Ulster,* Mercier Press, Dublin, 1995
Orr, J.C.D., *Servants of Christ, a Short History of the Bishops of Derry since the Reformation, 1605-1995,* Dublin 1997
Patton, Henry E., *History of the Church of Ireland for use in Schools,* A.P.C.K., Dublin 1907, 5th ed. 1943
Rankin, Peter, *Irish Building Ventures of the Earl Bishop of Derry,* U.A.H.S., 1972
*Raphoe Diocesan Magazine*
Rowan, Alistair, *North West Ulster* in *Buildings of Ireland Series,* Penguin Books, 1979
*St. Columba, Derry and Raphoe Celebrations 1963,* Ecclesiastical Press, Glasgow, 1963
Swan, Henry Percival, *'Twixt Foyle and Swilly,* Hodges and Figgis, Dublin, 1948
*The London Companies and the Irish Tenantry,* Reprint of article in *The Freeman's Journal,* Dublin 1888
Thomas, Colin and Fielding, Aubrey, eds., *Register of the Cathedral Church of St.Columb, 1703-1732,* Dublin, 1997
Walker, Simon, *Historic Ulster Churches,* The Institute of Irish Studies, Queen's University, Belfast, 2000
Wallace, Valerie, *A Life of the Hymn Writer Mrs Alexander, 1818-1895,* The Lilliput Press, Dublin, 1995
Witherow, Thomas, *Derry and Enniskillen in the year 1689,* William Mullan, Belfast, 1873

## PARISH HISTORIES

### *Diocese of Derry*


|  |  |
|---|---|
| Ardstraw | Gebbie, J.H., *Ardstraw, 1600-1900,* 1968 |
| Ardstraw, Baronscourt and Badoney Union | Ferguson, Eric, *Parish History,* published by the Select Vestry, 2001 |
| Ballynascreen | King, Robert, *The Old Church of Ballynascreen 1854,* Moyola Books and Braid Books, 1988 |
| Camus-juxta-Mourne | Lovell, E.W.O'M., *Christ Church, Strabane Centenary, 1879-1979,* 1979 |
| Castledawson | Parish Centenary booklet, 1975 |
| Castlerock | Chamberlain, A.P., *Short History of Castlerock Parish* |
| Christ Church, Londonderry | Hannon, B.D.A., *Milestones - Ministers - Memories 1830-1980,* 1980 |
| Clanabogan | Benson, T.W., *Clanabogan Parish Church* |
| Desertmartin | *Desertmartin Parish Recalled;* published by the Select Vestry, 1991 |
| Donagheady | Dundas, E.T., *The History of Donagheady Parish* |
| Drumachose | Knowles, G.W.A., *The Parish of Drumachose,* 1969 |
| Drumclamph | Creighton, F.D., *The River Flowing By - History of Drumclamph and Clare Parish,* 1996 |
| Drumragh | Taylor, R., *One Hundred Years 1871-1971 - Centenary of St. Columba's Parish Church, Omagh,* 1971. |
| Dunboe | Chamberlain, A.P., *History of Dunboe Parish* |
| Dungiven | Kelly, James, *The Parish of Dungiven - Memoirs of Bygone Days,* 1935 |
| Edenderry | Law, H.I., *The Parish of Edenderry,* Dungannon, 1952 |
| Errigal and Desertoghill | Kennedy, J.E., *Errigal and Desertoghill, 560-1970,* 1970 |
| Faughanvale | *Canice, Saint of the Roe Valley,* published by St. Canice's Jubilee Committee, Eglinton, 2000 |
| Killowen | Abbott, W.C., *A Short History of Killowen Parish,*<br>Maconachie, A., *The Church on the West Bank of the Bann, the Story of Killowen Parish,* 1997 |
| Kilrea | Parke, E.G., *Notes on the Parish Church of Kilrea, (St. Patrick's)* |

|  |  |
|---|---|
| Langfield | Creighton, F.D., *A Brief History of Langfield Parish,* 1992 |
| Leckpatrick and Dunnalong | Roulston, W.J., *The Parishes of Leckpatrick and Dunnalong, Their Place in History,* 2000 |
| St.Anne's, Six Towns | McKnight, T.R., *The Little Church in the Valley,* 1983 |
| St.Augustine's | Kelly, James, historical notes |
| Strathfoyle | Walker, Florence, *Strathfoyle Church of Ireland and Methodist Church; List of gifts donated during 1970-1999.* |
| Tamlaghtfinlagan | Gough, Harold, *Tamlaghtfinlagan, An Historic Church, 1995* |
| Templemore | Lawrenson, L.R., *Guide to Derry Cathedral,* 9th edition, 1965, |
| | St. Columb's Cathedral, Londonderry, *A Historical Guide,* 1987 |
| | St. Columb's Cathedral, Londonderry, *Millennium Historical Guide,* A.S. Ball Publishing, 2001, |
| | Ross, Linda and McDaid, Marta, *Memorial Tablets of St. Columb's Cathedral* |

## *Diocese of Raphoe*

|  |  |
|---|---|
| Clondevaddock/Portsalon | McDonald, G.A., *Gospel in Glass, A History of All Saints, Portsalon,* 1976 |
| Clonleigh | Edwards, W.M., *The Rectors of Clonleigh since the Reformation,* Lifford, 1884 |
| Conwall | Lawrenson, L.R., *A History of Conwall, Leck and Aughanunshin Parish,* 1943, |
| | Slater, Joan, ed. Barrett, P.F., *Conwall Parish, Letterkenny Church, 1636-1986,* 1986 |
| Donagh | Sharon Carey, Russell Turner and Pamela Crowe, Sunday School Children's Historical notes on Donagh Parish |
| Dunfanaghy | Pritchard, R.E., *Holy Trinity Church, Dunfanaghy Centenary, 1874-1974,* 1974 |
| Kilbarron | Dundas, E.T., *A Short History of Kilbarron Parish* |
| Kilmacrennan | Smeaton, W.B.A., *The Parish of Kilmacrennan Now and Then,* 1996 |
| Kilteevogue | Clark, J.R.L., *St. John's Church, Kilteevogue, 1879-1979,* 1979 |
| Laghey | Trimble, T.H., ed., *The Legend That is Laghey Community and Church,* 2000 |
| Lough Eske | Trimble, T.H., *Historical Meanderings Around Lough Eske,* 1996 |
| Mevagh | Lucas, Leslie, *Mevagh down the Years,* Record Press, Bray, 1962 |
| | Lucas, Leslie, *More about Mevagh,* Donegal Democrat, 1965 |
| | Lucas, Leslie and Smeaton, W.B.A., *The People, the Church, the Parish,* 1996 |
| Raphoe Cathedral | Good, G.F., *A Short Guide* |
| Taughboyne, Craigadooish All Saints and Killea | Crooks, D.W.T., *In the Footsteps of St. Baithin,* A History of Taughboyne Group, Donegal Democrat, 1992 |
| Tullyaughnish | Smeaton, W.B.A., *The Parish of Tullyaughnish,* 1997 |

# Arms of the Sees of Derry and Raphoe

IT SEEMS THAT the original arms of the Bishopric of Derry were a figure of St. Columba imparting a blessing. After the time of the Reformation, the arms used were *Azure,* three episcopal mitres, *Or* - a device, which, it is possible, alluded to the three Dioceses of Derry, Raphoe and Clogher being held together.

After the great Siege in 1689, Bishop William King obtained from Sir Richard Carney, Ulster King-at-Arms, a grant of the Arms which have since been borne by the See. These are the same as those of the See of London, with a harp added.

The Arms of the See of Derry are, *Gules;* two swords in saltire proper, the hilts in base *Or;* on a chief the arms of Ireland; *Azure;* a harp or stringed Argent.

The Arms of the See of Raphoe are, *Ermine;* a chief per pale *Azure* and *Or;* the first charged with a sun in splendour of the last; the second with a cross patée Gules.

The Arms illustrated are those of Archbishop King, Bishop of Derry from 1690 to 1702 when he was translated to Dublin, with the Arms of the Diocese of Derry. Note the position of the crozier.

# A Brief History of the Dioceses of Derry and Raphoe

THE IRISH CHURCH originated with the mission to Ireland of St. Patrick, who arrived in 432 A.D. Over the next three-and-a-half centuries, the Church spread and was consolidated. The great Celtic monasteries such as Clonmacnois, Clonard, Glendalough, Kells and Moville, were established, as well as many smaller ones all over the country. Manuscripts like the Book of Kells, the Book of Durrow and the Book of Armagh were produced. It was from Ireland, the Land of Saints and Scholars, that missionaries set out to re-convert Europe to Christianity after the fall of the Roman Empire.

The north-west produced its fair share of saints and scholars, the greatest of whom was Saint Columba of Gartan in County Donegal. His establishment at Iona became the base for the conversion of Scotland. A generation later, his monks were in the north of England, and not long afterwards, other Irish missionaries were on the Continent. Other great saints of the north-west were Eugene about 540, Baithin, Columba's younger cousin, Fiacra in the 7th century and Eunan at the end of the 7th century.

The Celtic Church was based in the monasteries. The Abbot was head of the community, and the bishops were subject to him. Eugene established a primitive "diocese" at Ardstraw in Co. Tyrone about 540, but this would not remotely resemble a modern diocese. It was, rather, a very early example of the emergence of a bishop from the monastery, taking charge of territory. This

*St. Patrick Window, All Saints Church, Londonderry.*

"diocese", as such, lasted until about 1150, when Maurice O'Coffey moved to Maghera. About 1280, the See was transferred to Derry. Meanwhile, though, for over a century before that, there were bishops based in the great Abbey at Derry. The first of these was Flahertach O'Brolchain about 1158.

The dioceses as we understand them today, were created after the Synod of Rathbreasil in 1111 and Kells in 1152. Derry Diocese was created out of most of County Derry, west Tyrone and Inishowen in Donegal. Raphoe Diocese consisted of almost all of the rest of County Donegal.

Raphoe had a Chapter in the 13th century, which consisted of a Dean and an Archdeacon, and the four Prebendaries of Clondehorkey, Drumholm, Inver and Killymard. The Chapter of Derry under James I consisted of a Dean, an Archdeacon and three Prebendaries, Aghadowey, Cumber and Moville. This was later altered to Dean, Archdeacon and eight canons. These prebendal titles lapsed at the Disestablishment of the Church of Ireland, but they are still nominally retained.

The Reformation, the Plantation of Ulster and the Great Siege of Derry were all landmarks in the history of the Dioceses of Derry and Raphoe. More detail about some of these and other historical events, and of prominent people, can be found in the insets throughout this book. Derry and Raphoe Dioceses were united in 1834 upon the death of William Bissett, the last Bishop of Raphoe as an independent diocese. The last bishop of Derry as an independent diocese was the Hon. Richard Ponsonby, who then became the first bishop of the united Sees. In the late 1960s, a few parishes in east Donegal were transferred from Derry Diocese to Raphoe Diocese, and in 1978, the parishes in Inishowen were added to Raphoe Diocese.

# The Diocese of Derry

## THE CATHEDRAL CHURCH OF ST. COLUMB, LONDONDERRY PARISH OF TEMPLEMORE

*St. Columb's Cathedral.*

DERRY, *"the oak grove"*, is for ever associated with St. Columba, who was born at Gartan in County Donegal in 521, and who went to Iona in 563. There, he and his twelve companions began the conversion of Scotland. He founded a monastery in Derry in 546, as well as the church which became known as the *Dubh Regles,* or Black Church. There were numerous monastic foundations over the centuries in the area, including an Augustinian friary which was on the site now occupied by St. Augustine's Church. In 1164, the Teampaill Mór, or Great Church was founded. This was destroyed in 1568, and was later replaced with the present cathedral.

In 1600, Queen Elizabeth I sent Sir Henry Dowcra to Ireland to garrison the north-west. Docwra chose Derry for his headquarters, and proceeded to rebuild the city. In 1613, King James I by Charter, formed the new County of Londonderry. The Honourable, the Irish Society was founded to promote religion and industry. The London Guilds came over and established themselves and their various trading companies around the county. The walls of Derry were built and completed by 1618. By 1628, the remains of the old cathedral and its neighbour, St. Augustines were incapable of accommodating the congregation.

St. Columb's Cathedral, within the walls of Derry, was begun in 1628. Its completion in 1633 is marked by an inscription from the foundation stone, which can be seen in the porch, and which reads,

*"If stones could speak then London's*
*prayse should sound,*
*who built this church and cittie*
*from the ground".*

***Foundation Stone with the small stone at the top from the original Columban Church of 1164.***

The foundation stone of the original cathedral, the Teampaill Mór, is built into, and can be seen in the foundation stone of the present building. The stone is signed, "Vaughan aed." Sir John Vaughan was the Governor of the city at the time of the building of the Cathedral.

The Cathedral was central to the events of the great Siege of Derry which lasted for 105 days in 1689. The besieged citizens held out against the forces of King James II, until they were relieved by the arrival of three ships carrying provisions. The Apprentice Boys' mound in the Cathedral graveyard commemorates these momentous events.

The Catheral grounds are entered through two magnificent gates on London Street. These were presented by the Irish Society in 1933 on the occasion of the tercentenary of the Cathedral. They have been restored recently to their former glory. Derry Cathedral was built in what was known as Planters' Gothic style. It consists of a tower and spire, a nave, aisles and chancel. There are turrets on the north and south aisle walls, and a chapter house in the south-west corner. There are battlements all along the exterior aisle and nave walls and chancel. The original spire was replaced by Bishop Hervey in 1776 with one which was too big for the tower. The tower and spire had to be demolished in 1802. They were replaced with the present tower and spire in 1822. The tower is four storeys high, and contains windows in the upper storeys. There are battlements and finials on the top.

Inside, in the nave, the Georgian galleries round the aisles were removed, the oak pews were installed, and the Bishop's throne and the western screens were provided during extensive renovations between 1855 and 1862. In 1887, during the incumbency of Dean Smyly, the chancel was built, and the organ was installed. There have been numerous renovations in recent times, including the complete restoration of the roof, the spire, and the turrets on the exterior nave walls.

***Nave and Chancel looking east***

The Cathedral is entered by the great west door in the base of the tower, or by a door in the north side of the tower. There is a spacious porch with an elegant staircase leading to the gallery. There is a mortar shell in the porch which was fired at the besieged defenders of Derry in 1689 containing terms of surrender which were not accepted.

In the tower, there is both a bell dated 1614, and the oldest peal of eight bells in Ireland which date from 1614 to 1671. They were recast in 1929, when five new bells were added.

*Mrs. C. F. Alexander Memorial Baptistery.*

Passing through the interior entrance oak doors which commemorate Sir William Miller, five times Mayor of Derry, one enters the vestibule. To the left is the baptistery, which commemorates the hymn writer, Mrs Cecil Frances Alexander (1818-1895), whose husband was Bishop of Derry and Raphoe, and later, Primate. The font is dated 1747. The stained glass window in the west wall commemorates Dorothea, wife of the Very Rev. Richard King, Dean of Derry, 1921-1946. The window in the north wall commemorates Mrs Alexander, and depicts some of her hymns. The tiling in the baptistery was presented by the Right Rev. Joseph Irvine Peacocke, Bishop of Derry and Raphoe from 1916 to 1945. There is a lectern with the naval crest of *Sea Eagle,* and a lovely tile and mosaic monument which has inscribed upon it, a prayer for the Cathedral by Mrs Alexander. There is a monument to the Rev. Robert Higinbotham, Curate of Templemore from 1850. He is also commemorated by the font in the north-west corner of the nave, the cover for which was presented by the branches of the Girls' Friendly Society of Derry and Raphoe in 1887.

To the right of the vestibule, there is a room which was formerly the choir robing room, and is now used as an office. It contains a stained glass window which commemorates the Siege of Derry. The window in the vestibule to the left of the office entrance shows Jesus as a child. It was the gift of Miss M. Magee. At the entrance to the Chapter House, there is a window which depicts the life of Jesus, His birth, baptism, Palm Sunday, the Last Supper, Gethsemane, and the Crucifixion. It is in memory of Dean King. The gallery over the vestibule contains an organ case which was presented by Primate Stone in 1747, when he was Bishop of Derry. There is a window with lattice glass on each side of the gallery west wall.

The two-storey nave has seven bays and a fine hammer-beam ceiling of 1823. The clerestory windows each have three lights and lattice panes. The corbels at the base of the roof support pillars, represent heads of former bishops and deans. The pew end carvings are all different - no two are alike. They were carved by a father and son named Alford.

The nave is flanked by north and south aisles. The chancel, with the choir stalls on each side, leads into the sanctuary. The marble floor in the chancel was laid during renovations in 1925. The

*Nave looking west.*

carpet depicts coats of arms of the Irish Society, of the See of Derry and of the Cathedral. On the east wall are six mosaics, three on each side of the high altar, with marble panels below. These mosaics depict the four Evangelists with St. Patrick and St. Columba. Behind the high altar, there is a fine reredos, the central section of which depicts the Lamb of God. It was presented in 1887 by clergy who had been ordained in the Cathedral. The solid silver altar cross was the gift of Sir Basil McFarland in 1966. There are four prayer desks in the sanctuary.

The pulpit is situated just outside the chancel. It is made of Caen stone and Cork marble, and dates from 1887. It commemorates William McCormick, M.P. for the City, 1860-1865. The organ chamber is to the left of the chancel, and the three manual console is to the right of the chancel opposite. The Bishop's throne is outside the chancel on the south side. It is a magnificent object, which is surmounted by a steep, tapering spire which reaches almost to the apex of the arch above. Dating from 1861, it contains a Chinese Chippendale chair, which is about one hundred years older. The brass lectern adjacent, was the gift of James Gilmour in 1868. There is a wooden eagle lectern adjacent to the pulpit, opposite, which was given in memory of John McKillip in 1935.

*Bishop's Throne.*

To the right of the chancel, raised four steps above the south aisle is a small side chapel for daily services. It is separated from the chancel by a finely carved wooden screen. The chapel contains an altar, and seats along the walls on each side. It was refurbished in memory of Mary Irvine who died in 1972.

*The Promise Chalice, 1613*

The Cathedral possesses some very fine and ancient Communion vessels. The oldest pieces are the "Promise Chalice", and a paten, dated 1613, so called, because the chalice was sent from London on the basis of a promise that the Cathedral would be built. A silver gilt insignium for the use of the Deans was presented by the Irish Society in 1963 to mark their 350th anniversary.

There is a yellow flag on each side of the east window in the sanctuary. The original flags were captured from the French army during the siege. On the sill of a window behind the chapel in the south aisle is a large plaque which states that in 1839, the ladies of Derry renewed the banners in the Cathedral which had been restored at the centenary of the Siege in 1789. The staves are original. The other flags in the chancel are the King's Colours of the 8th and 10th Royal Inniskilling Fusiliers. There is also an Ensign which was presented by the Royal Air Force, and there are Canadian and U.S. Ensigns, which were presented to commemorate their naval presence in Londonderry. There are also flags of other regiments, including the Londonderry Regiment.

St. Columb's Cathedral is lit by some excellent stained glass windows. The clerestory windows have already been mentioned. There are six windows of four lights in the south aisle. Starting from the west, the first of these depicts our Lord in the Garden of Gethsemane, and it commemorates Henry McCay, LL.D., who died in 1884. The second window shows the four Evangelists, and commemorates Thomas Gough, Dean of Derry from 1820 until his death in 1860. The third window illustrates the Raising of Lazarus, and commemorates Sir Robert Ferguson, Bt., M.P., who died in 1860. The fourth window commemorates Hugh Tighe, Dean of Derry 1860-1874, the year of his death. The four lights illustrate, the call of Samuel, Jesus blessing the children, Jesus calling the children, and the Bible as a source of instruction. The fifth window commemorates Canon Dougherty, Rector of Lower Fahan, who died in 1890, and it shows Jesus with the little children. The sixth window shows children crying in the Temple, "Hosanna to the Son of David". This window, along with the clerestory windows in the chancel, commemorate Dean Smyly, who was responsible for the erection of the chancel. He was Dean of Derry from 1883 to 1897. There are two stained glass windows at clerestory level on each side of the chancel, all of which depict angelic figures.

In the south wall of the chapel, the window depicts in its three lights, the text, "God also to the Gentiles hath granted repentance unto life". The window commemorates the Venerable Edward James Hamilton, Archdeacon of Derry, 1873-1896. A brass plaque on the window sill describes and commemorates the great Siege of Derry. The window in the area behind the chapel depicts in its three lights, St. Columba departing for Iona, St. Columba at the Council of Drumceatt in 575, and the death of St. Columba. It commemorates William Phillips, JP, who died in 1924. On the sill of this window, a plaque describes the restoration of the flags on the east wall of the sanctuary.

There are five windows in the north aisle wall, each with three lights. From the west, the first window shows the Empty Tomb. The second illustrates the text, "In that he liveth, he liveth unto God". The third window shows Jesus before Pilate, and it commemorates Brutus Babington, Bishop of Derry for a very short time before his death in 1611. The fourth window depicts Caleb, Joshua and Gideon, and it commemorates the Rev. George Walker, Governor of Derry during the Siege. It contains amongst others, Diocesan and City crests. The fifth window shows, on the left, the dedication of Stephen, in the middle, the text, "silver and gold have I none but such as I have give I thee", and on the right, St. Peter being released from prison. It commemorates Canon Richard Babington who died in 1893.

The east window has five lights and elaborate cusped tracery. The top section depicts the Ascension, and the bottom, our Lord's command to the Apostles to baptise the nations. The tracery contains various figures and floral designs. The

*Turret on North Wall.*

window commemorates William Higgin, Bishop of Derry and Raphoe, 1853-1867. In the east wall, to the right of the sanctuary, there is a window which depicts the ascended and exalted Christ. It commemorates Bishop Alexander who died in 1911.

Derry Cathedral contains over eighty monuments, memorials and brass plaques, more than any other church in Ulster. Quite a few are very fine, classical pieces of sculpture. No attempt is made to describe them all here. They are catalogued in a volume which can be seen at the Cathedral Office. They commemorate Derry's association with the London Guilds and the Irish Society, as well as former bishops, deans, dignitaries, benefactors and famous citizens. In the porch, there are memorials to, amongst others, Thomas Gough, son of Dean Gough who was killed at Sevastopol during the Crimean war in 1855, and to Bishop William Higgin who died in 1867. In the north aisle, there is the monument to John Elvin, Mayor of Derry, who died in 1676 aged 102 years. There is the memorial to those who fell in the Great War, and a monument commemorating the men of the 9th Londonderry Heavy Anti Aircraft Regiment who served in the second World War. Another classical monument commemorates Hugo Edwards who died in 1667. In the south aisle, there are monuments to William Knox, Bishop of Derry who died in 1831, and to William Hogg who died in 1770. In the chapel, there is a monument to Bishop Richard Ponsonby who died in 1853. On the east wall, behind the chapel, Bishop Charles John Tyndall, Bishop, 1958-1969, who died in 1971, is commemorated. There is a nice tiled memorial to Daniel Jones, Organist of the Cathedral, who died in 1911. Other former Organists are commemorated there. There are numerous brass plaques, for example, on the organ case which forms the north wall of the chancel. There are memorials to most of the recent Deans of Derry in the chancel and sanctuary.

The Chapter House in the south-west corner of the Cathedral was built in 1910 to a design by the architect, Sir Thomas Drew. It was the gift of Mrs F.

*Tomkins and Elvin Monument, St. Columb's Cathedral.*

*The Chapter House.*

Corscadden in memory of her husband. The Chapter House has some interesting furniture, including Bishop Hervey's writing desk and chair from Downhill House. It also houses relics and memorabilia from the Siege. These include the locks and keys of the original gates of the City walls which were built in 1618. There are swords, cannon balls and mortar shells, as well as the swords of the Rev. George Walker and of Adam Murray, one of the thirteen Apprentice Boys. Murray's watch and snuff box, and Walker's Bible are on display, as well as the Earl Bishop's pistols. There is a sea chest from 1625. Amongst the many interesting rare books, there is a "Breeches Bible" of 1583, so-called because of its rendering of Genesis 3:7, where the Authorised Version has, "aprons". There is a copy of Mrs Alexander's "Hymns for Little Children", and other papers. There are several fine portraits. Mrs Corscadden, painted in 1910 by F.M. Lutyens, hangs over the fireplace, above the roll of Bishops. There are portraits of past Bishops and Deans, including Primate Alexander, Bishop Higgin, and Dean Berkeley, the great 18th century Philosopher who became Bishop of Cloyne in 1732. There is a portrait of Mrs Alexander.

The Deanery on Bishop Street is a three storey Georgian-style house with basements. It was built in 1833. The Bishop's Palace opposite, was built about 1761, and was sold in 1945. The Cathedral Schools were built in London Street in 1891, and have recently been replaced by a new primary school which incorporates other schools in the area. Outhouses in the Cathedral grounds behind the Deanery were converted and renovated in 1981 in memory of Mrs Alexander for use as choir practice and music rooms.

## The Great Siege of Derry in 1689

THERE WERE ACTUALLY three sieges of Derry during the 17th century. The first took place during the Rebellion of 1641, and the second during the Civil War of the 1650s. The third was the Great Siege of Derry in 1689.

The Stuart King James II came to the English throne in 1685, and proceeded to advance Roman Catholics to positions of power and influence as quickly as possible. His manner of doing so caused great alarm, as it was thought that he was undermining the Protestantism which had been established in England. Thus, he was deposed and replaced in 1688 by William and Mary.

In Ireland, the people saw James as an opportunity to make a new attempt to gain independence. They lived in a land in which Protestants held all the main high offices of State from the Viceroy to the judges. James set about deposing Protestants from high office and replacing them with Roman Catholics wherever possible. Fears were raised that the Irish were soon going to attack Protestants in another rebellion, similar to that of 1641. Things came to a head when in December 1688, the regiment of the Roman Catholic Earl of Antrim arrived in Derry to replace the largely Protestant garrison there. They were barred by thirteen Apprentice Boys who closed the Ferry Quay Gate in the City walls against them. The other three gates were closed soon afterwards.

Lieutenant-Colonel Robert Lundy was appointed Governor of Derry in March 1689, having taken the oath of allegiance to William and Mary. One of King James' army captains, Richard Hamilton, clashed with Lundy's forces in a skirmish on the banks of the River Finn, 25 kilometres south of Derry. Lundy's forces were so easily defeated, that Lundy was suspected of having Jacobite sympathies. He later defected, and was replaced by the Rev. George Walker as Governor.

Meanwhile, James had landed at Kinsale in March 1689. He arrived in Derry on 18th April. His call for allegiance was met with shouts of "No Surrender". Resistance hardened, and the siege defences were strengthened. Whereas hitherto, there had been some coming and going in and out of the gates, the gates were from now on firmly and finally closed. The besieged Protestants held out under increasingly awful conditions for a total of 105 days. There is a list of the items available to them for food in the

Chapter House of St. Columb's Cathedral. The menu consisted of horses, dogs, cats, rats and mice and anything else that was around. One pound of horse flesh cost 1/8d, one quarter of a dog, 5/6d, a cat, 4/6d, a rat, 1/0d and a mouse, 2d. Provisions could not be brought into the city because of the boom of timbers and cables which had been placed across the River Foyle. The citizens were rallied and encouraged by the sermons of Governor Walker in the Cathedral.

*Rev. George Walker, D.D. (died 1690).*

The end finally came when three ships, laden with provisions, led by the *Mountjoy,* finally broke through the boom under heavy Jacobite gunfire. James' army beat a retreat for Dublin, burning and pillaging as they went on their way. The Jacobite cause in Ireland came to an end with defeat at the Boyne in 1690. In Scotland, Bonnie Prince Charlie tried to maintain the cause well into the 18th century, but it all ended at Culloden in 1745.

*Walker Monument on the walls of Derry.*

It has been calculated that there were about eighty fatalities from the army in battle. Many thousands more soldiers later died of wounds and famine. As many as 10,000 people altogether may have perished. What is known is that bodies were being removed from cellars for months afterwards. Today, the Great Siege of 1689 is commemorated by the Apprentice Boys' Order in two annual events, the Closing of the Gates and the burning of Lundy's effigy on 18th December, (according to the new calendar of 1752), and the Relief of Derry on 12th August.

## AGHADOWEY, St. GUAIRE

AGHADOWEY, *"the black field",* or possibly, *"the field of Duffy",* is a parish which lies along the River Bann in County Londonderry. The parish church is ten kilometres south of Coleraine. St. Guaire founded a church in the area in the 7th century. This was connected with his abbey at Agivey nearby.

At the time of the Plantation of Ulster at the beginning of the 17th century, the Ironmongers' Company and the Mercers' Company received land in the Aghadowey area. The Ironmongers maintained the old church at Agivey. This church was described in the Royal Visitation of 1622 as, "a Peculiar which is neither a parish or belongs to another parish". Agivey church was in due course served from Aghadowey, and its ruins can still be seen.

In 1622, Aghadowey became one of three prebends in Derry Cathedral, the others being Cumber and Moville. In that year, the church was reported to be in ruins, but there were plans to repair it from funds provided by recusants, that is, people who were fined for not attending church. The church was repaired about 1760, and rebuilt in

1797, with a tower and spire which were provided by the Earl Bishop of Derry, the Hon. Frederick Augustus Hervey. The spire was struck by lightning in 1826, and substantial damage was done to the church. The tower was rebuilt, but the spire was not replaced. There is an old bell which was presented by Queen Anne to her chaplain, the Rev. Robert Gage, who was Rector of Aghadowey at the end of the 17th century.

*Aghadowey Church.*

Aghadowey Church is entered through a louvered west tower. The organ was built in 1871 by a Mr. Fred Holt, and placed in the gallery in 1907. An old font beneath is decorated with family crests. The wooden eagle lectern on the right side of the nave, commemorates the Hon. Edward Hewitt, 1931, Edmond Stronge, 1911 and his wife Charlotte, 1900. Sir Norman Stronge, who was murdered by terrorists at his home, Tynan House in Co. Armagh in 1981, had lived at Lizard Manor in the parish of Aghadowey at one time. The lectern was presented in 1934. In the chancel, the prayer desk is situated to the right. The pulpit on the left has a plaque in the reading desk which notes that it was erected by Canon Smyly, Rector of Aghadowey, 1869-1880, and later Dean of Derry, in memory of his wife Eliza, and daughter, Joanna, 1875. The vestry room is to the left of the chancel. Both it and the chancel were built about 1850. There is a porch to the right of the chancel.

There are three windows in the south wall of the nave. The first of these has yellow and clear lattice glass. The second depicts an angel and flowers, and shows Jesus calling a little child. It is in memory of Alexander McCrae Maddison who died in 1868, and Alexander Maddison who died aged five years also in 1868. The third window illustrates the theme of faith, with the text, "fight the good fight of faith", and it commemorates Catherine Lopdell who died in 1921. The first and second of the three windows in the north wall also has both yellow and clear lattice glass. The third window depicts the Good Shepherd, and is in memory of the Rev. Robert Alexander, Rector and Prebend of Aghadowey, 1832-1869. He was the father of Bishop, later Primate Alexander, husband of the hymn-writer, Mrs Cecil Frances Alexander. The east window is a triple lancet with three circles above. On the left is the text, "I am the Vine, ye are the branches". In the middle there are the combined coats of arms of the Diocese of Derry and of Bishop William Alexander. On the right, there is the text, "glory to God in the highest, and on earth, peace, good will towards men". The whole window is elaborately coloured.

On the west wall, there are memorials to Mrs Orr who died in 1883, and to James Lancey, JP, who died in 1859. On the north wall, Hester, wife of George Barklie who died in 1868, and George, who died in 1882, are commemorated on a memorial. There is a classical monument to Alicia Orr who died in 1854. Henry Keown, Captain in the King's Hussars who died in 1872, and his wife Dorothea, daughter of the Rev. Robert Alexander, and their son Robert, are commemorated. There are memorials also to Robert Hezlet, JP, who died in 1872, and his wife, Elizabeth, who died the same year, and to Lt. Col. Richard Hezlet, Royal Artillery who died in 1925, and his wife Emily who died in 1944. On the east wall, there is a monument to Robert Knox who died in 1876. To the right of the sanctuary, on the east wall, Major Andrew Orr, Royal Artillery who died in 1870, and his wife Lucy, daughter of the Rev. W. Acworth, are commemorated. On the south wall, there are memorials to Francis Bennett who died in 1833, and his children, and to Lt. Col. Thomas Stirling who died in 1857. There are memorials to the Stirling family and to May Creery who died in 1933, and also, Captain John Stirling who died in 1841, and his son Henry who died in 1857, are commemorated, along with William and Annie Milliken and their children. On the floor of the sanctuary, there are two brass plaques. One commemorates Mary, wife of John Knox of Rushbrooke who died in 1844, and John Knox, who died in 1854, and other members of the family. The other commemorates Robert Knox of Rushbrooke who died in 1876.

## AGHANLOO

*Aghanloo Church.*

Aghanloo, "the little ford of Lugha", is a small parish to the north of Limavady in County Derry, on the Castlerock road. The patron saint was Lugha. At the time of the Plantation, it was granted to the Haberdashers' Company. The old church was reported to be ruinous in the 1622 survey. It was still in bad repair by 1693, but was rebuilt about 1700. The grassy mound nearby is the remains of this church.

The present church was consecrated on 2nd July 1826. It is a small, hall church, with a tower and chancel, typical of the design of John Bowden. The large basalt blocks of which the church is built, are striking.

Inside, there are rooms at either side of the chancel. There are three diamond-paned, clear windows, with cusped Y tracery in the south wall. The east window has three diamond lights with tracery. The font is in the north-west corner of the nave, the pulpit is on the left, and the prayer desk is on the right. The prayer desk and chair are in memory of Anna Lane Megeath and Dr James Lane. The brass eagle lectern commemorates Joseph Irwin who died in 1919.

On the north wall, there are monuments to Dr Benjamin Lane who died in 1922, and to the Rev. William Smyly, Rector of Aghanloo from 1827 until his death in 1835. His wife Charlotte who died in 1855 is also commemorated. There is a monument to Anna Lane Megeath and her brother Dr. James Lane, 1925, and to Samuel Martin who died in 1831 and to Arabella, his wife, and their daughter. A memorial commemorates Major John Percival Young of the Royal Pakistan Engineering Regiment who was killed in a mountaineering accident in Pakistan in 1948. The Youngs of Aghanloo House, a former Rectory, are a prominent land-owning family in the parish. On the south wall is a large memorial to the Rev. George Vaughan Sampson, Rector of Aghanloo 1794-1807, who translated the Epistle to the Hebrews. He was a well known historian and antiquarian. On the east wall, left of the sanctuary, there is a memorial to the Rev. George Craig, Rector 1853-1880, and to his wife who died in 1880.

## ARDSTRAW, NEWTOWNSTEWART, St. EUGENE

The parish of Ardstraw at Newtownstewart in County Tyrone has very ancient roots. In the north-west, the territory of *Cinel Eoghain* in Inishowen and Tyrone, was *Ard Sratha,* which means, *"the height of the bank"*, or *"strand"*. It gained prestige because of its associations with St. Eugene who founded the Diocese of Ardstraw about 540. It remained the seat of a monastic bishop until about 1150 when Bishop Maurice O'Coffey transferred the See to his native *Rath Luairg,* (Maghera).

The chief planter family in the 17th century were the Stewarts who gave their name to the village. In 1622, the church was in ruins. However, it was in good repair in 1693.

The present church was built in 1724, according to a date stone below the east window. It stands at the top of Newtownstewart's main street, overlooking the town. It is approached up steps through an 18th century gateway. There is a louvered tower which is surmounted by a spire and

*Ardstraw Church.*

finials. The spire was erected in 1806. There are lean-to porches on each side. There is a font in the porch, and a stair to the gallery.

The interior of the church was altered in 1858 and 1867, and the chancel was re-ordered in 1909. Over the west end of the nave is the gallery, which contains a two manual Conacher organ with pedals. This was presented by Thomas Noble Mitter, a friend of the American philanthropist and patron of Music, Andrew Carnegie of Pittsburgh, USA, in 1907. A space adjacent to the north wall of the nave is used for daily services. The pulpit is to the left of the chancel, and there is a prayer desk on each side. The sanctuary is raised above the chancel, and there are vestry rooms on each side.

There are three round-headed windows in the south wall, and two in the north wall. The first window in the south wall under the gallery, has clear, square glass. The second window has coloured glass, and commemorates Fanny Fulton, 1905. The third window has coloured glass, and the text, "the memory of the just is blessed". It is in memory of George Bates who died in 1890. In the north wall, the first window, which was erected in 1979, depicts the Good Shepherd, and is in memory of Mary Tipping who died in 1975. The second window commemorates Peter Scott Martin, aged fourteen years, who died in 1952. It depicts the text, "Blessed are the pure in heart". On the sill, a plaque commemorates his parents, Commander Ralph Martin, DSC, RN, and Doreen Martin. The east window has three lights and tracery. It depicts the Ascension, and commemorates the Rev. James McIvor, Rector of Ardstraw, 1847-1886. Dr. McIvor was a Fellow of Trinity College, Dublin, and Professor of Moral Philosophy.

Ardstraw church has some fine classical monuments. In the porch, two plaques record the covering of the stairway in memory of Thomas and Mary Ann Clarke, and the installation of the sound system in memory of Tommy and Jennie Doonan, 1998. There is also a plaque with a list of benefactors. The memorials to those who fell in the two World Wars are on the west wall on either side of the entrance. On the north wall, there is a memorial to John Fowler who died in 1907, as well as a classical monument to Major Jones Crawford who died in 1839, and a memorial to John McKeown who died in 1917.

Several monuments in the church commemorate distinguished academic clergy who were Rectors of Ardstraw in the eighteenth and nineteenth centuries. They held professorships or other senior positions in the University of Dublin along with the incumbency of Ardstraw. This was possible, as the patronage of the parish was held by Trinity College, Dublin until the Disestablishment of the Church of Ireland in 1870. The Rev. Thomas Wilson, DD, Rector of Ardstraw, 1786-1799, is commemorated on the north wall. Dr. Wilson was Professor of Natural Philosophy and Archbishop King's Professor of Divinity in the University of Dublin. There is also a monument to the Rt. Rev. George Hall, DD, Provost of Trinity College, Dublin, Rector of Ardstraw, 1800-1806. He was elected Bishop of Dromore, and was consecrated on 17th November 1811. He died six days later on 23rd November 1811. He was Professor of Greek, Archbishop King's Lecturer in Divinity, Professor of Modern History, and Professor of Mathematics at various stages of his career in Trinity College, Dublin.

On the south wall, beside the prayer desk, a monument commemorates Sir I.A. Montgomerie, Kt., son of Viscount Montgomerie, and Katharina,

Lady Montgomerie, who died in 1634. There is a monument to the Rev. Richard Nash, DD, FTCD, Rector of Ardstraw, 1819 until his death in 1847, as well as a monument to the Rev. John Hall, DD, Rector of Raymochy (Manorcunningham, Co. Donegal), and Ardstraw, 1713-1735. He was Vice-Provost and Librarian of Trinity College. On the same wall, Lt. Frederick Fitzgerald who died in 1817 is commemorated, as is his father, the Rev. Gerald Fitzgerald, DD, Rector 1806-1819. He too, was a Vice Provost of Trinity College. Amongst his writings was a Hebrew Grammar.

## BADONEY UPPER, PLUMBRIDGE, St. PATRICK
## BADONEY LOWER, GORTIN, St. PATRICK
## GREENAN

Badoney, *Both Domnaich, "the tent of the Lord"*, or *"of the church"*, is a parish in the Sperrin Mountains in County Tyrone, which includes the villages of Plumbridge and Gortin. St. Patrick is supposed to have founded seven churches in the vicinity, of which Badoney was one. The Patron Saint was Aithgen. Two ancient crosses and two stones are preserved in Upper Badoney church. The parish was divided into Badoney Upper and Lower in 1730.

Badoney Upper Church, near Plumbridge, eleven kilometres from Newtownstewart, was built in 1784 on an ancient site. It is a small, three bay hall with a tower, and a sanctuary which was added in 1859. The vestry room is on the north side.

*Badoney Upper (Plumbridge).*

The tiles in the porch are in memory of Robert Watson who died in 1958, and there is a window in the west wall with a mixture of plain and coloured glass. The three windows on each side have diamond-paned glass, and the east window of three lights and tracery, has coloured glass, and along the base, the inscription, "worship the Lord in the beauty of holiness". There is a window with diamond coloured glass in the south sanctuary wall.

The font is in memory of Lillie Stack who died aged ten years in 1867. The prayer desk and lectern are to the left of the sanctuary, and the pulpit is to the right.

On the north wall, a brass plaque commemorates James McCullagh, Fellow of Trinity College, Dublin, who died in 1847. Adjacent to the church is the Staples Room, which was renovated in 1999.

*Badoney Lower (Gortin).*

Upon the division of Badoney parish, a church was built at Gortin in County Tyrone in 1730. The present church at Gortin, Badoney Lower, thirteen kilometres from Newtownstewart, was built in 1856. It is a spacious seven bay hall with a large porch and sanctuary. There is a bellcote over the west end of the nave. In the porch, a plaque records the installation of the electric lighting in memory of those who fell in the second World War. It was switched on on Easter Day 1951. There is also an old font in the porch.

The baptistery is at the west end of the nave. There is a prayer desk on each side of the chancel. The pulpit is below, to the right, and the lectern is on the left. The altar is in memory of Alexander and

Mary Campbell, and was dedicated in 1969. There are vestry rooms on both sides of the chancel.

There is a window in the porch, and two windows in the west wall of the nave. Seven round-headed windows of two lights each light both sides of the nave. On the north side, the sixth window is of unusually delicate glass. On the left, the text, "glory to God in the highest", is illustrated, and on the right, "I am the Resurrection and the Life". It is in memory of Catherine Cole-Hamilton, 1869. On the south side, the fourth window illustrates on the left, the text, "this is my beloved Son", and on the right, "this do in remembrance of me". It commemorates the Rev. William Montgomery Beresford, Rector of Badoney Lower from 1866 until his death in 1868. He was a grandson of Marcus, 1st Earl of Tyrone. The east window, of three lights, has coloured diamond panes. All the other windows have clear, diamond-paned glass.

There are several monuments in the church, most of which commemorate the Cole-Hamilton family. The memorial to those who served and fell in the Great War is on the west wall. On the north wall, monuments commemorate Charles Cole-Hamilton, RN who died in 1911, and Arthur Henry Cole-Hamilton, Rector of Castle Ashby, Northamptonshire, who died in 1889. On the south wall, Jane Laughlin who died in 1932, is commemorated.

On the north wall of the sanctuary, there is a memorial to Letitia, daughter of Major A.W. Cole-Hamilton, and sister of the Rev. Arthur Cole-Hamilton above, of Beltrim, Co. Tyrone, who died in 1888. There are also memorials to Emily Catherine, wife of Arthur Cole-Hamilton of Beltrim who died in 1869, to Captain W. Cole-Hamilton, Royal Inniskilling Fusiliers who died in 1903, and to William Claud Cole-Hamilton who died in 1882. On the south wall of the sanctuary, Arthur Richard Cole-Hamilton who was killed at Gallipoli in 1915, is commemorated.

*Badoney Lower (Greenan).*

Greenan Church, deep in the Sperrins, thirteen kilometres from Gortin on the Draperstown road, is a chapel of ease for Lower Badoney. It was built in 1852. It is a small, three bay rectangular building. The porch was extended in 2001, and contains a vestry room There are three clear lattice windows in each side wall, and three clear lattice windows in the sanctuary, the middle one of which is higher than the other two. The font is outside the chancel on the left. The pulpit is on the right, and the prayer desk is on the left.

## BALLYNASCREEN, DRAPERSTOWN, St. COLUMBA
## SIX TOWNS, St. ANNE

Ballynascreen, *"the town of the shrine"*, is the ancient name of the Plantation town of Draperstown in south County Derry. In ancient times, there was a large and elaborate shrine nearby, of which the Patron Saint was Columbcille. At the time of the Plantation of Ulster in 1609, the area was developed by the Drapers' Company, hence the name change to Draperstown.

A church was built on the village green in Draperstown in 1760 with financial support from the Earl of Bristol, the future Bishop. A tower and spire were added in 1792. The present church was built in 1887 by Thomas Drew, and consecrated on All Saints' Day, 1st November 1888. The tower and the octagonal spire of the old church were retained. This church is one of the most beautiful in the Diocese of Derry, as much because of its situation as because of its design.

Ballynascreen church is entered through an open porch near to the south-west corner. Inside, the base of the tower forms an alcove to the west of the nave, which contains the baptistery. The font

*Ballynascreen Church.*

is in memory of the Rev. Robert Chichester, Rector of the parish from 1874 until his death in 1878. Also in the baptistery are some stones from the old church, as well as the old weather vane which was replaced at the time of the rebuilding of the tower in 1992. The two transepts are each bisected by transverse arcades. The vestry room is north of the sanctuary, and there are rooms to the left of the north transept. The stone reredos behind the altar

*Chancel.*

depicts the Lamb of God, and the north wall of the sanctuary contains an aumbry.

The pulpit is on the north-east corner of the nave. The prayer desk on the right side of the chancel commemorates the Venerable Charles Galwey, Archdeacon of Derry, 1860-1873. A Corkman, Archdeacon Galwey studied Medicine, but gave it up because he was so revolted by what he saw in the dissecting room! He then studied Mechanics, but was persuaded by his mother to study for Ordination, a more gentlemanly career! A double lectern is placed at the crossing between the nave and the chancel. The organ in the north transept has two manuals and pedals, and commemorates Robert Torrens O'Neill.

Ballynascreen Church has some very fine windows. The window in the baptistery has two

*Window in south wall.*

lights. The left side has the text, "love thou me", and the right side, "feed my sheep". It commemorates the Rev. Samuel Montgomery, Rector from 1843 until his death in 1874. He was a cousin of Primate Alexander. There are three windows in the south nave wall, the first two of which have pink and opaque glass. The first window also has a family crest. The third window, which commemorates S. R. Morewood who died in 1887, depicts the cleansing of a leper. The first two of the four windows in the north wall of the nave have square panes of pink and opaque glass. The third window depicts Jesus walking on the water, and it commemorates Arthur, son of the Rev. William Baron O'Neill. He died at sea in 1870. The fourth window illustrates the Song of Simeon, St.Luke 2:29-32, and is in memory of the Ven. John Torrens, Archdeacon of Dublin who died in 1857. The windows in both the west and east walls of the north transept each have opaque and pink square patterned glass. The same is true of the window in the south wall of the south transept. There are three windows in the east wall of the south transept. These together illustrate the Gospel account of the Resurrection of our Lord. The left window commemorates the Rev. William Chichester, 1st Baron O'Neill, (1813-1883), and his wife Henrietta who died in 1887. He was ordained in 1837. He came into possession of the O'Neill estates in Co. Antrim on the death of John, third Viscount O'Neill. In 1868, the Peerage was restored and awarded to Chichester under the title of Baron O'Neill of Shane's Castle. The Reverend Baron was a gifted violinist, an organist and a composer of considerable ability, and he used to give recitals in the two Dublin Cathedrals.

The east window is a triple lancet, the central section rising above the other two. On the left is the text, "behold the Lamb of God who taketh away the sins of the world". The crucified Christ is in the centre, and there are Passion scenes on the right. The window commemorates Robert Torrens of Derrynoyd, Justice of the Common Pleas, Dublin, who died in 1856.

On the north wall, there is a memorial to William Galwey Dysart, JP, who died in 1896. On the east wall of the north transept, a monument commemorates Robert Torrens O'Neill who died in 1910. On the east wall of the south transept, John Rowley Miller who died in 1862, is commemorated. There are memorials on the west wall of the south transept to Anne, wife of Judge Torrens who died in 1832, and to the Rev. Thomas Torrens, DD, FTCD, Rector of Ballynascreen from 1785 until his death in 1797. The tablet was erected by three nephews, Archdeacon John Torrens, Hon. Robert Torrens and Sir Henry Torrens, Knight of the Bath, and Adjutant-General of the British Army.

St. Anne's Church, Six Towns is close to the Plumbridge road, seven kilometres south-west of Draperstown. It was built as a chapel of ease in the parish of Ballynascreen, and it was a trustee church. The foundation stone was laid in 1840. Judge Torrens, the Drapers' Company and others contributed towards the cost. The church was consecrated by Bishop Ponsonby on 10th August 1843. The first curate was the Rev. Thomas de Vere Coneys, Professor of Irish at Trinity College, Dublin.

*Sixtowns Church.*

St. Anne's Church is a three bay hall with a three storey tower. Inside, there are raised pews on the north side of the west end of the nave, and the vestry cubicle is opposite. The font is in the centre of the nave in the aisle. The prayer desk is to the left of the sanctuary, and the pulpit is to the right. The church is lit by three windows of square-paned clear glass on each side of the nave. The east window is a triple lancet with clear glass. The church has no electricity, and is lit by oil lamps.

The only monument in the church, which is of classical design, was erected by John Stevenson of Fort William in memory of his wife Rebecca, daughter of Alexander Clarke of Maghera who died in 1842. John Stevenson gave the land for the building of St. Anne's Church in 1839.

St. Anne's Church has the distinction of having no parishioners. It is used twice a year for a Harvest Thanksgiving service and for a Christmas Carol service.

# Some Luminaries of Derry and Raphoe

OVER THE CENTURIES, the Dioceses of Derry and Raphoe have produced many great thinkers, writers, poets and churchmen. Apart from the Earl Bishop and the Alexanders, there were, George Berkeley, John Bramhall, William Archer Butler, Nicholas Forster, Ezekiel Hopkins, William King, Andrew Knox and John Leslie.

**George Berkeley (1684-1753),** was Dean of Derry from 1724 to 1732, and Bishop of Cloyne from 1732. He travelled widely on the Continent, and attempted to set up a missionary college in Bermuda in 1725. He was a writer and philosopher of the first rank, and was known and respected in the highest literary circles.

**John Bramhall (1594-1663),** was perhaps the greatest holder of the See of Derry. Appointed Bishop of Derry in 1634, his first act was the consecration of the new Cathedral of St. Columb. He provided churches and rectories for the newly re-organised parishes which were being rapidly populated by the incoming planters. He gained the sum of £40,000 for diocesan funds. Bramhall was forced to flee Ireland during the 1641 Rebellion, and lived in the Netherlands for the next 29 years. During this time, he wrote many fine books in defence of Anglican polity, including, *"Just Vindication of the English Church"*. After the Restoration, he became Archbishop of Armagh. During his primacy, he was responsible for re-organisation of the Church of Ireland.

**William Archer Butler (1812-1848),** was one of the most distinguished thinkers, writers, preachers and philosophers of his time. He was for a time, Professor of Moral Philosophy in the University of Dublin. He was Rector of Raymochy from 1842 to 1848. His all too short life ended upon his death of famine fever in 1848.

**Nicholas Forster (1663-1743),** was Bishop of Raphoe from 1716 to 1743. His memorial is in the many buildings which were erected during his episcopate. Amongst the schools which he endowed, was the Royal School at Raphoe, which had been founded in the reign of King James I in 1618. He built what is now the school boarding house in 1737. He provided the Volt House in Raphoe as a residence for clergy widows, as well as the tower of the Cathedral and the Diocesan Library. He left money for the Bluecoat Hospital and for Stevens Hospital. His remains are buried under the altar in Raphoe Cathedral.

*Rev. Archer Butler Memorial, Raphoe Cathedral.*

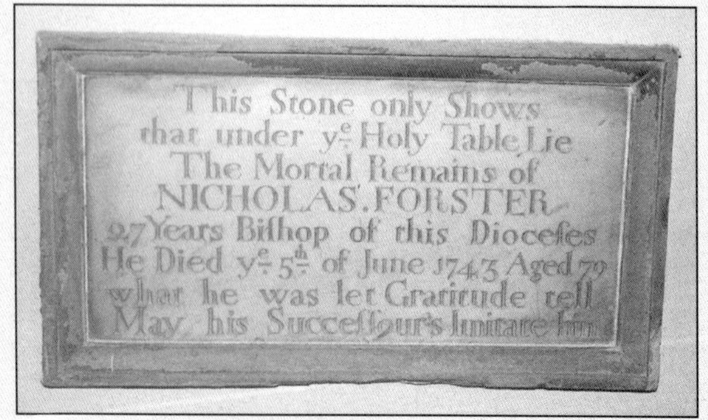


*Bishop Nicholas Forster Memorial, Raphoe Cathedral.*

**Ezekiel Hopkins (1634-1690),** was Bishop of Raphoe from 1671 to 1681, and then Bishop of Derry from 1681 until his death in 1690. He was inside the walls of Derry during the shutting of the gates at the beginning of the Great Siege in 1689. He was a man of learning, a poet and the author of a number of erudite writings and sermons.

**William King (1650-1729),** was born a Scottish Presbyterian, whose family came to Ireland early in the 17th century. He was a staunch Williamite, and following the Battle of the Boyne, he became Dean of St. Patrick's Cathedral, Dublin. Later that year, he was promoted to the Bishopric of Derry. During his episcopate, he restored the fortunes of his Diocese, and built and repaired many churches. He also provided the Diocesan Library, which today, possesses many fine old volumes. He became Archbishop of Dublin in 1702.

**Andrew Knox (1559-1633),** was translated from the Diocese of the Isles to Raphoe in 1611. He was one of the most distinguished bishops of Raphoe, and his descendants over the centuries were a noted family in the north-west.

**John Leslie (1571-1671),** was born in Aberdeen. He spent much of his youth on the Continent where he was ordained. He was consecrated Bishop of the Isles in 1628, and was translated to Raphoe in 1633. He built Raphoe Castle as much for defence as for living in, and he held out successfully during the 1641 Rebellion. He was a staunch defender of the Prayer Book during the Commonwealth period. As such, he had to defend Anglican principles against Cromwell. Again, he was able to hold out against Cromwellian attack in his fortress at Raphoe! Leslie was translated to the Bishopric of Clogher at the age of ninety years in 1661. He held the office until his death five weeks before his 100th birthday in 1671. He was one of the most colourful characters in the history of Raphoe Diocese.

There were, of course, many other great bishops of Derry and Raphoe. For further information, Jonathan Orr's *"Servants of Christ"*, gives an excellent acount of the Bishops of Derry from 1605.

## BALLYSCULLION, BELLAGHY, St. TOIT or St. TIDA

BALLYSCULLION PARISH is situated to the north of Lough Neagh, around the village of Bellaghy, in east Co. Londonderry. The name means, *"the town of Scullion"*, or, *"O'Scullion"*. The ancient name was Inistoide, or Toit's island. The original church was situated on an island in Lough Beg, north of Lough Neagh. This church was ruinous in 1622. It was replaced in 1625 with a new one by the Vintners' Company which had come over at the Plantation. The Earl Bishop built a tower and spire adjacent to the church in 1788, which he intended to be seen, and to look impressive from nearby Ballyscullion House. The old church was rebuilt in the village of Bellaghy in 1794. The Downing family, at one time resident in the parish, gave their name to Downing Street in London. Their mausoleum in the churchyard dates from 1776. The Earl Bishop also built a fine edifice in Bellaghy in 1787. This was never completed, and its grand portico is now the facade of St. George's Church, High Street, Belfast.

*Ballyscullion Church.*

Ballyscullion Church is an impressive building. It consists of a three bay nave with a three-storey tower and a tall, slender spire. There are two doors in the tower, and a window with square clear glass and Y tracery. Inside the nave is a large gallery at the west end. Underneath to the left is the baptistery. The church is lit by three round-headed windows on both sides of the nave. They have square-paned coloured glass on the bottom, and coloured lattice and Y tracery on the top. The third window in the south wall commemorates Andrew Spotswood who died in 1877, and the middle window in the north wall commemorates Joseph Johnston who died in 1918. The east window has coloured panes, with Jesus in the centre, and farmers gathering sheaves. It has three lights, and it commemorates Richard and Edyth Lee, 1990.

The sanctuary is separated from the nave by a broad archway, over which is the inscription, "Glory be to Thee, O Lord Most High". The vestry room is to the left. The panelling in the sanctuary was presented by Richard Lee in memory of his parents and sisters, 1966. The Holy Table is in memory of David Kelly and his wife Clara. The prayer desk on the right of the sanctuary is in memory of Jeannie Lee, 1966, and the chair adjacent to it commemorates Private David McQuillan, 5th Co. Londonderry Battalion, Ulster Defence Regiment, who was killed in 1977. There is a memorial to him on the north wall in the baptistery. The credence table on the right is in memory of Francis and Mary Milligan, and the credence table on the left is in memory of Sarah Dawson, 1966. The chair on the left side of the sanctuary is in memory of the Rt. Hon. Henry George Hill Mulholland, PC, HML, 1st Baronet of Ballyscullion Park who died in 1971, and the Communion rails, 1956, commemorate James Burnside, who died aged three months in 1953.

Outside the sanctuary, the pulpit on the right is in memory of Annie Wilson, 1979, and the lectern commemorates John Hill, JP who died in 1887, and his wife Mary who died in 1880. The prayer desk on the left is in memory of Jane Leonard. The front pew end on the right commemorates Andrew McQuillan, 1993.

There is a brass plaque in the baptistery in memory of the Rev. John Boyle, Rector of Ballyscullion, 1930-1949. On the north wall, memorials commemorate the Rev. Edward French, Rector 1849 until his death in 1863, and his wife Mary who died in 1881, and Mabella Hill Gordon, daughter of John Hill of Bellaghy Castle, who died in 1854. On the north wall of the sanctuary, there is a Latin inscription which was erected in 1712 by Simon and Anna Rowe, to commemorate their children. It has the family crest above. On the east wall of the sanctuary, there is a Latin memorial to Simon Rowe, 1731, and others.

When the Earl Bishop died in 1803, his cousin, Harry Bruce inherited the Bishop's Ulster estates of Downhill and Ballyscullion. He became a baronet in 1804 with the name Sir Henry Hervey Aston Bruce of Downhill. His son, Admiral Sir Henry Bruce, KCB of Ballyscullion, who died in 1863, is commemorated on a monument on the east wall of the sanctuary. On the south wall of the sanctuary, there is a memorial to the Rev. Thomas Spotswood, Rector of Ballyscullion, 1795-1833, and to Martha his wife who died in 1833. The Rev. William Kelly, Rector 1909-1926 is also commemorated. On the south wall of the nave, there is a monument commemorating George Hill, third son of John Hill of Bellaghy Castle who died in 1853. There is also a memorial to Thomas Spotswood Ashe, Manor House, Bellaghy who died in 1907, his wife Eliza who died in 1923, and their son, Captain Andrew Spotswood Ashe of the Cheshire Regiment who died at sea in 1904.

## BALTEAGH, St. CANICE

BALTEAGH PARISH is situated just to the south of Limavady. The name means, *"the town, or hut of the two ravens"*. The Patron Saint was Canice. In the 1622 survey, it was reported that the church was in ruins. These ruins can still be seen opposite the present church. By 1768, the church was in good repair.

The church which exists today was built in 1815. It is a typical hall and tower church, which is entered through a porch in the base of the tower. The main door is in memory of Hadessa Hylands who died in 1983. Inside, the baptistery is in the north-west corner of the nave. The font has a brass bowl and a beautiful covering which has a gold leaf bird on top. The baptistery and the font bowl and lid commemorate Jill, infant daughter of Sir Patrick and Elizabeth Macrory, who died in 1947 aged two months. The pulpit on the right of the chancel has

*Balteagh Church.*

three decorated panels, the centre one of which illustrates the Good Shepherd. It dates from 1896, when renovations to the church were made during the incumbency of the Rev. (later Dean) R.G.S.King. These renovations included the tiling of the church and the fine oak panelling in the sanctuary. The Holy Table and reredos are finely carved. The credence table is in memory of Annie and Henry Rodgers, and there are fine wrought iron communion rails with gilded patterns. The wooden eagle lectern reflects the pulpit. The prayer desk on the right, adjacent to the pulpit, is in memory of Dean King, Rector of Balteagh, 1896-1899. The organ, which is set in a chamber to the left of the chancel, was installed in 1913. It was built by the firm of Evans and Barr of Belfast to a design of the Rev. Wilfred Dixon, Rector 1910-1942. It has one manual and pedals. The lighting in the church was installed to commemorate Sir M. Macrory in 1951. The vestry room is behind the sanctuary to the right.

There are four windows in the south wall, which have diamond-paned, clear glass and Y tracery. The fourth window has a coloured inset. The two windows in the north wall were installed in 1896, and have square-paned clear glass. There is a little window in the organ chamber with coloured glass.

*The Pulpit.*

A monument on the west wall commemorates the Rev. William Horatio Stack, Rector of Balteagh from 1852 until his death in 1863. On the north wall, the Rev. Samuel J. Heaslett, Rector, 1946-1977, is commemorated, and on the south chancel wall, there is a memorial to John Buchanan, organist of Balteagh who died in 1924.

## BANAGHER, FEENY, St. MORESIUS

Banagher Parish is situated around the village of Feeny near Dungiven in County Londonderry. The name Banagher means, *"the place of the pointed hills, or peaks"*. The Patron Saint was Moresius, or Muiredach O'Heney. Interesting remains of an old church dating from about the 10th century survive. These include Muiredach's tomb. At the time of the Plantation, the Skinners' Company was established in the area. In 1622, Banagher Church was reported to be in ruins.

*Banagher Church.*

The present church was built by the Earl Bishop between 1780 and 1784. It was renovated in 1869 when the plaster ceiling was replaced with the present wooden one. Banagher Church is situated amid trees on top of a small hill near the village of Feeny. It is entered through a porch at the base of the tower. The tower is surmounted by a spire. Inside the porch are stairs to the gallery. There are three windows in the north nave wall. The first of these has clear diamond glass. The middle window depicts Jesus with the text, "who crowned thee in loving kindness", and is in memory of Violet Smyth of Altmover who died in 1962. The third window shows Jesus calling the children, and it commemorates the Rev., later Canon James Bedell Scott, Curate of Banagher, 1851 to 1868, then Rector until he died in 1897. He succeeded his father, the Rev. George Scott, Rector from 1850 to 1868, who then became Curate to his son! On the south side there are three windows, the first two being of clear diamond glass. The third window illustrates the text, "Blessed are the pure in heart" from the Beatitudes, St. Matthew 5:8. It is in memory of Alithea Marie Forwood who died in 1903. The east window has three lights and tracery. It depicts the Last Supper, and is in memory of the Stevenson Family of Knockan, Feeny, 1889.

The font is in the centre of the aisle. The pulpit on the left commemorates the Rev. Alexander Ross, Rector of Banagher from 1810 to 1850. The prayer desk on the right was given in 1884 by Canon J. B. Scott in memory of his father who died in 1879. The altar is in memory of the Rev. Charles Rutledge, Curate of Banagher 1887, then Rector, 1897 to 1931. The credence table commemorates Matthew Bolton and Martha Meenagh. The chair on the right of the sanctuary is in memory of the Rev. Leslie Stevenson who died in 1961, and the chair on the left is in memory of John Stevenson who died in 1918. The Communion rails are in memory of Margaretta Tate and Alexander Stevenson who died in 1898. The 1973 Walker organ on the right of the nave has two manuals and pedals, and it commemorates Miss B.B.Stevenson, 1984.

A Roll of Honour commemorating those who fell in the Great War is on the north wall, and it commemorates Corporal John McSparron. Also on the north wall, a plaque records the installation of the gates in memory of William and Mary Jane Irwin, 1971. There is a memorial to Anna Hunter who died in 1837 and to Lt. Nathaniel Hunter who died in Aden in 1844 and to Richard Hunter who died in 1855. Also commemorated are James Stevenson of Knockan in whose memory the doors of the church were renewed in 1966, and Kathleen Stevenson, in whose memory the walls were renovated in 1950. On the east wall, left of the sanctuary, there are memorials to Lt. Henry Stevenson who died in 1916 during the Great War, to 2nd Lt. Samuel Bristow Stevenson who died at Salonika in 1916, and to Lt. William Henry Stevenson, Canadian Scouts who died in 1902. On the south wall, there is a memorial to Ellen Jane, widow of the Rev. Canon James Scott, and daughter of Hugh Lyle of Knocktarna, who died in 1905.

## BARONSCOURT

BARONSCOURT was originally a district curacy in the parish of Ardstraw. The parish church, high in the west Tyrone hills six kilometres to the south west of Newtownstewart, was consecrated on 24th March 1858. It has one of the two lych gates in the Dioceses of Derry and Raphoe, the other being at All Saints, Newtowncunningham, Co. Donegal. It was erected by the second Duke of Abercorn in

*Baronscourt Church.*

memory of his mother. Over the gate are inscribed the words, I am the Resurrection and the Life saith the Lord".

The church is more English in style and character. It is entered through a porch in the south wall. The entrance doors commemorate Samuel and Margaret Crompton, 1993. The window in the west wall has coloured lattice glass. There are two windows in the south wall, which have two lights and geometrically patterned lights above, and richly coloured lattice panes. In the north wall, the first window depicts St. Matthew and St. Mark on the left, and St. John the Baptist and St. John the Evangelist on the right. It commemorates Louisa Jane, Duchess of Abercorn who died in 1905. The second window depicts King David and the Prophet Micah on the left, and the Prophets Isaiah and Zechariah on the right, and is in memory of James, 1st Duke of Abercorn who died in 1885. In the ceiling, there are two gables on each side of the church, containing dormer windows of three lights each and lattice panes. The east window has three lights and tracery. The left section depicts Faith, and commemorates Ronald Douglas Hamilton who died in 1867. The central section, Charity, is in memory of Beatrix Frances, Countess of Durham who died in 1871, and the right section, Hope, is in memory of Kathleen Elizabeth, Countess of Edgecombe.

The vestry room is north of the chancel. In the sanctuary, the Ten Commandments are inscribed on each side of the east wall. These, and the tiling of the chancel, commemorate Louisa Jane, Duchess of Abercorn. The pulpit is on the left and the prayer desk is on the right. The brass eagle lectern was presented by Bishop William Alexander and others in memory of James, 1st Duke of Abercorn, K.G. The beautifully decorated chamber organ also

*The Chancel.*

commemorates Louisa Jane, Duchess of Abercorn. It was built by the Positive Organ Company of London.

There are numerous monuments in the church which commemorate the Hamilton Family, Dukes of Abercorn. Baronscourt House, surrounded by its estates and gardens, is amongst the grandest neo-classical houses of its kind in Ireland. It was built between 1779 and 1781 by James Hamilton, eighth Earl of Abercorn. He died in 1789, and was succeeded by his nephew, John James who became the first Marquess of Abercorn in 1790. Following the destruction of Baronscourt by fire in 1796, the house was completely rebuilt. It has been altered a number of times since.

The Hamiltons have lived at Baronscourt since before 1566. Their ancestry can be traced back far further. For example, an ancestor, James Hamilton was 1st Earl of Arran at the beginning of the 16th century. The first Earl of Abercorn, James Hamilton, was a grandson of the second Earl of Arran. He died in 1617. Another ancestor, James Hamilton (1559-1643), was Viscount Clandeboye. James Hamilton, the sixth Earl of Abercorn (1656-1734), took part in the Siege of Derry in 1689, and was created Viscount Strabane in the Irish Peerage.

James Hamilton, (1811-1885), eldest son of James, Viscount Hamilton, was the first Duke of Abercorn. He succeeded to the title of Marquess of Abercorn in 1818 on the death of his grandfather, the first Marquess. He was Lord Lieutenant of Ireland, and as such, he presided over the installation of the Prince of Wales (the future King Edward VII), as a Knight of the Order of St. Patrick in 1868. He was raised to the Dukedom as the first Duke of Abercorn on 10th August 1868. The third Duke was the first Governor of Northern Ireland from 1922 to 1945. His Grace, the fifth Duke of Abercorn, the present holder of the title, was made a Knight of the Most Noble Order of the Garter by Her Majesty the Queen in June 1999.

Returning to the church, on the south wall, monuments commemorate Sgt. S.Price, who died in 1926, S/Constable J. Blair, 1930, and Constable T. Mawhinney of the Governors Guard, and Frances Hamilton who was killed by a falling tree in 1928. She was the only daughter of Canon Frederick Hamilton, Rector of Baronscourt from 1898 to 1938. On the south chancel wall, there is a memorial to the Very Rev. Edward Bowen, Rector from 1855 to 1867, and later Dean of Raphoe. On the east wall to the right of the sanctuary, Frederick Spencer Hamilton, son of James, 1st Duke of Abercorn is commemorated. He was responsible for the adornment of the church, and died in 1928.

A fine monument on the south wall records the erection of the tables of the Ten Commandments and the paving of the chancel in memory of Louisa Jane, Duchess of Abercorn, by her grandchildren, great-grandchildren and great-great-grandchildren and their wives and husbands. They are all named on the monument, 1906, and the Abercorn family crests appear on it. There are also two brass memorials to those who fell in the Great War, as well as a memorial to Georgina Susan, Countess Winterton, fifth daughter of James, 1st Duke of Abercorn, and wife of Edward, 5th Earl of Winterton. She died in 1913.

*Abercorn Memorial.*

On the west wall, Alexandra Hamilton who was drowned aboard SS *Leinster* in 1918, is commemorated, along with Gladys Mary, Countess of Wicklow who died in 1917. There is a memorial to James, 2nd Duke of Abercorn, K.G., who died in 1913, and to Mary Anna, Duchess of Abercorn who died in 1929. Arthur John Hamilton, Captain in the Irish Guards, who was killed at Ypres in 1914 is commemorated. His monument records his last words which were, "I am going - tell my mother how I died and pray for me". The inscription concludes, "and he died with a smile on his lips".

## BOVEVAGH, St. EUGENIUS

Bovevagh, *"Mevagh's hut"*, is a parish eight kilometres to the north of Dungiven in County Derry. A monastery was founded in the area by St. Columba in 557. St.Adamnan and St. Eugene are variously claimed as patron saint. The ancient ruins of a mediaeval church can be seen nearby.

Bovevagh church was ruinous in 1622, but was in good repair by 1768. The present church was

*Boveagh Church.*

built in 1823. It is a hall and tower church to a design by John Bowden.The tower is louvered and topped by pointed finials. The porch at the base is entered through doors which were given in memory of Hamilton and Mary Connor and Nenian and Margaret Dunlop, 1973. The window of coloured glass has a dove inset, and is in memory of the Kerr family, 1976.

There are three windows in the south wall of the nave. The first has coloured square glass panes with the Lamb of God inset. The second window has the crest of the Royal Ulster Constabulary, and is in memory of Constable Robert John McPherson, 1976, and the third window depicts the Holy Bible. A window in the north wall depicts the Empty Tomb, and it commemorates Canon John Howard Kingston, Rector, 1950-1970. The east window was installed in 1914. It depicts the Ascension of our Lord, and is in memory of the Stevenson family.

The baptistery is by the north wall, before the chancel. The font was presented by the McClelland families. The pulpit on the left of the chancel was the gift of the Quigley family, 1973. The prayer desk on the right commemorates Samuel Robinson, 1973, and the lectern was given in memory of James Stevenson Hunter, who died on board the ship, *Bowfell* off the Cape of Good Hope in 1867. The chancel contains the choir seating which is in memory of Mary Ferguson, 1976. The choir stall and the panelling in the sanctuary were made and presented by W. J. Quigley in 1986. The Holy Table commemorates George and Margaret Scott, 1955, and the credence table is in memory of Jackie McMullan, 1947. One of the three chairs in the sanctuary is in memory of Emily Fulton, 1922. The vestry room is to the left.

## CAMUS-JUXTA-BANN, MACOSQUIN, St. MARY

MACOSQUIN, *"the plain of the conquest"*, and Camus-juxta-Bann, *"the bend next to the Bann"*, are the two names of a parish which is ancient and historic. Today, Macosquin is a village five kilometres to the west of Coleraine, just off the main Londonderry road. A monastery is said to have been founded by St. Comgall in 780 at Camus. St.Colman, who died in 699, was abbot of an earlier monastery. At the turn of the 13th century, the O'Cahan family, chieftans in the area, founded a Cistercian house at Macosquin which was known as *"de Claro Fonte"*.

At the Royal Visitation in 1622, it was reported that the old monastery was in ruins, and that the Merchant Taylors' Company, which had come to the area at the time of the Plantation, petitioned the Primate for the building of a new church on the ruins of the monastery. This would unite both the churches at Camus and Macosquin, which existed by 1600. The church was duly built, and was reported to be in good repair in 1693, and again in 1768.

The present church in Macosquin was rebuilt in 1827. A stone on the west wall of the tower records this. A carved stone in front of the tower came from the Cistercian abbey. The tower is of three stories, and has a window of clear lattice glass in the west wall. There is a clock in the second level, and louvered windows at the top level. The tower is

*Camus-Juxta-Bann (Macosquin) Church.*

battlemented with corner finials. A plaque in the porch records the donation of the clock in memory of James Sinclair, 1899. The interior entrance doors commemorate Alexander and Anne McAllister. The chancel and vestry room to the north of the nave were built by Welland and Gillespie in 1867.

There is a stained glass window in the west wall of the nave to the left of the entrance. It depicts the boy Samuel with Eli in the Temple, and it commemorates Mr and Mrs Samuel Smyth. The nave is lit by three windows of two lights and small overhead windows on each side. In the north wall, the first window depicts, on the left, the text, "the children of Israel brought an offering unto the Lord", and on the right, Dorcas (Acts 9:39). There is an angel in the upper section. The window commemorates Katherine Sinclair of Dundarg who died in 1906. This is recorded on a brass plaque adjacent. Mrs Sinclair was the daughter of the Rev. Robert Alexander, Rector of Aghadowey, 1832-1869, and sister of Bishop, later Primate Alexander. The middle window has the Lamb of God on the left, and, "behold I stand at the door and knock", on the right, with a dove above. This window commemorates the McMath family, 1991. The third window has, "I am the Way and the Truth and the Life" on the left, and floral patterns and family crests on the right. It commemorates H. Richardson Scott who died in 1876.

In the south wall, the first window depicts, on the left the text, "the souls of the righteous are in the hands of God", and Mary with the Baby Jesus, and on the right, Jesus calling the little children. It commemorates Dorothea Alice Sinclair who died aged eleven years, and Isabella Ann Sinclair who died aged five years. The font, which is adjacent to this window in the south-west corner of the nave, also commemorates these two little girls. The middle window shows the Good Samaritan, with "the Word of God" in the small light above, and it commemorates Alfie McClements, 1991. The third window depicts, on the left, Mary with the infant Jesus, and on the right, Joseph in the Carpenter's shop. The fifth Commandment is written overhead. A plaque adjacent records that the window is in memory of Thomas and Agnes Oliver, 1999. The east window is a triple lancet with cusped tracery containing a dove. It has nine illustrations of our Lord, depicting various parables and Gospel stories. It commemorates John Baillie, 1972.

The altar is in memory of Major John Arthur O'Neill Torrens, Royal Scots Greys who died in 1936. A credence table and three chairs are adjacent. The reredos commemorates John Robert Baillie and his wife Mary Louise, 1962, and the panelling in the sanctuary is in memory of William and Annie Oliver, 1962. The pulpit, which is to the left of the nave below the chancel, is in memory of Katherine, wife of James Sinclair of Dundarg. The prayer desk on the left below the pulpit commemorates James and Isabella Stirling, and their son Robert and his wife Ellen, 1987, and the prayer desk on the right is in memroy of James Sinclair of Dundarg. There is a fine brass lectern.

On the west wall, Rolls of Honour commemorate those who served and fell in the two World Wars. A plaque records the installation of electric lighting in 1960 in memory of those who fell in the second World War, and another plaque records the present lighting system in memory of Malcolm and Gwen

McQuigg, 1980. On the north wall, there are memorials to James McLernon of HMS *Briton* who was killed in action in Egypt in 1884, and to James Wilson and his wife Maria. Also commemorated are Henry Richardson who died in 1786, and his sons John and Henry. A monument commemortaes Hatton Elizabeth, wife of the Rev. Thomas Richardson, Rector, 1821-1837. She was the daughter of the Rev. George Young, Rector 1787-1797. She died in 1855. The next monument is in memory of Thomas Rumbold, 1st Regiment, Life Guards who died in 1868, and his mother, the Lady Emily Kerr who died in 1874. There is a memorial to Mary, daughter of the Rev. Thomas Richardson, and to the Rev. Thomas Richardson himself, and his son Henry who died in 1849. Another daughter, Barbara, wife of the Rev. Henry Torrens, is commemorated.

On the south wall, a monument commemorates Thomas Bennett, JP, who died in 1858, and other members of his family. The family crest is above the monument. A plaque records the installation of the amplification system in memory of Thomas and Jeannie Campbell, and John and Ellen Gault, 1989. The flags of the local branch of the Royal British Legion are placed to the left and right of the chancel arch.

## CAMUS-JUXTA-MOURNE, STRABANE, CHRIST CHURCH

*Camus-Juxta-Mourne Church.*

THE TOWN OF STRABANE, Co. Tyrone, stands on the River Mourne, where it joins with the Foyle. The name of the parish, Camus-juxta-Mourne, means, *"the bend next to the Mourne"*. St. Conall was patron saint. In Lewis' Topographical Directory, it is reported that the Earl of Abercorn built a chapel of ease for the new town of Strabane in 1619. The ancient church of Camus was in ruins by 1622, so the parish with its new church, was united with neighbouring Leckpatrick.

The present church was consecrated by Bishop (later Primate) Alexander in 1879 on a site which he had donated. His wife, the hymn-writer Mrs Cecil Frances Alexander, came from the town. The church is a cruciform building with a three bay arcaded nave, aisles and transepts. There is a tower between the north transept and the chancel, which is surmounted by a spire. The spire is a pyramid at the base which becomes hexagonal at the top. The church is entered by a porch at the base of the tower, or by a porch in the north-west corner. The peal of eight bells in the tower dates from 1920. In the north-west porch, a stone records the munificence of William Hamilton, 1640. A replica of this stone is adjacent. There is a window depicting St. Patrick in memory of Alfred McIntyre who died in 1998, and a window depicting St. Columbcille, the gift of Canon F. W. Fawcett, Rector 1987-1999. A brass plaque in the porch records the donation of the heating system in memory of Maude Boggs, 1968.

*The Chancel.*

The baptistery at the west end of the nave was furnished in memory of Robert Wray who died in 1990. The window in it, which depicts the Baptism of Jesus, was restored in memory of Thomas and Catherine Harpur and family, 1999. There is an aisle on each side of the nave, with three clerestory windows above the aisles and nave. The windows in the aisles are richly coloured. The window in the west wall of the south aisle, and the window in the west wall of the nave, which has three lights, illustrate hymns of Mrs Alexander, in memory of Thomas McNeill who died in 1994, and his wife Kathleen. In the north aisle, the first window, in memory of Kathleen, Isobel, Thomas and John Harpur, depicts Jesus calling the children, and the second shows Mary and Jesus in the manger in memory of Catherine Harpur. The north aisle also contains a small chapel for daily services. The altar in it is in memory of Doris Wilson who died in 1975. In the south aisle, William and Frances Boyd are commemorated in a window. The next window was given by Nicholas and Jane French, and the third one shows the Good Shepherd.

The window in the north transept has five lights, and commemorates James Hunter McClay who built the church, and who died in 1924. The window in the south transept also has five lights, and it depicts Dorcas in the Book of Acts. It commemorates Kathleen McNeill who died in 1978. The stained glass east window with five lights and cusped tracery, is an elaborate and beautiful depiction of the Last Supper. It commemorates John and Elizabeth Humphreys, the parents of Miss C.F. Alexander, and dates from 1879.

The font is in the north transept. Opposite in the south transept is the three manual organ. The organ chamber is behind, to the south of the chancel. It was installed in 1937 in memory of William Lawson and his wife. The stone pulpit is to the left of the chancel entrance, and there are prayer desks on each side. These and the stone eagle lectern commemorate Samuel and Jane Colquhoun. There is another prayer desk in memory of Lt.Col. J.R.A.McFerran who died in 1969. The oak panelling in the sanctuary marks the jubilee of the church, and was erected by John Claudius and Maud Harriett Herdman in 1929. The cross on the altar commemorates Annie Louisa Campbell, 1965, and the book stands are in memory of Thomas Boles who died in 1958, and Charlotte Boles who died in 1976. The vestry room is to the right of the chancel.

Those who fell in the two World Wars are commemorated on monuments in the north transept. There is also a plaque which records a benefaction in memory of the McKinley and Thompson families, 1990. In the south transept, there is a memorial to James Thompson who died in 1904, and to Elizabeth McFarlane who died in 1914. A memorial in the south wall of the chancel records the donation of the public address system in memory of Canon Ernest Lovell, Rector, 1956-1986. In the north porch at the base of the tower, there is a monument to the memory of the Rev. Stewart Hamilton, Rector, 1804-1832. A brass plaque records the building of the church in memory of the Rev. James Smith, Rector, 1835-1860, who died in 1870. Catherine Skipton who died in 1850, and Rosamond Leslie who died in 1869, and others are also commemorated.

Next door to the church is the John Perry Memorial Hall which was built in 1966. The modern rectory is nearby.

# William and Cecil Frances Alexander

WILLIAM ALEXANDER and his wife, Mrs Cecil Frances Alexander, were two of the great figures of the 19th century in Derry and Raphoe. William was born in Derry on 13th April 1824, the son of the Rev. Robert Alexander, Rector of Aghadowey. He was educated at Tonbridge School and Exeter College, Oxford. While at Oxford, Alexander came under the influence of John Henry Newman and the Tractarians, the party in the Church of England which wanted to bring the Church back to a more catholic position. When Newman became a Roman Catholic in 1845, Alexander contemplated following, but after much soul-searching, he remained an Anglican.

*William Alexander.*

Alexander was ordained deacon in Muff Church on 19th September 1847. He was curate of Templemore, then successively, Rector of Termonamongan (1850-1855), Fahan, (1855-1860) and Camus-juxta-Mourne, Strabane, (1860-1867). He was consecrated Bishop of Derry and Raphoe in Armagh Cathedral on 6th October 1867. He was elected Archbishop of Armagh and Primate of All Ireland on 25th February 1896. He remained Primate until his retirement in 1911, and he died a few months later at Torquay on 12th September 1911.

William Alexander was a truly outstanding Bishop at a time of great uncertainty and change for the Church of Ireland. He vigorously opposed Disestablishment, speaking eloquently against it in the House of Lords, but to no avail. After Disestablishment, Alexander set about guiding his Dioceses of Derry and Raphoe as the Church came to terms with its new position. He went to America in 1891 to raise funds for the Cathedral schools.

*Cecil Frances Alexander.*

William Alexander was a great scholar, and he had an illustrious academic career. In Oxford, he won the Denyer Prize for an essay on the Divinity of our Lord. He was also awarded the University prize for a poem. He graduated in 1867 with a Doctorate in Divinity. He was a prolific author and an eloquent preacher. Thousands flocked to hear him when he preached in the English cathedrals. He was Select Preacher at the Universities of Oxford, Cambridge and Dublin for a number of years, and he was the Bampton Lecturer in 1876. He published numerous books and sermons, amongst which were, *Leading Ideas of the Gospels,* London 1872, and, *The Epistles of St. John,* in *The Speaker's Commentary.*

William Alexander married, in October 1850, Cecil Frances, daughter of Major John Humphreys, J.P., of Milltown House, Strabane. Mrs Alexander was born in 1818, and was thus, six years older than her husband. Her hymns, which are world-renowned, include such favourites as, *Once in Royal David's City, Jesus Calls us o'er the tumult, The Golden Gates are lifted up, There is a green hill far away, All things bright and beautiful,* and, *In the roll-call of God's sons.* Her poem, *The Burial of Moses,* is considered to be one of the finest in the English Language, upon reading which, Alfred Lord Tennyson expressed the wish that he himself had been its author.

William and Cecil Frances Alexander had four children, two boys and two girls. Mrs Alexander died on 12th October 1895, while her husband was still Bishop of Derry, thereby predeceasing him by nearly sixteen years. She is buried in the City Cemetery. Portraits of Bishop and Mrs Alexander by C. N. Kennedy hang in the entrance hallway of the Deanery. The window in the east wall of the chapel in the Cathedral, which depicts the ascended Christ, commemorates Bishop Alexander. The Baptistery in the Cathedral is Mrs Alexander's memorial.

## CAPPAGH, St. EUGENE

CAPPAGH, *"a plot of land laid out for tillage",* is a parish which is situated in mid-Tyrone. The parish church is five kilometres to the north of Omagh, close to the Gortin road. The 16th/17th century ruins of Dunmullan old church are still preserved.

Cappagh Church is pleasantly situated close to Mountjoy Forest on the River Strule. It was built in 1768 at the expense of the rector, Dr. Wood Gibson. At the west end, the tower is flanked on the left side by the room which contains the stairs to the gallery, and on the right, by the vestry room. The tower is surmounted by an elegant spire. On either side of the west door are blind windows. The general style of the facade is classical. The main entrance door commemorates Samuel Dodds, 1991.

Inside, the baptistery is beneath the gallery. Round each side of the square black marble font are memorial inscriptions to Tempe Bagot Stack, daughter of the Rev. Edward Stack and his son, the Rev. Richard Stack. Richard was curate of St.Peter's Church in Dublin. He died in 1851 aged 36 years. On the font is the inscription, "his end was hastened by the too laborious duties of a large city parish during a period of famine and pestilence". Bessie, second daughter of the Rev. Edward Stack who died in 1853, and his son, Capt. George Stack, are also commemorated.

The pulpit is to the left of the chancel, and the prayer desk is on the right. It commemorates Rebecca Elrington who died in 1899. The brass eagle lectern is in memory of the Rev. James Scott, Curate of Cappagh in the 1860s. The Holy Table commemorates the Rev. Gerald Moriarty, Rector of Cappagh, 1898-1927, and his wife Mary. It was dedicated in 1946. The sanctuary is a three-sided apse by Welland and Gillespie which was added in 1870.

There are nine fine stained glass windows in the church, three in the north wall, three in the sanctuary, and three in the south wall. Each has two lights and tracery. The first window in the north wall depicts, on the left, Faith, and on the right, Hope, and is in memory of Charles Rowe

*Cappagh Church.*

Scott who died in 1868, and his wife Anne. The second window illustrates a variety of New Testament stories, including the Prodigal Son. It commemorates the Rev. James Scott, Curate of Cappagh who died in 1874. The third window shows the boy Jesus with the doctors in the Temple on the left, and the Risen Christ appearing on the Emmaus road on the right. It commemorates David Auchinleck who died in 1849.

The first window in the sanctuary has, on the left, "feed my sheep", and on the right, "I will make you fishers of men", and is in memory of the Rev. Richard Stack, DD, FTCD, Rector from 1806 until his death in 1812. The centre window has the verse from the Te Deum, "make them to be numbered with thy saints in glory everlasting". It commemorates those who fell in the second World War. The third window has on the left the text, "I know that my Redeemer liveth", and on the right, "I am the Resurrection and the Life", and it commemorates the Rev. Thomas Stack who died in 1839, and his wife Margaret. Thomas's daughter married a cousin, Charles Maurice Stack, son of the Rev. Richard Stack.

In the south wall, the first window shows our Lord on the left, and Mary and Martha on the right. It commemorates the Rev. Matthew Moriarty, Rector of Killaghtee in Co. Donegal who died in 1888. He was father of the Rev. Gerald Moriarty, Rector of Cappagh. The window also commemorates William Courtenay who died in 1897, and his wife Elizabeth. The second window shows the Risen Christ, and is in memory of the Rev. Gerald Moriarty who died in 1927. The third window shows, on the left, Jesus calling the children, and on the right, St.Columba. This window was copied from one in St. Columb's Cathedral, Londonderry, and it commemorates Isabella Craig who died in 1996.

In the porch, over the door, a plaque lists bequests to the church from 1872 to 1947. There is also an old stone which was taken from Dunmullan old church in 1968 to mark the bi-centenary of Cappagh Church. On the west wall, five marble plaques commemorate the men who were killed while serving with the Royal Ulster Constabulary, or with the Ulster Defence Regiment. These are Private JJ Graham, UDR, 1979, Constable Kenneth Sheehan, 1977, William Hutchinson, 1974, Constable Christopher Kyle, 1981 and Constable Andrew Woods, 1981. There is also a memorial to Charlotte Houston who died in 1879, and a plaque records the carpeting of the choir stalls and other gifts in 1972.

On the north wall of the nave is the memorial to those who fell in the Great War. A monument commemorates Lt. Col. Robert Pierce of the Royal Inniskilling Fusiliers who was killed at the Somme in 1916, and another commemorates Richard Stack, son of Rev. Richard Stack who died in 1832. The Rev. James Wright, Rector of Cappagh, 1935-1958, and the Rev. Henry Harte, Rector of Cappagh from 1831 until his death in 1849, are also commemorated. On the north wall of the sanctuary, there is a memorial to the Very Rev. James Byrne, Rector, 1849 to 1897, the year of his death. He also held the Deanery of Clonfert in Co. Galway from 1866 to 1897.

## CARRICK

Carrick, *"the rock"*, is a small parish south of Limavady on the Dungiven road. It was created in 1846 as a perpetual curacy out of the parishes of Balteagh, Bovevagh and Tamlaghtfinlagan. The church, which is pleasantly situated on the banks of the River Roe amongst trees, is a beautiful but simple little building. It was built in 1846, and consecrated on 25th May 1847.

The church is entered through a west porch which has two small windows. Inside, the nave is a four bay hall, with gabled transepts at each side of the west end, which do not protrude from the walls. There are four windows of two lights in both north and south nave walls. Each window has Y tracery and clear, diamond paned glass. The east window has three lights and tracery. It depicts an angel with other figures. It commemorates those who fell in the Great War.

*Carrick Church.*

The pulpit is on the north side, the lectern is in the centre, and the prayer desk is to the right. The Holy Table came from St. Elizabeth's Church, Dundonald, Belfast. The vestry room is to the right of the chancel.

On the west wall, a monument records the restoration of the church in 1907 during the incumbency of the Rev. George Moriarty, Rector, 1889 to 1907, and a brass plaque records the incumbency of the Rev. Samuel Heaslett, Rector, 1946 to 1977. On the north wall, there is a memorial to the Rev. Richard Benson, Rector, 1908 to 1923, and to his wife. 1st Lt. William John Campbell, 5th Fusiliers, who died in 1843, in whose memory the church was endowed, is commemorated, as is George Williams who died in 1972. On the south wall, Bernard and Ellen McIlmoyle are commemorated.

## CASTLEDAWSON, CHRIST CHURCH

The Parish of Castledawson in east Co. Londonderry, was created in 1875 from parts of the neighbouring parishes of Magherafelt in the Diocese of Armagh, and Ballyscullion. The old church, which was built in 1760, by the Dawson Family of Moyola Park, replacing an earlier church of 1710, was enlarged and consecrated on 7th November 1876 with the dedication Christ Church.

Castledawson Church has a nave, chancel and a large north transept. The vestry room is to the left of the chancel. The porch is in the north-west corner of the nave. An external extension of it has balustrades on both sides. The porch, and the window in it which shows Christ, the Light of the World, were the gift of Lady Spencer Chichester in

*Castledawson Church.*

1912. There is a large bellcote over the west wall of the nave. Between the porch and the transept is a new committee room, which was opened on 26th May 1996. Its furnishings were donated by parishioners. The door is in memory of Alexander Pickering, and the windows were donated in memory of Stanley Alexander Inglis and Olive Johnston. The vestry room door is in memory of Thomas Moorhead Adamson who died in 1953, and his brother, Claude who died in 1936. It was presented by Miss N.Adamson in 1960.

The baptistery is in the south-west corner of the nave. The carpeting in it and in the sanctuary is in memory of Robert Ditty, 1980. The pulpit lights commemorate Mr and Mrs R. Lennox and Robert and Thomas Lennox, and the wooden eagle lectern is in memory of Adolphus John Spencer Churchill Chichester. These, along with the beautifully carved oak Communion Table, two chairs and the Communion rails, and the carvings on the sanctuary walls, were provided in 1851 by George Robert Dawson. Mrs Chichester-Clark gave a new pulpit in 1929. The Communion rails were presented by Matthew McCombe. The brass plaques on them state that the rail on the right was made by Robert McCombe in 1929, and that the rail on the left is in his memory, 1939. The prayer desk in the sanctuary commemorates Ruby Chambers who died in 1972. It was dedicated in 1979. There is a prayer desk on the left. The chair commemorates Charles Francis Clarke and his wife Eliza Ann Ogilby Olivia Clark of Moyola Lodge. The book stand at the west wall is in memory of Richard Lennox who died in 1978. There is a one manual chamber organ in the transept.

*The Chancel.*

The window in the west wall has three lights, with lattice and square clear glass. In the south wall, there are four round-headed windows. The first illustrates the text of Acts 9:36, "full of good works". The second is, "in thy presence, the fullness of joy, and at thy right hand there are pleasures for evermore". A plaque on the sill commemorates the Hon. Mary Elizabeth Dawson, wife of Col. Peel Dawson of Moyola Park, and daughter of the first Lord Lurgan, who died in 1888. The third window is in memory of the Rt. Hon. George Robert Dawson, 1858. The fourth window, which illustrates the texts, "my peace I give unto you", and, "consider the lilies of the field how they grow", is in memory of Col. Robert Peel Dawson, Lord Lieutenant of Londonderry, and Member of Parliament for the county. He died in 1877. The two windows together in the west wall of the transept, both depict angels. The one on the left is in memory of Lt.Col. Robert Peel Dawson Spencer Chichester, DL, MP for South Derry, of Moyola Park, Irish Guards and 14th Royal Irish Rifles who died in 1921. The window on the right is in memory of Robert James Spencer Chichester who died in 1920. The windows were erected by Dehra Chichester, wife of Robert Peel Dawson Spencer Chichester. The round-headed east window has three lights and is filled with coloured glass.

Numerous monuments and memorials in the church commemorate the Dawson and Chichester-Clark families. The Dawsons of Moyola Park, in whose grounds the church is built, are an old family. They gave their name to Dawson Street in Dublin. The Chichesters were also an old family who were very much involved in the political life of Northern Ireland. Arthur, Lord Chichester of Belfast (1563-1625), was Lord Deputy of Ireland, and may have commmanded a ship during Drake's last voyage at the time of the Spanish Armada. Arthur Chichester (1606-1675), was first Earl of Donegal.

Major James Chichester-Clark was one time Prime Minister of Northern Ireland. They and the Dawsons were also related to the Spencers of Althorp in Northamptonshire, the family of Lady Diana Spencer, late Princess of Wales.

In the sanctuary, the first four Commandments are inscribed on the north wall, and the other six, on the south wall. The Lord's Prayer is on the left side of the east wall, and the Creed is on the right. They are surrounded by fine wood carvings, and in the sanctuary panelling, there are finely carved wood square panels. There is a wooden eagle over the east window. On the east wall, left of the sanctuary, there are memorials to Marion Caroline Dehra Chichester of Moyola Park who died in 1976, and to Capt. James Jackson Lenox-Conyngham Chichester-Clark, RN, DSO and Bar, who died in 1933. On the other side of the sanctuary, Canon Henry Egan, Rector of Castledawson, 1937-1975, who died in 1986, is commemorated. On the south wall, there are memorials to Henry Mann who died in 1908, D.Campbell Gaussen, JP who died in 1900, Alexander Clark, DL, OBE who died in 1952 and his wife Anita who died in 1959, and to Margaret Bates, daughter of Richard Dawson who died in 1838. A plaque states that the walls and gate at the entrance were presented in memory of the Blakeley family by Anne Blakeley in 1973. There are memorials to Alexander Clotworthy Dawson, RN, and to Elizabeth Ewing who died in 1938.

On the west wall, a monument commemorates Mary, daughter of Sir Robert Peel, Bart., wife of the Rt.Hon. George Dawson, who died in 1848. The brass genealogy of the Dawson family adjacent to the door, states that the Dawsons first settled in the parish of Temple Soerby in Westmoreland, and afterwards, in Castledawson. It gives members of the family as far back as 1170. The carved wooden frame in which it is set, was brought from Malines Cathedral in Belgium by George Robert Dawson in 1847.

On the north wall, there are memorials to Admiral John Dawson who died in 1836, and his wife who died in 1852, and to Anne, wife of the Rev. J. Wrixon, and daughter of Rear Admiral John Dawson, who died in 1901. The north wall is dominated by a huge monument to the Rt. Hon. George Robert Dawson of Moyola Park, (1790-1856), Privy Councillor of Great Britain, MP for Londonderry, 1815 to 1830, and then, for Harwich in Essex. It contains two brass plaques, and is thought to be a large wooden chimneypiece. The

*The Dawson Monument.*

carving in it is of very high quality. A classical monument commemorates Capt. Harry Brereton Trewlany of the Grenadier Guards who died in 1851. Flying Officer William Mann of the Royal Air Force who was killed in 1944, and Richard Mann who died in 1955, are commemorated.

On the east wall of the transept are monuments which commemorate Edward Donnelly who was drowned at Portrush in 1891, and Lt. Augustus John Bruce Macdonald Dawson Chichester, son of the Rt. Hon. Lord Spencer Chichester, who died in 1902. On the north wall of the transept, there is a memorial to Arthur Dawson who died in 1822, and to his wife, Katherine, daughter of George and Lady Araminta Monck, who died in 1838. A plaque at the junction of the transept and the nave east wall commemorates Ivor Wilson who died aged nineteen years in 1979. He was a Scout, and was killed in a traffic accident while at a Scout camp in France. The light in the reading desk was given in his memory.

## CASTLEROCK, CHRIST CHURCH

CASTLEROCK is a seaside resort on the north coast of Co. Derry. The parish was created out of neighbouring Dunboe as a perpetual curacy in 1867. The church, one of the most beautiful in the Diocese, was built between 1867 and 1870 from endowments granted by Sir Hervey Bruce and the Clothworkers' Company. The Clothworkers' Company had been established in the area at the time of the Plantation of Ulster at the beginning of the 17th century. The

*Castlerock Church.*

Hervey Bruce family was prominent in the area. They lived at Downhill House, just east of Castlerock, which had been built by their ancestor, the Hon. Frederick Augustus Hervey (1730-1803), the Earl Bishop of Derry 1768-1803. Bishop Hervey was a notable traveller, and he built several churches in the Diocese. He was also responsible for the building of the Mussenden Temple at Downhill on a cliff overlooking Lough Foyle.

Christ Church, Castlerock, was consecrated by Bishop (later Primate) William Alexander. For the occasion, his wife, Mrs Cecil Frances Alexander, wrote a hymn, which was set to music by Canon James Armstrong, first Vicar of Castlerock. The porch in the north-west corner is at the base of the tower. The tiling in the porch is in memory of Robert Nicholl who died in 1984. The tower is capped by a spire, at the base of which is a clock with four faces. It was built in 1909. The peal of eight bells dates from 1891. They are a memorial to Sir Hervey and Lady Bruce.

The church is cruciform with transepts, a chancel and a three-sided sanctuary. The interior is of a deep red brick, which creates a warm and solemn atmosphere. Over the entrance door are the words, "Depart in Peace". The west window is of three lights. It commemorates Dame Mary Anne Margaret Bruce, daughter of Sir L. G. Clifton, Bart., of Clifton Hall, Nottingham, and wife of the Rt.Hon. Sir Hervey Bruce, Bart., of Downhill who died in 1891. It depicts scenes from the Parable of the Sheep and the Goats, (St. Matthew 25:31-46). The font is at the base of the window.

There are three stained glass windows in the south nave wall. The first, dated 1918, depicts St. Patrick and St. Columb, and marks the fiftieth anniversary of the incumbency of Canon James Armstrong, first Vicar of Castlerock, from 1868. The middle window depicts Melchizedek and Elijah, and is in memory of William Armstrong who died in 1860, and the third depicts Aaron and Samuel, in memory of Frances Armstrong who died in 1883. The three windows in the south transept wall illustrate the theme of Jesus' favour with God, and the Ascension, and they commemorate Col. Robert Bruce who died in 1899. The three windows in the north transept depict the Sower, the Light of the World and the Good Shepherd, and are in memory of the Rt.Hon. Sir Hervey Bruce, Bart. of Downhill who died in 1907. In the north nave wall, the two windows depict Mary and Joseph at the Manger, in memory of Andrew Mitchell who died in 1974, and Jesus with the little children in memory of Robert Stanage who died in 1911, and his family. There are three windows of two lights each in the sanctuary. The outer ones are of finely coloured glass, and the central window depicts, on the left, the Ascension, and on the right, the Empty Tomb. It commemorates General Sir Arthur Benjamin Finton, K.C.H.

The vestry room is to the left of the chancel, and the organ chamber is opposite. The organ, which has two manuals and pedals, was built by the firm of Gray and Davison in 1870 to a design of Canon Armstrong. The original water pump for the bellows, now restored, is on display in the church. The pulpit to the left of the sanctuary was the gift of Sir John Musgrove, Bart., a member of the Clothworkers' Company, 1870. There is a prayer desk on each side of the choir. The lectern on the right, was presented by William White in 1870. The wooden cross behind the altar came from the crypt of St. Martin-in-the-Fields, London. It commemorates the Rev. Charles ffolliott Young, Rector 1948-1959. The words, "Holy, Holy, Holy, Lord God Almighty which was and is to come", are painted over the sanctuary. The stencil work and fleur-de-lys patterns in the south transept are thought to have been painted by Canon Armstrong. There are elaborate brass candelabra.

On the west wall, a brass memorial to Lady Bruce who died in 1891, states that the peal of bells was given in her memory. A plaque records the munificence of Miss E. K. Stinson who died in 1987, and there is a memorial to William George Simpson who died in 1985, in whose memory the entrance doors were erected in 1987.

*Organ Water Pump.*

A brass memorial on the north wall commemorates Samuel Carson, RN, of Downhill who drowned at Madras, India in 1948. The memorial to those who fell in the Great War is also on the north wall. In the north transept, there is a memorial to the Rt.Hon. Sir Hervey Bruce, Bart.

## CHRIST CHURCH, LONDONDERRY

CHRIST CHURCH, LONDONDERRY is a benefice in the parish of Templemore. It originated in 1830 when the Free Church was built on Northland Road to accommodate the poorer people of the area. It was called "the Free Church", because there were no pew rents. The cost, £760, was borne by the Bishop, the Hon. William Knox, and it was consecrated on 22nd August 1830. The congregation of the area expanded so rapidly that it was necessary to build a gallery in 1832.

In 1882, the church was enlarged again with the erection of north and south transepts and the chancel. The name, the Free Church, was abandoned, and the church was given the

# The Earl Bishop

*Frederick Hervey, Bishop of Derry, from the portrait by Pompeo Batoni. (By kind permission of M.A. Nicholson, Esq., Q.C.).*

THE HON. FREDERICK AUGUSTUS HERVEY, 4th Earl of Bristol, was born on 1st August 1730. He was the third son of John, Lord Hervey, whose father, also John, had been created Baron Hervey of Ickworth, Suffolk in 1703, and Earl of Bristol in 1714. He became the 4th Earl upon the death of his brother George in December 1779. Frederick was educated at Westminster School and Corpus Christi College, Cambridge. In 1747, he enrolled at Lincoln's Inn to study Law.

Hervey decided to take Holy Orders, and was ordained for Ely Diocese in 1754. In 1763, he was appointed chaplain to George III. He was appointed Bishop of Cloyne in Co. Cork in 1767 by the favour of his brother, George, Earl of Bristol. Hervey was anxious, however, to become Bishop of the wealthy See of Derry. He achieved his ambition upon the death of Bishop Barnard in 1768.

Hervey was an eccentric and colourful character. At first, he governed the Diocese of Derry wisely and conscientiously. He was ahead of his time in that he favoured Roman Catholic emancipation. He likewise pitied the Presbyterians, who also suffered religious discrimination, and he got on well with all denominations. John Wesley admired him. He built several Roman Catholic churches, including the Long Tower church in Derry.

Hervey had two great passions, building and travel, and he was a great patron of art and literature. He built and enlarged several churches in Derry Diocese. He also built Downhill House with the Mussenden Temple overlooking Lough Foyle near the village of Castlerock, which incidentally, did not exist in his time. Another of his great houses was Ballyscullion, near Bellaghy, the classical facade of which is now at St. George's Church in Belfast. He also enlarged the ancestral house at Ickworth near Bury St. Edmunds in Suffolk. He built a spire at Derry Cathedral, which had to be dismantled a few years later, as it was too heavy, and he also built many of Derry's fine buildings, and a bridge across the Foyle. Because of this, he earned the nickname, "the Edifying Bishop".

Hervey travelled more and more widely on the Continent as the years went by, collecting art. The Bristol Hotels in many European cities are named after him. Hervey's marriage to Elizabeth, daughter of Sir Jermyn and Lady Davers, broke down. He quarrelled with her incessantly, and did not see her for twenty years before her death. Hervey was absent from the Diocese for the last eleven years of his episcopate. He died of gout at Albano in Italy on 8th July 1803.

In his will, Hervey left Downhill and Ballysculllion, and his collection of art treasures to his nephew, the Rev. Hervey H. Bruce.

*Mussenden Temple.*

*Christchurch.*

dedication, Christ Church. This was because Bishop William Alexander believed that churches should have no other dedication, and so several other churches in the diocese, including Limavady, Castlerock and Strabane are thus dedicated. The consecration of the extensions was held on 30th March 1882. In 1886, the church was enlarged yet again to its present size. At this time, a new three manual Conacher organ was installed. The Choir vestry room on the west side of the north transept was built in 1953.

A Mission Church in connection with Christ Church was dedicated at Claremont on 19th December 1903. This continued in use until its closure in 1967. The closure of the Mission Church was due to the building of St. Peter's Church at Belmont, which was consecrated in 1966. St. Peter's was at first, a daughter church for Christ Church. It was detached from Christ Church and united with Muff and Culmore in 1978, with parish status. Upon ceasing to be used for worship, the Mission Church was used for Scouting and other youth activities. It was destroyed by fire in 1976.

Christ Church, though dwarfed by St.Eugene's Roman Catholic Cathedral across the road, is a large cruciform church with a wide four bay nave, transepts and chancel and sanctuary, and a tower at the west end. At its base is the entrance porch which contains stairs to a spacious gallery. There are two doors in the tower, and a two-light window in the west side. The interior entrance doors have glass panels with inscriptions recording the re-hallowing of the church in 1998. The font is in the south-west corner of the nave. The east wall of the sanctuary is covered with mosaic tiles in memory of Canon Joseph Potter, Rector of Christ Church, 1878-1903, and Dean of Raphoe from 1903 until his death in 1905. The panelling on the north and south sanctuary walls commemorates the Rev. Alexander Spence, Curate, 1914-1916, who as chaplain to the Ulster Division, was killed in 1918 near the end of the Great War. The high altar is finely carved, and dedicated by "a Bishop who had been Curate", in memory of Elizabeth Sophia Percy, 1923. The coats of arms of the Diocese and of the City are engraved at opposite ends. It was carved by Canon Duncan, Rector of Clonleigh (Lifford), and presented by Bishop Robert Miller, a former curate. Two curates of Christ Church became Bishops, Robert Miller, curate 1892-1894, later Bishop of Cashel, and William Hardy Holmes, curate 1896-1898, and later Bishop of Tuam, then Meath. There are two prayer desks and chairs in the sanctuary. Those on the left were presented in memory of Robert Ree who died in 1959, and those on the right, in memory of Robert Grandsen. The pulpit of Caen stone on the right of the chancel was erected in 1887 in memory of the Earl of Enniskillen, and the brass eagle lectern is in memory of Mary Emma, Countess of Enniskillen. The prayer desks and chairs in the chancel were presented by a lady friend of Christ Church in 1923. The choir stalls were erected in 1898. There is a small chapel for daily services in the south transept, which was laid out in 1970. It has an altar, prayer desk and lectern.

There are four windows of two lights and Y tracery in both the north and south walls. In the south wall, the second window illustrates the text, "Peace on earth and good will to men". It commemorates those who fell in the second World War, and their names are recorded on the sill. In the west wall of the south transept, the window of two lights illustrates the loaves and fishes in the story of the feeding of the 5,000. It is in memory of Adam Riddel who died in 1948, and of his son, the Rev. John Riddel who died in 1964. There are two windows in the south wall of the transept. Both have coloured glass. The one on the left has the text of the Fifth Commandment. The window on the right has the text, "The Lord is my light and my salvation", and "Thou art my helper and my redeemer". The windows commemorate Thomas Wylie who rented the ground for the Mission

Church, and his wife, Elizabeth, 1882. The window over the small altar in the south transept, east wall, has stained glass, and commemorates Capt. C. B. Williams of the Royal Irish Rifles who was killed in 1915, and his brother Alfie of the same regiment, who was killed in 1916. Each of these windows has circular lights above.

In the north transept, there are two windows in the west wall. The one on the left illustrates the text, "the wages of sin is death", and the one on the right, the text, "for as in Adam, all die". It was erected by Minchin Percy Lloyd and Margaret Davidson in memory of their parents, brothers and sisters. Overhead is a circular window which has a Bible open at Psalm 23. The choir vestry is beyond the west wall of the north transept, and the vestry room is opposite. The organ chamber is left of the chancel at the corner of the north transept.

The east window has five lights and tracery, the central light being the full height of the window. The whole window depicts the Ascension, and is in memory of Caroline, wife of Dean Potter, who died in 1881, and of Caroline, their daughter, wife of the Rev.John Wilson McQuaide, Rector of Christ Church, 1913-1930. Caroline McQuaide died in 1941.

Christ Church has a number of monuments. In the porch there is a memorial to Lt. Robert Ramsay, RN, who died in 1850. In the south transept on the east wall, there is a memorial to Lt. Ernest Williams of the Royal Irish Rifles who was killed in 1918. The east window in the transept commemorates his brothers who also perished in the Great War. On the east wall of the nave, to the right of the chancel, Robert Algeo who died in 1915 is commemorated, along with his son William, Surgeon on S.S. *California,* who died when the ship was torpedoed in 1917. A plaque in the north transept records the erection of the Choir Vestry in memory of James and Pauline Roden in 1953, and its extension in memory of Elizabeth Price and Thomas Taylor, 1967.

Christ Church was badly damaged by fire in an arson attack on 27th September 1996. The Conacher organ of 1886 and the east window were completely destroyed. The east window has been replaced with an exact replica, and a new three manual organ with pedals, costing £200,000, has been built by the Wells Kennedy Partnership of Lisburn and completed in 2001. This splendid

*New Wells Kennedy Organ, Christ Church, Londonderry.*

instrument, with its beautiful case, will assist Christ Church to maintain its long-established choral tradition of Music of the highest quality. During the renovations, which cost £760,000, the floor of the church was entirely re-tiled. Also, at the time, the door leading into the gallery was re-instated. It contains some of the glass which was salvaged from the east window. The church was re-hallowed on 1st May 1998 by the Rt.Rev. James Mehaffey, Bishop of Derry and Raphoe.

The Craig Hall across the road from the church was built in 1878, and commemorates the Rev. William Craig, incumbent of the Free Church 1853-1873. Christ Church also had a school which originated in 1810, before the Free Church. This was later merged with the Model School, and over the years, it has occupied various buildings.

## CLANABOGAN

SET IN A VALLEY, seven kilometres south of Omagh, just off the Enniskillen road, is the beautiful parish church of Clanabogan. The architects were Welland and Gillespie.

The parish originated as a perpetual curacy which was formed in 1863 out of the parishes of Drumragh (Omagh), and Donacavey and Dromore in Clogher Diocese. The Galbraiths of Clanabogan House were the main land-owning family.

*Clanabogan Church.*

A brass plaque in the porch records the consecration of the church on 22nd December 1863. Behind the porch, in the south-west corner, is a tower which is surmounted by an octagonal spire. There is a wide, spacious nave and a chancel and sanctuary with a vestry room to the left. The gallery is over the west end of the nave.

There are two windows with clear, lattice glass in the west wall, three windows in the south wall, and four in the north wall. Each has two lights, and a small circular window above. In the south wall, the first window has clear, lattice glass. The second window has floral designs, and the text, "ye that hath pity upon the poor lendeth unto the Lord". It commemorates John Galbraith who died in 1903. The third window has coloured glass, and contains various texts. It commemorates Major Samuel Galbraith of the Madras Staff Corps, who died at Suez in 1872. There is a window in Cumber Lower Church at Killaloo near Londonderry in his memory. The first two windows in the north wall have clear lattice glass. The third window has the text, "behold an Israelite indeed in whom is no guile". It commemorates the Very Rev. George Galbraith, Dean of Derry who died in 1911. The east window contains crests and shields of the Galbraith family, and is ornately coloured. Above it is the text, "glory to God in the Highest". It has three lights, and there are three circular lights above. It commemorates Samuel Galbraith who died in 1812, his daughter Katherine who died in 1832 and his son Samuel who died in 1864.

Clanabogan Church is noted for its spectacular marble. The furnishings and fittings are made of a rich variety of marbles in many colours, from many parts of Ireland and elsewhere. The sanctuary and chancel were decorated by the Galbraith Family in 1894. The architect was Sir Thomas Drew. The east

*Marble Sanctuary.*

wall of the chancel has mosaic squares outlined with strips of Connemara and Sienna marble. The reredos is of alabaster. The text, "this do in remembrance of me" is carved in the centre, and there are also shamrocks and three crowns, signifying the Holy Trinity. The Communion rails are made of a French marble, *"rouge royal"*. The plinth is of Kilkenny marble, and each rail is supported by three pillars of Connemara marble, with a base and chapiter of Cork marble. The chancel steps are of Galway grey marble, which in a certain light can appear green. The word "faith" is carved on the first step, "hope", on the second, "love", on the third, and below the Communion rails, "repent ye".

*Marble Pulpit.*

The pulpit is set on a square base. The upper part is hexagonal, with three larger panels and two smaller ones, as well as the entrance. Each panel has yellow, green, black and white insets of marble, with circles and diamond patterns within. The top layer is a rare brown and yellow Brocatello Italian marble. The pulpit book rest is of carved red alabaster. The eagle lectern is of Carrara marble. The eagle stands on a marble orb, and the supporting pillar is of polished white marble with Connemara insets. The base is of Sienna marble on a sub-base of black marble. The initials SJG and the date 1875 are carved on the lectern. The font, which is situated in the south-east corner of the nave, is of white marble. It was given in 1875 in memory of Samuel Galbraith who built the church. A marble step at the vestry door has the words, "faith's journey" carved upon it. There is a niche in the west wall with a marble frame. Carved in this are the words, "Praise the Lord upon earth", and "Fire and hail, snow and vapours, wind and storm fulfilling his Word".

The altar, which is made of carved oak, is in memory of Canon Walter Henry Scott, Rector of Clanabogan, 1872-1903. It was given to the church in 1913. The credence table is of bog oak, which was carved from a large log which was unearthed nearby. Several of the roof beams are from the same log. The prayer desk on the right of the chancel is also made of carved oak. The organ was presented by Samuel Galbraith in 1863. It has one manual and pedals. In the porch, there is an unusual object - a stand for coffins which can swivel so that manoeuvering coffins inside and outside the church is made easier!

On the south wall over the entrance door, there is a memorial to Margaret Mitchell who died in 1858. On the east wall, to the left of the chancel, a monument commemorates the Rev. John Buchanan, Honorary Canon of Gibraltar who died in 1864, and his wife Matilda, daughter of Baron Friedrich de Breton, who died in 1837. On the east

***Galbraith Monument.***

wall, to the right of the chancel, there is a memorial to Ambrose Bole who died in 1879. On the north wall of the sanctuary, Katherine, wife of Canon Scott and daughter of Samuel Galbraith is commemorated. She died in 1910. On the south wall of the sanctuary, there is a very fine classical monument to Lt. Col. James Galbraith, 66th Royal Berkshire Regiment. He was a son of Samuel Galbraith of Clanabogan, and he was killed in 1880. The monument was designed by Thomas Brock, who designed the monument to Queen Victoria which stands in front of Buckingham Palace in London. It contains military figures in high relief. A brass plaque records the donation of the chancel lighting in memory of Robert McKinley who died in 1942.

## CLOONEY, LONDONDERRY, ALL SAINTS STRATHFOYLE

CLOONEY, *"the meadow"*, is a large parish in the Waterside of Londonderry. In ancient times, there was a chapel of Clooney in Glendermott parish. This was rebuilt before 1600, but was in ruins in 1692. A perpetual curacy was established in Glendermott parish for Clooney district in 1863. James Murray of Caw, Londonderry, granted a site for the church, which was dedicated to All Saints in 1867.

*Clooney Church.*

Clooney church is well sited above the east bank of the River Foyle in the Waterside, at the hairpin bend junction of Bond's Hill and Clooney Terrace. The tower in the north west corner is surmounted by a short octagonal spire. The spire is flanked at its base by four small steep pyramids. Beneath it, steps descend to Bond's Hill below. On the Bond's Hill north side of the church at basement level, are three blind arcades. Round the corner from the west wall with its imposing west door entrance, is a porch which protrudes from the south aisle. The refurbishment of the entrance stonework is in memory of Isobel Lowry, 1983. The list of Rectors of Clooney in the porch was donated by Dick and Dorothy Harvey, 1979. The little window on the left of the porch depicts St.Patrick with a shamrock, and the window opposite depicts St. Columba. These were installed during further renovations in 2000.

The interior of the church is most impressive, as indeed is the whole building. The central nave is flanked by two arcaded aisles with short transepts contained within the line of the east end of the aisles. Three marble steps lead into the chancel, beyond which is a three-sided sanctuary. Beneath the north aisle, there is a basement which contains choir vestries and other rooms.

There is a small prayer desk at the west door which commemorates James Gibbons, 1969. Above the west door, there is a rose window. Above that are two stained glass windows, and over them again, a single circular window in the apex of the roof. In the west wall of the south aisle, there is a small window of coloured glass, depicting a dove, and beside it is a window depicting praying hands, the gift of the McCorkell family. On the other side of the west wall, a window depicts the Good Shepherd in memory of Thomas and Margaret Alexander and their parents, George and Mary, 1968. The baptistery is at the west end of the north aisle. The window in it depicts Jesus gathering the little children, 1898. There are two pairs of windows in the north aisle. The first pair is of opaque diamond glass. The first of the second pair is in memory of soldiers of the 5th Londonderry Battalion of the Ulster Defence Regiment who were killed or who died between 1970 and 1992. It contains the City crest and the badge of the U.D.R., and the Bible. The other window has opaque diamond glass. In the south aisle, there are also two pairs of windows. The first pair has one window which was presented by the Brownies to mark sixty years of their existence in the parish, 1932-1992. Their motto, "lend a hand" is inscribed. The other window is of opaque diamond glass, as are both windows in the neighbouring pair. The nave and aisles are separated by four arches above which are three clerestory windows of two lights on each side. The window in the south transept contains various figures in stained glass, and has tracery above. It commemorates Henry Lane, 1894. The opposite window in the north transept illustrates the "Nunc Dimittis", (St. Luke 2:29-32) on the left, and, "behold the Lamb of God", on the right. The left section is in memory of the Rev. Edward Stewart who died in 1883, and the right section commemorates his son, the Rev. John Stewart, Vicar of Clooney, 1872-1880. The three windows in the sanctuary have two lights each, and are inserted in the three sections of the apsidal east sanctuary wall. Each window has three levels. The twelve Apostles are depicted in the top two levels, and there are various Biblical scenes in the bottom levels. Memorial inscriptions at the base of the whole window record that it was erected in memory of W. S. Harvey, who died in 1870, to the Glory of God at the desire of and by the bequest of James Nesbitt. It is altogether, a magnificent set of stained glass windows. Round the base of the sanctuary is a fine marble reredos.

*The Sanctuary.*

The altar is finely carved. Two of the four chairs in the sanctuary are in memory of Canon William Garstin, Curate of Clooney, 1905-1908, and Rector, 1914-1920. The prayer desk in the sanctuary is in memory of Mary Campbell, 1958. There is a prayer desk at each end of the choir stalls. The vestry room is to the left of the chancel, and the organ chamber is to the right. The organ is of two manuals and pedals, and its detached console is in the north aisle. The pulpit on the right is of brown marble. The small prayer desk beside it was made in 1996. A small font adjacent commemorates James Moore who died in 1987.

The two memorials to those of the parish who fell and served in the Great War and in the second World War are on the east wall of the north transept. A monument on the north wall of the north aisle commemorates Lt. William Gilliland of the Royal Inniskilling Fusiliers, who was killed in action at Galipoli in 1915. Margaret Gilliland who died in 1938, and Joseph Cooke who died in 1918 are commemorated on other memorials on the same wall. On the south wall of the south aisle, there is a memorial to Sgt. Major John Lowry who died in 1936, and a memorial to Martha Plummer who died in 1940.

A joint Methodist and Church of Ireland worship centre and hall was opened and dedicated in Strathfoyle, just off the main Limavady road, on 21st

*Strathfoyle, joint Church of Ireland/Methodist Church.*

March 1970. It is a rectangular building with an extensive entrance porch. Inside the porch, there are kitchens to the left and toilets to the right. The large white wooden cross over the exterior west wall was donated by Brian and Willa McMorris and family. Inside, the sanctuary, which can be closed off, is three steps above the main hall. The frontal and lectern on the Holy Table were the gift of the Diocese of Limerick. The cross on the Holy Table was presented by Mervyn Montgomery, and the prayer desk, which is on the right side of the chancel, was presented by the Government Training Centre at Maydown, nearby. The font bowl was given by James and Marion Hughes, 1974, and the font stand, on the left of the chancel, was the gift of the Rev. W. A. Agnew, 1974. A brass plaque on the west wall states that the aisle carpeting was given in memory of Samuel Butler.

## CUMBER UPPER, ALLA, CLAUDY
## CUMBER LOWER, KILLALOO, CLAUDY, HOLY TRINITY

THE NAME CUMBER comes from the Irish, *com*, together, and *bior*, water, so the name suggests the meeting place of two waters, the Rivers Glenrandle and Faughan, in the vicinity of the village of Claudy, some thirteen kilometres east of Londonderry, just to the south of the main Belfast road. According to tradition, St. Patrick founded a church in the area. In 1622, the church was ruinous. It was in reasonable condition by 1693, and was rebuilt in 1757. The parish was divided into Cumber Upper and Lower in 1798.

*Cumber Upper Church.*

Cumber Upper Church at Alla, two kilometres south of Claudy, was built in 1860. It is a three bay hall with a north aisle. The lean-to and gabled porch is in the south wall, and the tower is in the corner of the south and west walls. The copper spire was erected in 1960. Inside the porch are stairs into the gallery, below which are the vestry rooms. These rooms, as well as the public address system and the rose window in the west wall, were donated by the Robinson family in memory of John and Annabella Robinson, 1995. There is another vestry room at the east end of the aisle. In the porch, the window commemorates Robert McFaul, a constable in the Royal Ulster Constabulary who died in 1984, and there is a plaque in memory of George and Jane McFaul.

There is a window of three lights and diamond glass in the west wall, with a rose window above. Both windows in the south wall have two lights. The first window illustrates Christ, the Light of the World, standing at the door and knocking, and is in memory of Samuel and Eileen Eakin, 1991. The second window has diamond opaque glass, with an inset illustrating the text, "and a little child shall lead them". It commemorates Kathryn Alexandra Eakin, aged eight years, who was killed in a bomb blast in Claudy in 1972. The window in the west aisle wall came from St. Nicholas' Church, Castlerickard in the Diocese of Meath, which was closed. It illustrates the text, "It is I, be not afraid", in memory of Richard Vernon Kellet. It was installed in the church in memory of James Whiteside, James McFaul and Samuel Craig, 1979. The baptistery is in the north aisle. The window in it shows Jesus welcoming the little children, and it is in memory of Paul Robinson, aged two years, 1964. The middle window in the aisle shows the raising of Lazarus, and is in memory of John Robinson who died in 1964. The third window, which was installed in 1994, shows on the left, the text "peace, be still", in memory of Joseph and Annie Haire, and on the right, Jesus giving a blessing, in memory of Annie Bonner who died in 1971. There are three windows in the sanctuary, which has three sides. The first window has, *Ave*

*Maria, gratia plena,* Hail Mary, full of Grace, the second has, *Ego sum Pastor Bonus,* I am the Good Shepherd, and the third has, *et Verbum caro factum est,* and the Word became Flesh. The windows are in memory of Mary, wife of Charles Robinson, and daughter of Canon John Beckett, Rector 1905-1943.

The altar, the reredos and credence table were presented by Claude Braddel in memory of his wife Eileen, 1959. In the chancel, the prayer desk on the right was given in memory of Robert and Jane Forsythe, 1959, and the prayer desk on the left, in memory of Edith Leslie, 1990. The pulpit on the left of the nave was erected by Ernest Browne and Constance Browne in memory of the Browne family of Cumber House, 1938. There is a brass eagle lectern. A new organ, was installed in the aisle in 1999. The detached console of two manuals and pedals is to the right of the nave.

A brass monument on the south wall commemorates Flight Sergeant William Harkness, RAF, who was killed in 1943, and a memorial records the life of the Rev. Thomas Lindesay, Prebendary of Cumber, 1847-1860. On the north aisle wall, there is a memorial to Canon John Beckett who died in 1949, and to his wife Violet who died in 1942. It was presented by their daughter, Dorothea Harvey in the church's centenary year, 1960.

***Cumber Lower Church.***

Cumber Lower Church at Killaloo is three kilometres west of Claudy on the main Londonderry to Belfast road. It was built in 1796, and dedicated to the Holy Trinity. There is a fine battlemented tower with two louvers in each wall of the upper storey. The central part of the exterior south wall projects slightly from the rest of the wall, and the roof section above is gabled. This architectural feature has caused the church to be a listed building. In the porch, there is a new staircase to the gallery. The tiling commemorates William Simpson who died in 1979. The baptistery is on the north side of the nave, below the gallery. In it, the chairs, prayer desk, font cover, books and carpet were the gift of Canon Gordon Anderson, Rector 1957-1994, and Mrs Anderson, in memory of their son, Gordon, who died in an accident on 13th May 1961. The vestry room is half way along the north wall. The window in it has rectangular panes, and the inscription, "thy Word is truth". The pulpit is on the left of the nave. The three choir pews on the left commemorate Rebecca Simpson, 1976, and the two on the right, James Anderson and David Miller, 1976. The lectern, which is a white marble eagle on a green marble orb, standing on a brown marble pillar, is both unusual and striking. The prayer desk on the right is in memory of Robert Glenn, 1967, and that on the left is in memory of William Thomas Bond, 1967. The organ, with one manual and pedals, is on the right side of the nave. The altar was presented by Mr and Mrs W.R. Hamilton in 1963, and the credence table was presented in the same year by Mr and Mrs S. Collins. There are two chairs in the sanctuary.

There are three windows in the south wall. Each window has two lights and a small circular light above. The first window has on the left, "The Holy Ghost came upon them", and on the right, "Sir, what must I do to be saved?" The second window illustrates the text, "Come unto me all ye that labour" on the left, and "He that liveth and believeth in me shall never die" on the right. The third window is beside the organ. It is in memory of Major Samuel Galbraith, Madras Staff Corps, who died in 1872. It was erected by his brother, the Rev. George Galbraith, Rector 1867-1883. The east window has three lights and tracery, and shows various figures, illustrating, on the left, *fides,* (faith), *caritas,* (charity), and *spes,* (hope).

On the north wall, there is a monument to Samuel Lyle of Oaks Lodge who died in 1868, and one to Acheson Lyle, HML, who died in 1870, and his wife Eleanor who died in 1876. Felton Hervey who died in 1861, and Colonel James Cox of the Royal Engineers who died in 1880, Samuel Lyle who died in 1815, his wife Esther who died in 1844, and

James Acheson who died in 1830 and his wife Sarah who died in 1836 are all commemorated. On the east wall, there is a monument to James Acheson Lyle, DL of the Oaks who died in 1907, and his wife Ida who died in 1904, and on the other side of the sanctuary, there is a memorial to Lt. Col. James Galbraith who died in 1880. The Acheson Lyle family mausoleum is in the adjoining churchyard.

## DERG, CASTLEDERG, St. JOHN

Derg, *"the oak wood"*, is a parish which is centered in the west Tyrone town of Castlederg. The ancient church was reported to be in ruins in 1619, when it was rebuilt by Sir John Davis. This was destroyed in 1641, and it remained in ruins until 1731 when the nave of the present church was built by Hugh Edwards of Castle Gore.

It is certain that the tower at the west end of Derg church is older than the nave, as it is more Elizabethan or Jacobean in architectural style. It presumably survives from the old church. It has a fine classical doorway which is flanked by free-standing Tuscan columns, and it is surmounted by a high pediment with a crest carved upon it.

*Derg Church.*

Inside the porch, the entrance door to the nave is surmounted by a round-headed archway with the Latin inscription, *"auspiciis Domini resurgo"*, which can be translated, "by the favours of God, I rise", and the date 1731. The architrave has floral patterns and acanthus leaves on an ogee moulding. The door is in memory of William and Fanny Harper, 1959. The sections of panelling in the porch were donated in memory of Mary Jane Bogle, Samuel and Rebecca Loughlin, Joseph and Elizabeth Milligan, Jack Cummings, Jack Cooper, Harry Dougal RN, and Samuel and Lilian Walls. The tiling on the floor of the porch was the gift of Colonel and Mrs Carr, 1971, the floodlighting is in memory of Ronald Finlay and the retaining wall in the churchyard is in memory of Leslie McNutt, 1992. To the left of the porch is the Smyly Room which was built in 1971 to commemorate John Denis Ferguson Smyly who died in 1941, and his father, uncle and grandfather.

The window over the west entrance to the nave depicts the Lamb of God. The nave is of five bays, and to the left is the north aisle. They are joined by four arches. On the south nave wall, the first window, which is in the baptistery, depicts St.John, and the second is of square-paned opaque glass with an inset depicting St.Luke. The third window was donated in 1959, and shows Jesus blessing the children. It is in memory of Andrew McCready who died in 1957. The fourth window depicts St. Mark, and the fifth, St.Matthew. In the west aisle wall, there is a round window, and there are five windows with opaque glass in the north aisle wall. The window in the east aisle wall has three lights and tracery. The east window has three lights of coloured diamond glass, and the middle section has an inset depicting the Lamb of God.

The baptistery is in the south-west corner of the nave. The font was presented by the children of the Sunday School in 1931. There is a stone pulpit on the right side, and a prayer desk on the left. The Conacher organ has two manuals and pedals. The blower was presented by the Mothers Union in 1954. In the sanctuary, the panelling on the south side commemorates those who fell in the Great War, and that on the north side, those who fell in the Second World War.

On the south wall, a monument commemorates the Rev. Edward Edwards, JP who died in 1881. He was perpetual curate of Derg, 1849-1880. Adjacent is an inscription in his memory which was erected by his daughter. On the same wall, a monument commemorates Lt. Col. Edwards and Lt. Edwards who died in 1884. It is surmounted by a crest. There is also a memorial to William King Edwards, DL who died in 1912. On the west wall, there is a brass memorial to those who were killed whilst serving in the Royal Ulster Constabulary and with the Ulster Defence Regiment. There is a record of the donation of £300 to the church by Major John Smyly in 1896. On the north wall, a memorial commemorates Sir Robert Ferguson Bart., MP for Londonderry who died in 1860, and other members of the family. On the aisle north wall, the Rev. Archibald Hamilton, perpetual curate of Derg, 1808-1849 is commemorated along with other family members.

## DESERTMARTIN, St.COMGHALL

DESERTMARTIN VILLAGE is near Magherafelt in Co. Derry. The name means, *"the desert"*, or *"hermitage of Martin"*. St. Martin is supposed to have been an uncle of St. Patrick. In 1622, the church was in reasonable repair, though its fortunes fluctuated during the 17th century. By 1818, the church was in bad repair.

***Desertmartin Church.***

The present church at Dromore, just outside Desertmartin, was built in 1820. It is entered through the porch at the base of the tower. The little window in the west wall of the porch has opaque lattice panes, with a Bible inset, and the words, "Thy Word is a lamp to my feet", (Psalm 119:105).

Inside, the wide north transept, with its big, four-light decorated window, was added by Welland and Gillespie in 1869. In the south wall of the nave, are four windows with two lights, and Y tracery. Each has clear lattice glass. Opposite in the north wall are two identical windows, as well as two with opaque lattice glass in the west wall of the transept. The east window has three lights and tracery, and depicts the Good Shepherd. It commemorates John Albert and Mary Jane McGuckin, 1979.

***The Chancel.***

The vestry room is to the left of the sanctuary. The wooden ceiling and its support pillars over the chancel, are striking. The stone reredos in the sanctuary contains niches, which continue on both sides right round the chancel. The font is in the transept. The bowl is in memory of Edward David Crosby, 1975. The Holy Table commemorates Henry and Margaret Charles, and was dedicated in 1968. The pulpit is on the left of the chancel. Adjacent to it is the lectern, and the prayer desk is on the right. The organ of 1970 commemorates the Rev. John Nesbitt, Rector of Desertmartin, 1944-1964.

The memorials to those who served in the first and second World Wars are in the porch. On the south wall, there is a memorial to those who fell in the Great War, as well as a memorial to Samuel Alan Victor Caskey of the Royal Ulster Constabulary who was killed in 1982. The picture

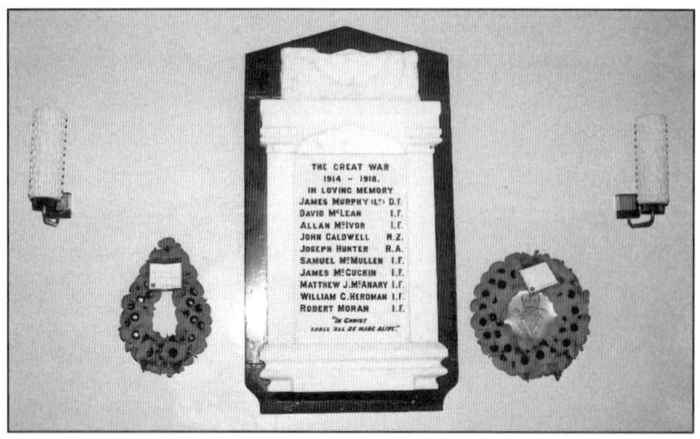


*World War I Memorial, Desertmartin.*

of the Last Supper over the west door, commemorates William Wallace who died in 1996. On the north wall, there is a memorial to L/Sgt. Allan Chambers of the Royal Ulster Rifles who was killed in Normandy in 1944. On the north wall of the sanctuary, a memorial commemorates the Venerable Edward James Hamilton, Archdeacon of Derry, and Rector of Desertmartin from 1868 until his death in 1896.

Desertmartin Rectory was built in 1831. It is a fine two-storey house with a basement and outhouses.

## DONAGHEADY, DONEMANA, St. JAMES

Donagheady, "the church of St. Caidinus", is a parish in north-west Co. Tyrone. The parish church is in the village of Donemana, eighteen kilometres from Londonderry. Caidinus was one of the companions of Columbanus. As was usual, the church was ruined at the time of the 1641 rebellion, but was in reasonable repair by 1768. A new church, dedicated to St. Michael was built in 1788 near the ruin of the old one. It had a small cupola and a bell. It was in bad repair by 1879.

*Donagheady Church.*

The present fine church was built in 1879, and was consecrated on 28th November that year by Bishop Alexander with the dedication St. James. It is cruciform, with nave, transepts and chancel. The three-storey tower with finials, and a tall slender spire stand at the junction of the north transept and chancel. The entrance porch is at the north-west corner. The vestry room is to the right of the chancel.

The window in the west wall has three lights, the centre light being taller than the other two. Each has both square and lattice opaque glass. In the north wall, there are two windows of two lights, the first of which depicts St. Barnabas, in memory of Christopher Danton, MRCVS. The second window has diamond, opaque glass. On the left is the text, "Thy Word is a lamp unto my feet", and on the right, "Thy Word is truth". It commemorates the Rev. John Boden, Rector of Donagheady, 1971-1977. In the south nave wall, are three windows with two lights each. The first, opposite the porch entrance door has both lattice and square-paned opaque glass. The middle window shows Jesus, with the text, "full of good works", and is in memory of Louise Danton who died in 1984. The left section also has Girls' Friendly Society emblems, and the right section has the Mothers' Union Logo. The third window has coloured and opaque latice glass. The left section depicts *Agnus Dei,* the Lamb of God, and the right section, the Dove of the Holy Spirit. It commemorates John McKeegan, A Company, 6th Co. Tyrone Ulster Defence Regiment, who was murdered in 1981. The window in the south wall of the south transept has three lights and tracery, with opaque lattice and square glass. The window opposite in the north transept is similar, and was donated by the parish Indoor Bowling Club, 1997. The east window is particularly fine. It depicts the Ascension, and consists of five stained glass lights, the central one of which is the tallest. There are two lights to the sides, and geometric tracery, all in stained glass round the top of the window. It was erected in 1894 in memory of James Clark, JP, father of Canon Frederick James Clark, Rector of Donagheady, from 1871 until his death in 1897. The Communion rails were also erected in 1894. Canon Clark built Dunnalong district church in 1865, during his time as curate of Donagheady from 1863 to 1865, then as incumbent of Dunnalong, 1865-1871.

The chancel ceiling is painted blue with gold stars as decoration. The panelling in the sanctuary was erected in 1894. The Holy Table commemorates James Dunn JP, and his wife, Rachel, 1964. The font is below the chancel steps to the right. On it is carved the name of William Hamilton, Church Warden, 1684. The pulpit on the left commemorates Canon Frederick Clark. The brass lectern beside the pulpit is in memory of the Rev. George John Thomas, Rector from 1860 until his death in 1871, and of his wife Harriet who died in 1883. There is a prayer desk on each side of the chancel. The chair on the right is in memory of Canon Samuel Chadwick, Rector 1943-1959. There is an electronic organ with two manuals and pedals, which was purchased "in memory of loved ones" in 1994.

In the sanctuary, on the north wall, there is a memorial to Louisa Augusta, wife of James Clark, JP, who died in 1878. On the south sanctuary wall, monuments commemorate Canon Clark's wife, Margaret Katherine who died in 1877, and their sons, James who died in 1898 and Frederick who died in 1911. On the south wall of the nave, there is a monument to William Hamilton, Medical Officer for Donemana district who died in 1932, and his wife, Jane, who died in 1936. A plaque records the installation of the lighting in memory of the parents of Margaret Hamilton, and there is a memorial to Margaret Katharine Hamilton who died in 1872. On the west wall, the list of the Rectors' and People's Church Wardens of Donagheady from 1988/89, was presented by the parish branch of the Mothers' Union on the occasion of their fiftieth anniversary.

On the north wall of the nave, there is a memorial to Captain J. Gatchell, MC, RAMC, son of the Rev. James Henry Gatchell, Rector 1897 to 1923, and Mrs Gatchell. Captain Gatchell was killed at Passchendaele in 1917 during the Great War. On the east wall of the south transept, is the memorial to those who served, and who fell in the Great War, and on the corresponding wall of the north transept is the memorial to those who served, and who fell in the second World War.

## DRUMACHOSE, LIMAVADY, CHRIST CHURCH

LIMAVADY, COUNTY LONDONDERRY, is an important market town on the River Roe, at the foot of the Sperrin Mountains. The name means, *"the leap of the dog"*. The parish name of Drumachose means, *"the ridge of the rent (or tithe)"*. The patron saint was Canice who was born in the area about 517 A.D. The Convention of Drumceatt which was held about 575, was attended by St. Columba who returned from Iona to be present. The ancient church was at Fruithill in the Drenagh estate, and its ruins are still visible.

*Drumachose Church.*

At the time of the Plantation of Ulster from 1609, Sir Thomas Phillips allocated lands in the Roe Valley to the Haberdashers', Fishmongers' and Skinners' Companies. He established a town called Newtown Limavady near the ancient settlement of Ballyclose. It received a charter in 1613.

In the 1622 survey, the church was in ruins. A church was built some time before the 1641 rebellion, but was badly damaged at that time. In records of 1736, the church is referred to as Christ Church. It was rebuilt on the same site in 1750.

During major renovations in 1881, the south transept, the chancel, organ chamber, vestry room and north porch were added to the church, along with several new windows. The old church walls were raised and a new roof was put on. It was consecrated on 1st December 1881.

Drumachose Church has a lofty, four-storey tower which was built in 1749. The north transept was built in 1824. There is a small circular window in the porch at the base of the tower. Inside is the stairway to the gallery. A plaque in the porch states that the lighting in the church is in memory of Major J. A. Ritter, and another plaque states that the bell was electrified in memory of Robert Connor, Rector's Churchwarden, 1954-1966. The table in the porch is in memory of Police Constable Norman Kennedy who died in 1987.

Inside, the church design is cruciform, with nave, transepts and chancel. The gallery over the west end has five depictions of scenes from the Passion of our Lord, made of sticks and pieces of metal on soft board background. On the north wall, are three windows with diamond-paned opaque glass and tracery. On the south wall, the first window is similar. The second window depicts, on the left, St. Columba, and on the right, St.Canice, and is in memory of Alexander Boyle of Bridge House who died in 1920, and of his wife. The third window depicts the Ten Commandments on the left, and the New Law on the right. It commemorates John, Alfred and Margaret Ritter, 1950. In the west wall of the south transept, there is a window with diamond opaque glass. The window in the south wall of the south transept has three lights, and depicts the Parable of the Good Samaritan. It is in memory of Samuel Alexander, D.L., of Roe Park, 1887. The window in the east wall of the transept depicts on the left, Christ the Light of the World, and on the right, the Raising of Lazarus. It is in memory of Conolly McCausland, JP, DL, of Drenagh who died in 1902.

In the north transept, west wall, there is a diamond, opaque window. The rose window in the north wall of the transept has floral patterns. At its centre is the Dove of the Holy Spirit. It commemorates Robert Macrory who died in 1890. The window in the north transept east wall depicts the raising of the widow's son at Nain, and is in memory of John Boyle and his mother, Mary Ann, both of whom died in 1890. The east window has three lights and shows, in the tracery at the top, the Ascension. Below, on the left side of the window, are the angels of the Nativity, in the middle, Jesus with the children, and on the right, the Risen Christ. The window commemorates William Ross and Mary Ross.

The baptistery is in the north transept. There is a second font in the south transept. The three marble steps up to the chancel are in memory of Frederick Trench of the London Scottish Regiment who was killed in 1916. The chancel is entered through a splendidly carved stone archway, which has upon it, various celtic figures and symbols. At the apex is a leaping dog, from which Limavady gets its name! The organ chamber is on the left, and the vestry room is to the right. The pulpit on the left is in memory of the Rev. John Olphert, Rector of Drumachose from 1820 until his death in 1851. The brass eagle lectern commemorates Hugh and Mary Lane, 1881. The prayer desk on the left of the chancel is in memory of members of the Ogilby Family, and the prayer desk on the right is in memory of Samuel Stirling, 1913. The panelling at the front of the pews in the south transept is in memory of Conolly McCausland and his wife, the Hon.Laura St.John 1828-1919. The panelling in the chancel and sanctuary is very fine. It extends to form a canopy over the vestry door, and altogether, it was carved by the Rev. Richard King, Rector 1904-1921, who became Dean of Derry. The Lord's Prayer is carved on the section of panelling by the organ chamber. The altar is particularly finely carved, and it commemorates Dean King's son, Robert, of the Royal Dublin Fusiliers, who was killed at Ypres in 1915. The cross on the altar was

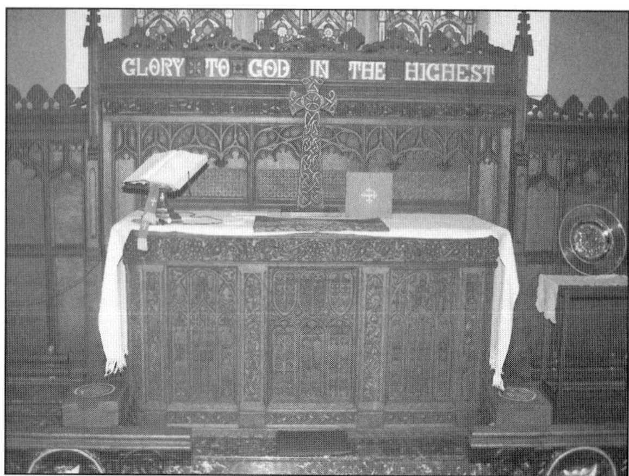

*Altar and Sanctuary.*

carved in 1967 by another son of Dean King, Major Travers King. The two small prayer desks in the sanctuary were given in memory of Sybil Hunter, 1989. The organ has two manuals and pedals, with a detached console. It was installed in 1881 in memory of Canon (later Dean) Andrew Ferguson Smyly, Rector, 1880-1883, and of his wife.

*1st World War Memorial.*

*Section of 1st World War Memorial Monument.*

There are several fine memorials and monuments. The monuments commemorating those who fell in the Great War are on the north wall of the nave in three sections. They are of Bath stone, and stand three metres high. The first section contains on the left, a general war memorial, and on the right, a memorial to Samuel Harrison who was killed in 1918. The second section contains on the left, a memorial to Frederick Trench who was killed in 1916, and on the right, J. Proctor who was killed in 1916, is commemorated. On the third section, there are four parts, commemorating James Bearley, 1915, William Predy, 1917, Robert King, son of Dean King, 1915, and Cecil King, who died in 1916. Over the top of each section are the names of Great War battles, and all who fell are commemorated on a frieze at the base which runs along the whole length of the monument. In the north transept, west wall, are memorials to Lesley Alexander who died in 1852 and to Robert Ogilby, M.D., 1817, and his wife and daughter. On the north wall of the north transept, Rev. George Stuart, Rector 1851-1869, and Rev. John Olphert, Rector 1820-1851, are commemorated. On the east wall of the north transept, Lt. John Olphert, R.N., son of the Rector, who died in 1844, and Henry Tyler who built the organ chamber, are commemorated.

In the south wall of the nave, there are monuments commemorating Conolly McCausland of Drenagh who died in 1902, Dr.Benjamin Lane who died in 1922, Capt. Anthony Boyle, Royal Inniskilling Fusiliers who was killed in the second World War in 1943, and Mary McCausland who died in 1790. On the west wall are memorials to Dr. Stanley Monck, Archdeacon of Derry, and Rector of Drumachose, 1751-1768, who died in 1785, and to Edward Boyle who died in 1925.

In the south transept, east wall, Samuel Maxwell Alexander, JP., DL, who died in 1886 is commemorated. There is a memorial to Thomas Fleming who died in 1890, and to Catherine King who died in 1865. On the south transept, south wall are memorials to Alexander Alexander who died in 1832, and to John Campbell who died in 1821, and to his wife. On the west wall of the south transept,

John Moody who died in 1840, and Marion, daughter of Henry Taylor, who died in 1843, are commemorated.

To the left of the north transept, there is a suite of rooms which were dedicated in 1967 in memory of Canon Douglas White, Rector 1936-1963. These contain a room which is used both as a chapel for daily services, and a choir practice room. The stained glass window in it is in memory of Norman Simpson, Organist of Drumachose for many years. The parish halls were built close to the church in 1969. Miss Jane Ross, who discovered and preserved the famous tune, "the Londonderry Air", is buried in the graveyard.

## DRUMCLAMPH, CLARE, St. ANDREW'S CHAPEL OF EASE

Drumclamph, *"the hill of the lepers",* is a parish in west Tyrone, near Castlederg, on the banks of the Derg River. It is also known as Crew. The parish was formed as a perpetual curacy out of its neighbour, Ardstraw in 1838, and it attained full parochial status in 1877.

*Drumclamph Church.*

Drumclamph church was built in 1846. It is entered through a porch in the west wall, which, along with the vestry room, was built in 1868. The window in the porch has coloured glass, with an inset depicting the sower sowing seed. Inside, the spacious gallery was erected in 1993. The stairs to it are to the left. The two windows in the north wall have insets depicting Jesus with the children, and Jesus, the Carpenter. The two windows in the south wall have insets depicting the Empty Tomb, and three crowns. The east window depicts, in the upper section, the Last Supper, and in the lower section, grapes, a cup and bread, the food and drink of the Eucharist. It is in memory of Andrew Scott who died in 1982.

The vestry room is to the left of the sanctuary. The window in it is in memory of Francis Hamilton who died in 1985, and it depicts the Good Shepherd. The altar has an inscrition, "for mercies received, F. M. Hamilton 1935". The pulpit on the right of the sanctuary was erected by Mrs Leitch in memory of her husband, 1935. The lectern on the left was presented by Col. G.Carr, M.C. in 1953. The font is adjacent to it. The prayer desk is on the left of the sanctuary.

There is a memorial on the north sanctuary wall to Thomas Martin Leitch who died in 1933. On the south wall, a memorial commemorates Private William Victor Foster, 6th Ulster Defence Regiment who was killed in 1986.

In the early days, just after the separation of Drumclamph from Ardstraw, there were two or more centres of worship in the area. One of these was at Clare. It is possible that worship was going on there as early as 1810 in a building which was used jointly as a school and as a chapel of ease. Until 1996, the parishioners at Clare worshipped in the upper floor of a building which had also housed the school until it closed in 1959. This was demolished and replaced

*Drumclamph/Clare Church (demolished).*

with a lovely new church, dedicated to St. Andrew, which was consecrated on 21st February 1997. At the west end is a tower which is capped by a pyramid. At its base is the entrance porch. Inside, there are four windows of clear glass on each side, and an east window of three lights depicting the Last Supper. The pulpit is to the left in the sanctuary. It was given in 1957 by parishioners of a redundant church. There are two prayer desks, one of which was donated by William and Valerie Crowe, 1981. The sanctuary chair commemorates James Rankin and his wife, 1988.

On the south side of the church, there is a suite of rooms which are used as a vestry, and for Sunday School and church meetings.

*Drumclamph/Clare Chapel of Ease.*

## DRUMRAGH, OMAGH, St. COLUMBA

*Drumragh Church, Omagh, before 1871.*

DRUMRAGH PARISH, whose name means, *"the ridge of the fort"*, is situated around Omagh, the County Town of Tyrone. The Drumragh and Camowen rivers meet in Omagh to continue north-westwards as the River Strule.

There was a Fransciscan friary dating from 1464 in the area. A mediaeval castle, the *Oigh Maigh*, which means, *"the virgin plain"*, gave its name to the town. In 1622, the church in Omagh was reported to be in ruins, but it was hoped that a new one would soon be built. However, with the 1641 Rebellion, no progress was possible. A church was erected in 1777 by the Mervyn Family. They had been granted land around Omagh by Charles I in 1631. This building was enlarged with the addition of a north aisle and galleries in 1820, at the expense of the Bishop of Derry, Dr. Knox.

The present Parish Church of Drumragh was consecrated on 20th October 1871 by Bishop William Alexander, with the dedication St. Columba. Standing at the highest point in the town of Omagh, it is an impressive building. It is cruciform, with nave, north and south aisles, transepts and chancel. The tower in the north-west corner is surmounted by a spire. There are two entrance porches, one at the base of the tower, and the other opposite in the south-west corner. Inside the church, the north and south aisles are separated

# Church Buildings and Furnishings

MANY CHURCHES ARE simple rectangular halls, whereas others are larger and more complex buildings. In this volume, technical architectural terminology has been kept to the barest possible minimum. A full and excellent glossary of such terms can be found in *North West Ulster* by Alistair Rowan, pages 509 to 534. The most usual features of the building are:

**Tower:** usually at the west end with a porch in the base. It can be of three or more storeys, with louvered windows, and finials, or little pyramids, and battlements along the top. Many towers are surmounted by a spire.

**Gallery:** a short upper storey over the west end of the nave, and sometimes along the sides of the nave, which contains pews. It is accessible by a staircase in the porch or west end of the church.

**Nave:** from the Latin *navis,* a ship, the main body of the church where the congregation worships.

**Transept:** an area to the right and/or left of the east end of the nave

**Crossing:** the area where the nave, transepts and chancel meet.

**Chancel:** the area to the east of the nave, usually raised above it by three or more steps, which contains the reading desks and choir stalls, and sometimes, the pulpit.

**Sanctuary:** the area to the east of the nave or chancel which contains the altar. It is usually separated from the rest of the church by the communion rails. Many sanctuaries have fine wooden or marble panelling.

**Vestry:** a room, usually to the side of the chancel, where the clergy robe.

Every church has most or all of the following items of furniture and other things which are necessary for the orderly conduct of the Divine Worship of Almighty God.

## Furnishings:

**Altar/Holy Table:** a table, usually placed against the east wall of the sanctuary, though sometimes free-standing, for the celebration of the Holy Eucharist or Communion. The use of the term *altar* implies the participation of the faithful in the once-for-all and irrepeatable Sacrifice of Christ upon the Cross.

**Aumbry;** a small recess in the sanctuary wall for the reservation of the Blessed Sacrament.

**Font:** a large bowl, usually of stone which holds water for Holy Baptism. Some fonts have carved wooden covers. Most are hexagonal in shape, and stand on a pillar. They are usually placed near the entrance of the church.

**Lectern:** a stand for the Bible, from which the Holy Scriptures are read. They are usually made of wood or brass, and many have eagles for the book rest, symbolising the swift carrying forth of the Word of God.

**Organ:** a keyboard musical instrument, sometimes with foot pedals, with one or more manuals. Some are pipe organs, others are electronic.

**Piscina;** a basin built into the wall for disposing of water which has been used for rinsing chalices, etc.

**Prayer Desk/Prie Dieu:** a desk, usually made of wood or stone, and normally placed in the chancel or choir for the reading of Morning and Evening Prayer. There are often small prayer desks in the sanctuary.

**Pulpit:** a structure of wood or stone from which the sermon is preached in church. Some pulpits are elaborately carved.

## Communion Vessels

These are almost always made of precious metal, silver, pewter or silver plate. Many are very old.

**Flagon:** a large jug which contains wine which at the Offertory, is poured into the chalice.

**Chalice:** a cup from which the congregation receives the consecrated Wine, the Blood of Christ, at Holy Communion.

**Paten:** a plate on which is placed the Bread for Holy Communion.

**Bread Box:** a box in which bread for Holy Communion is placed until required.

*Drumragh Church.*

from the nave by three arches. In the north transept, the choir seats are tiered upwards to the level of the transept window. To the left of the chancel, are various parish rooms, and to the right, is the vestry room.

The westwards extension of the nave contains both the font and a small altar for daily use. The font is in memory of Sub Lt. Anthony Bassett, RNVR who was killed in 1944. The panelling in this area commemorates Lancelot Studholme who was killed in 1916.

*Baptistry, Drumragh Church.*

The marble panelling round the chancel and sanctuary is in memory of Hans Beresford Fleming and his sister Harriette, 1923. The High Altar, and the reredos, which depicts the Last Supper, were erected in memory of Col. Lewis Buchanan. The prayer desks on either side of the sanctuary were donated by the parish Bowling Club in 1971.

*Drumragh Church, Omagh, interior.*

There are two prayer desks in the chancel. The pulpit on the right is in memory of Emily Brown, 1899. The brass eagle lectern commemorates Thomas Houston who died in 1855, Claude Houston who died in 1862 and Charlotte Houston who died in 1879. There is a three manual Conacher organ with pedals. The detached console is at the entrance to the north transept, and the organ is in the north transept.

Drumragh Parish Church has some very fine stained glass windows. The great west window has four lights with geometrically patterned circles above. It depicts eight of our Lord's parables from the New Testament. Below it are five small windows which depict from left to right, SS. Matthew, Mark, Paul, Luke and John. These windows commemorate Samuel Galbraith of Clanabogan who died in 1864. In the north aisle wall, there are three windows with coloured glass. One of these commemorates Hans Fleming, MD, 1887. In the west wall of the north transept, a stained glass window commemorates Charles and Margaret Stack, 1874. In the north wall of the north transept, the first window depicts St. John the Evangelist, and it is in memory of Edward Stack who died in 1867. The middle window, which has two lights, depicts St. Columba at the top. Amongst other figures in the window, there is a scribe. The third window depicts further Biblical scenes.

There are three windows in the south aisle. The middle one illustrates the theme of Love, and is in memory of Charlotte and Tempe Bagot. The other two have coloured glass. In the west wall of the south transept, the window depicts the Parable of the Sheep and the Goats, (St. Matthew 25:31-46), and is in memory of Ralph Stone who died in 1903. There are four windows in the south wall of the south transept. The first is in memory of Francis West, MD who died in 1880, and depicts the Good Samaritan. The second, which has two lights, depicts various New Testament scenes, and is in memory of Col. Montague Browne who died in 1919, and of his wife Meta who died in 1883. The third, which also has two lights, depicts more New Testament scenes, and commemorates Major Burleigh Stuart who died in 1905. The fourth window is in memory of Henry Thompson who died in 1875.

The east window has four lights and elaborate tracery. As it dates from 1862, it came from the old church. It depicts amongst others, four saints, and four of the seven acts of mercy, and is in memory of Thomas Stack who died in 1859.

On the south wall, a plaque records the donation of heating in memory of Kathleen Boyd, and the restoration of the windows in memory of Evelyn Diver, during the renovations to the church in 1990-1992. On the north wall, a plaque records the re-hallowing of the church on 20th October 1992, by the Rt. Rev. James Mehaffey, Bishop of Derry and Raphoe, following these renovations. On the first pillar of the north transept arch, a monument commemorates Constance Buchanan who died in 1935, and on the west wall of the north transept, there is a memorial to Canon Arthur McQuade, Rector of Drumragh from 1914 until his death in 1929. On the north wall of the north transept, there is a memorial to the Rev. William Chartres, Curate of Drumragh, 1859-1870, and Rector, 1875-1893. Canon Charles Cullimore, Rector of Drumragh from 1930 until his death in 1948 is also commemorated.

On the east wall, left of the sanctuary, the maintenance of the organ in memory of Georgina Adams who died in 1977, is recorded on a plaque. There are also memorials to those who fell in the two World Wars. The Second War memorial states that the organ was erected in memory of those who fell.

On the north wall of the chancel, a plaque states that the King's Colours of the 9th (Service) Battalion, the Royal Inniskilling Fusiliers, were raised in County Tyrone in 1914. In the south chancel wall, there is a memorial to soldiers of the 2nd Tyrone Regiment of the Ulster Volunteer Force, afterwards, the 9th Battalion, the Royal Inniskilling Fusiliers, who fell in the Great War. It was presented by Mercia Guy of Omagh in 1918. In the south transept, on the east wall, are two classical monuments. The first commemorates the Rev. William George Stack, Curate of Drumragh, 1833. He died in 1837. The second monument commemorates Dr John Hamilton, Omagh Fever Hospital, who died in 1856. On the south wall of the south transept, there are memorials to Henry Thompson who died in 1907, to Lt. Col. William Thompson, RAMC, who died in 1928, and to Edward Thompson, FRCSI, Surgeon, Tyrone County Hospital, who died in 1933. Emily, his wife, who died in 1938, Private JA Hannigan, who was killed in 1979, and L.Cpl. Newell, Royal Irish Regiment, who was killed in 1991, are also commemorated.

## DUNBOE, ARTICLAVE, St. PAUL
## FERMOYLE, THE CHURCH OF THE ASCENSION

DUNBOE, *"the fort of the cow"*, is a parish on the north coast of County Derry, eight kilometres to the west of Coleraine. The Patron Saint was Adamnan. St. Patrick visited the area, and found that Christianity had already been established, possibly by Scottish settlers. In Mediaeval times, the parish was permanently linked to the Archdeaconry of Derry.

The Clothworkers' Company established the Plantation village of Articlave in 1618-1621. In 1622, the church was reported to be in good order, having been repaired by them. The old church, being distant from the new village, was abandoned. Its ruins can still be seen to the west of Articlave. The present church in Articlave was built in 1691. This was extended by the addition of a pinnacled tower at the west end some time around 1800. Between 1821 and 1825, the walls were raised, the chancel was built, and a vestry room was added to

*Dunboe Church.*

the tower. The sundial in the south wall was installed in 1823. On it is the inscription, "'Tis greatly wise to talk with our past hours, and ask them what report they bore to Heaven". The windows in the north wall, and the gallery, were added in the 1830s.

St. Paul's Church is entered through a door in the south-west corner, which is in memory of Jane and Robert Johnston, 1991. There is a small round window over the door. The vestry room in the base of the tower is to the left, and at the end of the porch are the stairs to the gallery. The vestry door is in memory of Jonathan Wilson, 1991. Inside, the church is a three-bay hall, with the gallery over the west end. The baptistery is in the south-west corner. The pulpit on the left, the altar and reredos were all installed for the tercentenary celebrations of the church on 2nd June 1991. The lectern and organ are on the right side of the nave. The chairs in the sanctuary were the gift of Mrs Macafee in 1953.

The three windows in the north wall each have diamond-paned glass with coloured insets. The first window depicts a Bible and candle, the second, a lion and a lamb, and the third, a cross and crown. On the south side, there are also three windows. The first, by the entrance, has opaque glass. The middle window has an inset depicting the stoning of St.Stephen, and is in memory of Mr and Mrs W.Kennedy, 1991, and the third window depicts St. Paul in Athens in an inset, and commemorates Robert and Elizabeth Warke, 1991. The east window has three lights and tracery. The middle section depicts St. Paul in Miletus (Malta). The window commemorates James Coleman who died in 1934.

The memorial to those who gave their lives in the Great War is on the south wall. On the north wall, there is a memorial to Alexander Coleman who died in 1898, and to his wife and family. A brass plaque on the wall of the baptistery records renovations to the church for the tercentenary celebrations in 1991, which were made possible by a bequest from Miss E. Stinson.

In 1843, the district church of Fermoyle was established with nine townlands from Dunboe. Despite its location in the foothills of the Sperrin Mountains, it was envisaged that Fermoyle Church would be in a town which was to be built between Coleraine and Limavady. This did not materialise, largely due to the famine in the 1840s. Further townlands were detached from Dunboe in 1868 when the parish of Castlerock was established. Also, at Disestablishment in 1870, the Archdeaconry of Derry was separated from Dunboe.

*Fermoyle Church.*

Fermoyle, *"the exposed or abutting round hill",* is a simple church of four bays, which is entered through a small porch. It was dedicated to St.Matthew, but is known as the Church of the Ascension. The four windows on each side are all of clear glass. The prayer desk and lectern are to the left, and the pulpit is on the right. The font is in the middle, in front of the chancel. The chancel has five sides, and three plain windows surround the altar.

On the east wall, to the left of the chancel, there is a monument to the Ven. Thomas Bewley Monsell (1785-1846), who built the church in 1843. Fermoyle ceased to be a perpetual curacy, and was united with its mother church at Dunboe in 1873.

## DUNGIVEN

DUNGIVEN VILLAGE is in County Derry, 31 kilometres from Londonderry on the main Belfast road. One kilometre to the south of the town are the remains of St. Mary's Priory. It is thought that St. Neachtain founded a monastery as early as the 7th century. The O'Cahan tomb is in the ruin, and contains some of the finest mediaeval tracery in the north-west. The priory became Augustinian about 1140, and was suppressed by the beginning of the 17th century.

*Dungiven Church.*

At the time of the Plantation, a church was built by the Skinners' Company on the site of the priory. The fact that the name Dungiven means, *"the fort of the skins"* is coincidental. Its name has also been translated, *"the pleasant mount"*.

A new church was built at the head of the town in 1718. This was replaced by the present church which was built on the same site in 1816. It is cruciform, with nave and transepts, and a louvered tower at the west end. The bell in the tower was the gift of Edward Cary of Dungiven Castle in 1712. The entrance to the church is through the porch at the base of the tower. The window in the west tower wall illustrates the text, "follow me and I will make you fishers of men", and is in memory of Canon John H. Kingston, Rector of Dungiven 1950-1970. In the nave, there is one diamond-paned window with Y tracery on each side, and likewise in the west wall of both transepts. In the north wall of the north transept, a stained glass window of three lights depicts from left to right, Nehemiah, the Good Centurion and Ezra. It commemorates Robert Alexander Ogilby who died in 1902. Opposite in the south wall of the south transept, a window of two lights and tracery, shows the women at the Empty Tomb, in memory of Esther Gladys Ogilby, 1900. The window in the north wall of the chancel depicts Jesus gathering the little children, and it commemorates Jane King who died in 1890, and her daughter. The east window has three lights and tracery. It illustrates the parable of the Sheep and the Goats, and is in memory of James Ogilby who died in 1885.

The baptistery is in the north-west corner of the church. The Holy Table is in memory of John Trewlawny Ross, D.D., Curate of Dungiven from 1876 to 1879 and again from 1883 to 1886. The chairs in the sanctuary are in memory of George and Mary Sharp Ward, 1936. The pulpit is below on the left, and is in memory of Martha Cromie who died in 1944. The prayer desk on the right is in memory of Canon James Kelly, Rector of Dungiven from 1930 to 1950. It and the seat are finely carved, and incorporate the crest of the Diocese of Derry. The brass eagle lectern on the left commemorates the Rev. Alexander Ross, Rector of Banagher and Vicar of Dungiven, 1810 to his death in 1850. The panelling in the sanctuary is of good quality. The organ has two manuals and pedals, and was made by the firm of Forsters and Andrews of Hull in 1878. The cushions in the choir stalls and the lectern microphone were given in memory of Eric Scott who died in 1985.

On the west wall, a monument records various benefactors from the Ogilby family and from the Skinners' Company. The Ogilbys, an old family, resided at Pellipar House near Dungiven. The mausoleum near the main entrance to the church is one of their burying plots. On the south wall, there is a memorial to Lt. Samuel McDonnell Campbell of the 3rd Lancashire Fusiliers who was killed in action in 1916. There is a monument commemorating the Ross family of Springhill, Dungiven on the north wall of the nave.

On the west wall of the north transept, a monument commemorates Canon George Warren, Rector 1886-1930 and his family. On the east wall of the north transept are the memorials to those who fell in the Great War, and to John Semple Moore who died in 1899. On the south wall of the south transept, are the memorials to Mildred Morley, daughter of Robert and Helen Ogilby who died in 1945, and to Mabel Crocker, daughter of Captain R.Ogilby, who died the same year. On the east wall of the south transept, there are memorials to Michael King who died in 1899, to the Rev. Edward French, Rector 1823-1849, and to Esther Ogilby who died in 1900.

A memorial on the east sanctuary wall commemorates Michael King, son of the Rev. John King, Rector of Upper Fahan, who died in 1891, and his wife Matilda. A plaque on the same wall records renovations to the chancel in memory of Canon William Ross, Rector of Dungiven, 1850 to 1886, who died in 1891.

## DUNNALONG, BREADY, St. JOHN

THE PARISH OF Dunnalong is in County Tyrone, on the east bank of the River Foyle, half way between Derry and Strabane. Its name means, *"the fort of the ships"*, as a ferry used to cross the river at the village of Bready. The parish was formed out of the neighbouring parish of Donagheady, and the church was built in 1865. It was consecrated on 1st November 1866.

*Dunnalong Church.*

Dunnalong Church is a distinctive building. It is built of stone with coloured brick trim, and it has a steeply pitched roof. There is a bellcote at the west end. At the east end of the south wall, a transept is now used as a porch with a vestry room and other rooms above it. The transept has a double lattice window with a trefoil light overhead. There is a porch in the south-west corner.

In the west wall, there are two windows with opaque lattice glass, and four coloured panes, with geometric tracery above. The first of two windows in the south wall of the nave, has two lights and similar design. The second window has Psalm 150:6, "let everything that hath breath praise the Lord", and is in memory of Warren Wallace who died in 1990. The three windows in the north wall have lattice panes and four coloured panes each. The east window has three lights and geometric tracery, and the text, "follow me and I will make you fishers of men". Jesus is depicted alongside ships and fishing nets. The window commemorates Samuel and Isabel Sheerin, 1989.

At the west porch entrance, inside the nave, a wooden partition is surmounted by four glass sections. These from right to left are engraved with illustrations and texts, showing the Manger, Golgotha, the Empty Tomb and Christ's promise to be present until the end of the age. Opposite, in the north-west corner, is the baptistery. The font bowl was given in memory of George and Mary Fulton. The pulpit is on the left of the nave, and the prayer desk is to the right. Both are in the chancel, and below the prayer desk is the lectern. Beside the lectern is a new electronic organ with two manuals and pedals. In the sanctuary, above the nave, the altar is in memory of Samuel and Irwin Faulkner, 1999. The chairs in the sanctuary are in memory of Leslie Hamilton of the Ulster Defence Regiment, 1982.

The memorial to those who fell in the Great War is on the north wall, as is the memorial to Jim Ballantine who died at sea in 1893. On the south wall, there is a memorial to William McCrea who died in 1873, and to his wife who died in 1890.

Dunnalong Church underwent extensive renovations in 1998.

## EDENDERRY

EDENDERRY, *"the brow of the oak"*, is a parish just to the south of Omagh. The parish church is five kilometres from Omagh, close to the Omagh to Monaghan road. It was consecrated on 23rd June 1847, after the parish was separated from Cappagh as a perpetual curacy. The chancel was built in 1877.

Edenderry church is a three-bay hall with a bellcote, and a porch at the west end, and a sanctuary at the east end. The vestry room, with a lower basement floor, is to the left of the sanctuary. In the porch, there are doors on two sides, and the window, depicting the Wedding at Cana in Galilee was the gift of the Rev. Robert Clarke, Rector from 1987, and his wife Kay and their children. In the nave, the baptistery is in the north-west corner. The font is in memory of Major Thomas Auchinleck, DL, who died in 1893. The pulpit on the left, and the prayer desk on the right, commemorate the Rev. Matthew Francis Moriarty, Rector of Edenderry, 1898-1919. The lectern, which is in the centre, below the three chancel steps, is in memory of Catherine, wife of the Rev. W. Bond, Rector of Ballee, Co. Down, and mother of Alessie, wife of the Rev. Henry Faussett, Rector 1872-1885. She was a hymn writer, and she died in 1884. The table in front of the lectern is in memory of Rhona Moriarty, 1959. The Communion rails commemorate the Rev. Henry Faussett, and the hand rails on the chancel steps were presented in memory of John Anthony who died in 1992. In the sanctuary, the altar is in memory of Jane, wife of Major Thomas Auchinleck. The chairs in the sanctuary were presented by the Rt. Rev. Packenham Walsh DD, Bishop of Ossory, to the Rev. Henry Faussett. The small prayer desk and chair in the sanctuary were presented in thanksgiving for the Ordination of the Rev. Robert Lee in 1978.

The east window has three lights, the middle one being taller than the others, and there are circular lights on each side of it. Our Lord is depicted in the centre with the text, "he that believeth in me hath everlasting life", and it is in memory of Alexander Laughlin who died in 1951. In the north wall of the nave, the first window,

*Edenderry Church.*

which is in the baptistery, depicts a font. It commemorates Joseph Ewing who died in 1978, and his wife Maude who died in 1986. The second window depicts the River Jordan, which is inspired by the Camowen River in the parish. It illustrates the themes of Creation, Incarnation, the Cross and Resurrection, with a dove overhead. It was presented by the Pollock family. The third window shows the Good Shepherd, and commemorates Major Thomas Auchinleck who died in 1893. In the south wall by the entrance, the first window has square clear glass. The second window depicts a church, and is in memory of William Todd who died in 1999, and his wife Winifred who died in 1991. The third window shows the Sower sowing seed, and commemorates Armour Young who died in 1964. The nave windows all have Y tracery.

Several monuments in Edenderry Church commemorate the Auchinlecks, who were a distinguished military family. Their ancestral home was Crevenagh, Omagh. On the west wall, there is a brass plaque which records the installation of lighting in the nave in memory of Tom Todd, 1950. A brass plaque records gifts to the church in the year 2000. There is a memorial to Field Marshal Sir Claude John Eyre Auchinleck, GCB, GCIE, CSI, DSO, DBG, who died in 1981. On the north wall of the nave, there is a memorial to A. Auchinleck who was killed at the Somme in 1916, as well as a memorial to Brigadier General William Auchinleck of the Bengal Army. He served in the Indian Mutiny of 1858-1859. Memorials on the north wall commemorate Major Daniel Auchinleck, 21st Royal Scots Fusiliers who died in Burma in 1886, Lt. Col. Ralph Auchinleck Darling of the Royal Corps of Signals and the Royal Inniskilling Fusiliers and High Sheriff of Tyrone who died in 1958, and Daniel Eccles Auchinleck who died in 1849, and his wife Elizabeth who died in 1888.

On the east wall, left of the sanctuary, the Sebastopol Marbles, three stones which were brought from the Crimean War in 1856 by Captain Bond, were erected by his sisters in 1884. To the right of the sanctuary, a plaque records the donation of cushions in the choir pews in memory of William Knox who died in 1997. On the south wall of the nave, there is a memorial to Canon Joseph Davidson, Rector of Edenderry from 1919 to 1947, who died in 1951. A plaque records the restoration of the church in 1877 during the incumbency of the Rev. Henry Faussett. Below it is a plaque which contains in it, the collecting plate which Mr Faussett used whilst raising funds. The plaque also contains a poem by his wife, Alessie. The plaque which commemorates those who fell in the two World Wars, was erected to mark the year 2000.

## ERRIGAL, GARVAGH, St. PAUL DESERTOGHILL

ERRIGAL, *"the oratory"*, was in ancient times associated with St. Adamnan, or Eunan, who was its patron. The parish is situated in east County Londonderry, half way between Maghera and Coleraine. Its principal town is Garvagh. The ancient church was in the townland of Ballintemple nearby, close to St. Onan's (Eunan's) rock. St. Columba is supposed to have founded a monastery about 589, which flourished until the Danish invasions in the ninth century.

At the time of the Plantation, the old church was replaced with a new one in the Plantation town of Garvagh. As usual, it suffered considerable damage during the 1641 rebellion.

The present church in Garvagh was built by the Canning family in 1670. Their monuments are in the church. The church is entered through a small west porch, over the entrance door of which is the date of the erection of the church, 1670. The doors in the porch commemorate James and Martha Torrens. The chancel was built in the tercentenary year of the church, 1970, which was also the centenary of the Disestablishment of the Church of Ireland. It was consecrated on St. Columba's Day, 9th June 1970 by Bishop Cuthbert Irvine Peacocke. A plaque on the chancel arch records this. The gallery is over the west end, and the vestry room is to the left of the nave.

There are two small windows in the west wall, on either side of the entrance door, and a larger window over the door, which has two lights with coloured and patterned glass and Y tracery. There

*Errigal Church.*

is a bellcote over the west wall. In both north and south walls of the nave are three windows with two lights and Y tracery and clear lattice glass. In the south wall, the first window commemorates Robert Alexander and Robert McMillan. The second window commemorates James and Joanne Torrens, and the third window is in memory of Robert Watt and his son, Arthur. In the north wall, the first window commemorates Arthur and Margaret Church. The second window is in memory of Samuel and Annie McMaster, and the third window commemorates Thomas and Sarah Turner. The east window has three lights and double Y tracery. On the left is the text, "blessed are the dead which die in the Lord". The middle lancet has the text, "the wages of sin is death, but the gift of God is eternal life through Jesus Christ our Lord". The right section has the text, "the righteous shall flourish like a palm tree". The window as a whole has coloured glass with floral patterns, and it commemorates Dr. John Cochran and his family.

The font is on the right of the nave near the chancel entrance. It was presented by Mr and Mrs R. J. Gillanders in 1988. The old font is on loan to Garvagh Museum. The pulpit is on the left of the chancel. A plaque on the east wall adjacent states that it was dedicated in memory of Maria Moore who died in 1885, Eliza Moore who died in 1881 and Rebecca Moore who died in 1886. The prayer desk is on the right. A plaque on the chair states that it was given by Mr and Mrs W. J. Torrens in 1982. The Communion rails and panelling in the sanctuary commemorate William FitzSimons, and were presented by his wife. The altar was presented by Miss Anne FitzSimons in memory of her father, William FitzSimons.

There are numerous monuments in Errigal Church. On the west wall, Hanna Macausland and her sisters are commemorated, as are Martha, wife of the Rev. Redmond Macausland, Rector of Desertoghill, 1842-1856. She died in 1900. On the north wall, there is a memorial to Lt. Oliver Macausland of the Indian Army who was killed in action in 1915. The Canning family, a distinguished family in the parish, claimed descent from William Canynges of Bristol, (c1399-1474). An ancestor at the time of the Plantation of Ulster obtained the manor of Garvagh, and died there in 1646. There is a monument to the Rt. Hon. Charles Canning, 3rd Baron Garvagh who died in 1915, and to his wife, Alice Florence, Baroness Garvagh, who was born Baroness de Bretton. The next monument on the north wall commemorates the Rt. Hon. George Canning, Baron Garvagh who died in 1840, and his wife, Lady Georgina Canning who died in 1804. Also commemorated on the same monument, is George Canning, (1770-1827), who was Prime Minister. Canning began his Parliamentary career as a Whig, (Liberal), in 1793. Under the influence of William Pitt, he joined the Tories. He was noted as a great orator. He was Under-Secretary of State, and later, Treasurer to the Navy in Pitt's Government. He was Secretary for Foreign Affairs under the Duke of Portland. He became Prime Minister in 1827, and died four months later. Charles Canning, Earl Canning, KC, PC, GCB, son of George Canning, first Viceroy of India who died in 1862, and Stratford Canning, Viscount Stratford de Redcliffe, KC, PC, GCB, DCL, Ambassador, who died in 1880, are commemorated on the same monument. Also on the north wall, the Canning family crest appears on a hatchment.

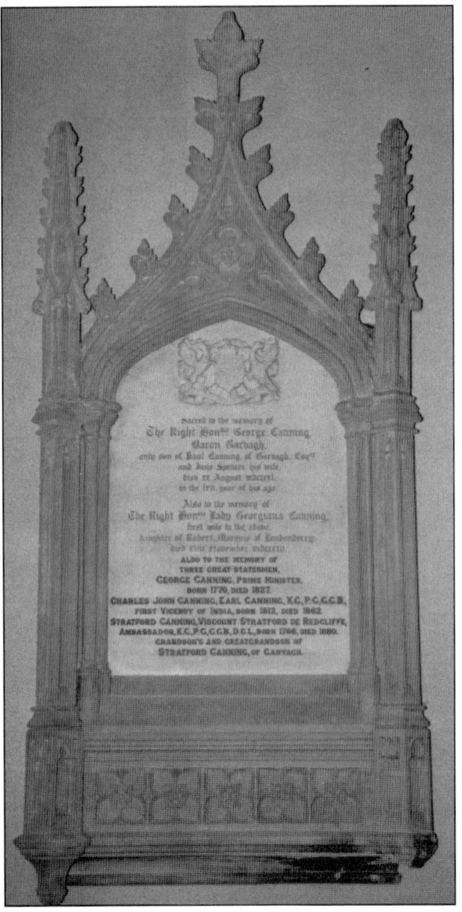

*The Canning Monument.*

On the south wall, there are memorials to the Rev. Mitchell Smyth, Rector of Errigal 1832-1879, and to his wife Elizabeth who died in 1875, and to members of the Garvagh detachment of the Ulster Defence Regiment who were killed through terrorism from 1970 to 1995. There is a memorial to Paul Canning Clinton who died in 1862, and there is both a memorial to those who fell in the Great War, and a Roll of Honour. Robert Ogilby who died in 1846 is commemorated.

The Parish of Desertoghill, *"the desert of O'Tuohill"*, is so closely associated with Errigal, that they are treated together. Rory O'Tuohill is traditionally considered to have been the last chieftan of the O'Tuohill clan. The original church was a Columban foundation, and Adamnan was the

*Desertoghill Church.*

Patron Saint. In the graveyard of the old church, there is an old stone with a hollow depression in it. According to legend, this is the mark of the knees of St. Columba at prayer!

The present church at Moyletra, five kilometres from Garvagh, was built in 1784 at the partial expense of the Bishop, the Earl of Bristol. It replaced an older church. At the west end, is a two-storey tower. There are two blind windows in the west wall. The three windows in the south wall all have square-paned clear glass, and double Y tracery, which contains some coloured panes. The east window is a triple lancet with double Y tracery. The centre section has square, clear panes, and there is coloured glass on either side. There are no windows in the north wall. The font is in the south-west corner of the nave. The pulpit is to the right of the sanctuary, and the prayer desk is to the left. The vestry room is left of the sanctuary. A monument on the east wall commemorates the Rev. Redmond Conyngham Macausland, Rector of Desertoghill from 1842 until his death in 1856.

## FAUGHANVALE, EGLINTON, St. CANICE

THE PRETTY LITTLE village of Eglinton in Co. Derry, is thirteen kilometres east of Londonderry, just to the south of the Limavady road. The parish name of Faughanvale derives from the Irish, *"nua chongbhail"*, new habitation, and has nothing more than coincidence to do with the name of the River Faughan which flows through it. The Patron Saint was Canice who was born about 517 near Limavady, and who died about 600. Canice founded a monastery in the area. He also founded one at Kilkenny, which means Canice's Church. He was one of the twelve companions of St.Columba on his journey to Iona. In Scotland, he was known as Kenneth. Ruins of Faughanvale old church can still be seen.

*Faughanvale old church ruin.*

At the time of the Plantation, in 1615, the Grocers' Company of London was granted a manor of 15,900 acres, (6,435 hectares) around the southern shore of Lough Foyle. The village which grew up was at first called Muff. The Grocers' Company built a new church on their estate in 1626. This lasted until 1820 when the Grocers' Company decided to replace it with the present church in Eglinton. Its ruins are adjacent to the church.

St. Canice's Church in Eglinton was completed in 1826 to a design by John Bowden. It was a rectangular, aisleless four bay hall. North and south transepts were added in 1856, and the chancel was built in 1899 by W.E.Scott of Willsborough in memory of his wife and daughter. The tower is topped by four pinnacles at the west end. At its base is the porch, inside which are stairs to the gallery and organ loft. The main entrance doors are in memory of the Doherty family, 1973, and the bell has an inscription in memory of the Rev. Arthur Dobbs, Rector, 1912-1930. Inside, the baptistery is to the right under the gallery, and there is a corresponding space opposite. The pulpit and prayer desk are to the left at the lower chancel

*Faughanvale Church.*

entrance, and the prayer desk and lectern are to the right. The organ, by Evans and Barr, has two manuals and pedals. The console is in the south transept. The marble steps in the chancel and sanctuary, along with the panelling, as well as re-construction of the tower, commemorate Thomas and James Gallagher, 1930. The vestry room and other rooms are to the left of the chancel.

In the south wall, the window, which has two lights and Y tracery, illustrates the 23rd Psalm, and is in memory of William and Elizabeth Michaels, 1936. Opposite in the north wall, a similar window ilustrates the encounter on the Emmaus Road, (St. Luke 24:29), in memory of Meta, Robert and Thomas Alexander Michaels, 1936. The window in the south wall of the south transept has tracery, and illustrates the Wise Men and the Shepherds at the Manger. It is in memory of James Gallagher of Belfast who died in 1929. Opposite, the window in the north wall of the north transept has three lights, and illustrates the Empty Tomb. It is in memory of Thomas Gallagher who died in 1927. The east window of three lights was given by Katherine Phillips in memory of her father, Edward Scott of Willsborough who died in 1913. On the left is St. Peter, St. John is on the right, and our Lord is in the centre.

On the west wall, a plaque records the re-hallowing of the church after extensive renovations on 16th October 1997. Another plaque adjacent records the installation of electric lighting in memory of Catherina Michaels in 1948. There is a memorial to Winifred Webster who died in 1992, and a plaque records the donation of the carpet in the area opposite the baptistery in memory of Alexander Thompson and his wife Lucinda. The memorials to those who fell in the Great War are on the north wall, and in the porch. On the south wall, Major William Quin of Campsie House, who died in 1922, is commemorated.

On the east wall of the south transept, there is a memorial to Anne, second wife of Thomas Scott of Willsborough who died in 1840, and to Katherine, his third wife who died in 1857, and to Thomas Scott himself, who died in 1872. Katherine Phillips who died in 1934, is commemorated, and a plaque records the installation of amplification in memory of the parents of Robert Carson and James Moore in 1984. On the west wall of the north transept, Edmund Lecky of Longfield Lodge, Eglinton who died in 1917 is commemorated, and on the east wall, there is a memroial to the Rev. James Christie, Perpetual Curate of Faughanvale from 1823 until his death in 1846.

In the chancel, on the north wall, there is a memorial to Elizabeth Burnside who founded the Sunday School in the parish, and who died in 1907, and on the east wall, a plaque marks the association of the North Irish Brigade with the parish from 1st April 1960 to 1st April 1964. On the south wall of the chancel, there is a memorial to Margaret Davidson who died in 1903, and on the east wall, a brass plaque notes the donation of the hymn board in memory of Mamie Ruth in 1987. In the upper section of the chancel, on the north wall, a monument records the erection of the chancel in 1899 in memory of Georgina Scott and Annie Scott, wife and daughter of W. E. Scott of Willsborough. Another plaque records the renovations already mentioned in memory of Thomas and James Gallagher, 1930. On the south wall of the inner chancel, there is a memorial to John Michaels who died in 1948, and to his brother who died in 1956.

There was a close association between the parish of Faughanvale and the nearby military airfield in the 1940s and 1950s. In August 1941, during the second World War, the airfield at Eglinton began to be used as an RAF fighter base. On 1st May 1943, RAF Eglinton was loaned to the Royal Navy, and on 15th May that year, it was commissioned as HMS *Gannet*. To acknowledge worship by personnel of the Royal Naval Air Station at Eglinton from 1943 to 1959, the ensign and crest of HMS *Gannet* are on the east wall of the chancel.

There were some distinguished families in the parish as can be seen from the windows and memorials. In 1696, the Rev. Gideon Scott, a chaplain in the army of William III, bought the Willsborough estate in the townland of Donnybrewer in the parish. The name Willsborough derives from the name of the King, who was apparently pleased by a sermon which he had heard Mr. Scott preaching! He was the ancestor of Major W. E. Scott of Willsborough. The Michaels and Gallaghers were benefactors of the church in the 1930s. Mrs Eliza Michaels who died in 1936, was a sister of Thomas Gallagher of the tobacco firm of Gallaghers. The large and prominent burial monument in the graveyard belongs to the Spencer family who lived in the 18th century. They had a direct ancestral link with the Spencers of Althorp, Northamptonshire, of which family, the late Diana, Princess of Wales, was a member.

# The Plantation of Ulster

IN ORDER TO secure the loyalty of a substantial proportion of the Irish population to the British Crown, two attempts were made at colonising, or planting large numbers of English people in Ireland during the 16th century, in the reigns of Queen Mary I and of Queen Elizabeth I. Both of these failed, mainly because they were attempted in the midlands and in Munster. However, during the reign of James I, (1603-1625), from 1609, following the Flight of the Earls, O'Neill and O'Donnell in 1607, Scottish and English settlers planted Ulster with much greater success.

In 1600, Elizabeth sent Sir Henry Dowcra to Ulster. Dowcra chose Derry as a suitable location for a settlement, because of the potential harbour there. Dowcra befriended the youthful Cahir O'Doherty, son of the chieftan of Inishowen, who fought on his side against O'Neill. For this, he was made Lord of Inishowen, and awarded the forts at Buncrana and Burt. In 1606, Dowcra left Derry, disappointed at his failure to establish a proper settlement there. His successor, George Paulett fell out with Cahir O'Doherty, who promptly raised an army and attacked and sacked Culmore Fort. He went on to capture Derry, for which he was condemned as a traitor. In the end, O'Doherty was defeated, and he was killed in 1608. It seemed to be the end of the attempt to set up a new city at Derry.

By this time, James I had come to the throne, and he was determined to make another attempt to garrison Derry. It was he who began the Plantation of Ulster in earnest, by sending people over to Ulster. The planted counties were Donegal, Derry, Armagh, Tyrone, Fermanagh and Cavan. The land was to be divided into lots which were to vary in size from 1,000 to 3,000 acres. Undertakers, who had taken the Oath of Supremacy, were allocated these lands. In time, little new towns with cobbled streets, and churches, houses and schools, appeared. Although the native Irish chieftans had been dispossessed and expelled, many Irish remained and worked for their new masters on the land.

The most important developments were the creation of the new City of Londonderry, and the County of Coleraine which was enlarged in 1613

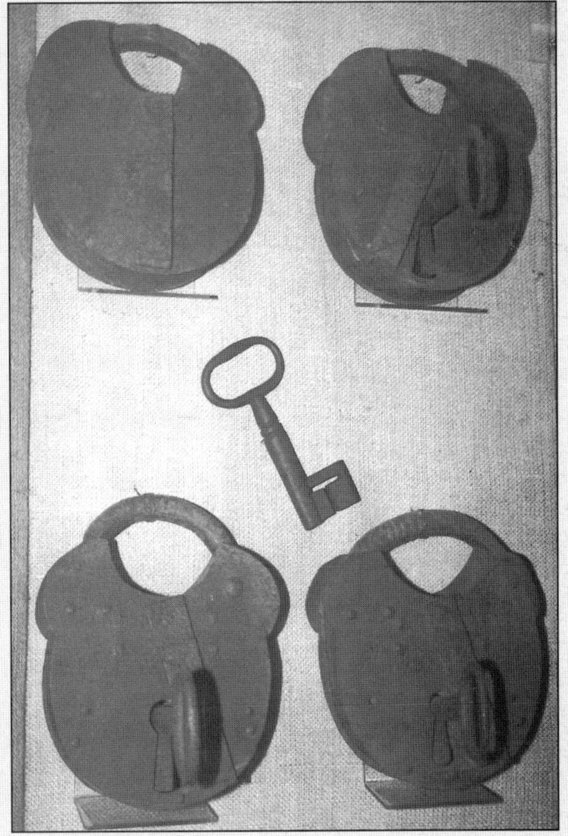

*Padlocks and Keys of the Gates of Derry's Walls, 1618.*

and re-named the County of Londonderry. The County of Coleraine stretched along the north coast as far as Lough Foyle. Sir Henry Dowcra came back to Derry, and strengthened the defences of the city. Later, in 1618, the walls were built, and the Cathedral of St. Columb was erected between 1628 and 1633.

In 1613, Londonderry was granted a Charter by King James I, and the Hon. The Irish Society was formed to promote religion and trade. The ancient mediaeval London Guilds came over and established themselves in the County. For example, the Grocers' Company was granted a manor of 15,000 acres along the south shore of Lough Foyle. They established the village of Muff (not to be confused with Muff, Co. Donegal), and built a church in what is now Eglinton. The Clothworkers' Company was established further along the coast where Castlerock is now, and the Skinners' Company set up in Dungiven. The Worshipful Companies of Mercers, Masons, Cooks and Broderers (embroiderers) were in Kilrea, and the Fishmongers' Company settled in Ballykelly. The Salters' Company built Magherafelt, and the Drapers' Company was set up in Ballynascreen, which was re-named Draperstown. Cookstown in Co. Tyrone was another Plantation town.

On the whole, the native Irish, once it was realised that they could not be totally expelled, were treated reasonably well at first. However, conditions for them deteriorated, and became so bad, that they rose up in a bloody rebellion in 1641. Nevertheless, by that time, the Plantation had taken root, and to this day, descendants of the original planters continue to live in Ulster. Their legacy is in the towns that they built, as well as in their religion, culture, industry and politics.

*Ferryquay Gate, Derry Walls.*

## GLENDERMOTT, LONDONDERRY, NEW BUILDINGS, THE CHURCH OF IRELAND CENTRE

GLENDERMOTT PARISH, formerly Clondermott, *"the tribe of Dermott"*, is located in the eastern suburbs of Londonderry. In ancient times, Saint Patrick, Saint Columba and St. Canice founded churches in the area. About 1622, just after the Plantation of Ulster, the Goldsmiths' Company built a church, which was known as the Ivy Church. The district was constituted a perpetual curacy in 1821, and in 1860, it became a parish. In 1863, due to population growth, part of the parish was separated to form the parish of Clooney.

*Glendermott Church.*

The present church dates from 1753. The tower was added in 1789. A wooden and copper spire was added to this in 1794, but it was blown down in 1831. The north aisle was built in 1861. The porch at the base of the tower was modified in 1982 so that now, one large porch at the west end connects both original porches. The west door was the gift of the Coyle family. Inside, the gallery is over the west end of the nave. To the left, at the west end of the north aisle is the baptistery. There is wood panelling on two sides, and it commemorates Edith Ross Smyth and Norah Ross Crawford of Ardmore. The vestry room is to the left of the chancel.

The panelling in the sanctuary is finely carved. This and the Holy Table are in memory of Alexander Anderson, J.P. who died in 1931. They were presented by his widow in 1935. The chair on

*Chancel and Sanctuary.*

the left commemorates Richard Coyle, 1967, and the chair on the right is in memory of Elizabeth Smallwoods, 1965. The prayer desk is in memory of Ross Thompson Smyth of Ardmore who died in 1881, and the chair commemorates James Moore, 1987. The prayer desk on the left side of the chancel is in memory of Robert and Elizabeth Gallagher, and the one on the right side commemorates Joseph Smallwoods who died in 1972. Another prayer desk is in memory of Jessie Brown. The stone pulpit, which was installed in 1896, commemorates the Rev. Richard Babington and Dora, his wife. He was Rector of Glendermott from 1889 to his death in 1893. The brass lectern is in memory of Anna Maria Knox. The public address system is in memory of William and Isabella Butler and family, 1985.

There is a two manual organ with pedals at the east end of the north aisle, before which is a small font. The ewer on it was given in memory of Georgina Nesbitt in 1984, and the curtains at the side of the organ commemorate Annie Adams who died in 1980.

Glendermott church has some good stained glass windows, some of which are new. On the left side of the porch, on the west wall, are two small lattice windows. To the right of the entrance, is a window of two lights, with on the left, "feed my lambs", and on the right, "feed my sheep", in memory of Thomas Montgomery who died in 1987.

*The new porch (1982) and the Milligan Memorial Window.*

On the south porch wall, a stained glass window depicting Christ, the Bread of Life, commemorates Kathleen Milligan who died in 1978. There are four stained glass windows, each of two lights in the south nave wall. The first depicts the sower sowing seed, in memory of Cecil and Kathleen Milligan. The second is, "Behold I stand at the door and knock", in memory of Wilhelmina Hempton, who died in 1986. The third window depicts our Lord teaching, and commemorates Col. George Knox, D.L. of Prehen, 1913, and the fourth window in the choir is, "suffer the little children", in memory of Rose Virginie Knox, 1906. Over the west aisle wall, there is a striking rose window in memory of Col. John Crawford of the Royal Army Medical Corps, 1982. It illustrates the Dove of the Holy Spirit. Of the three windows in the aisle, the first depicts the empty tomb in memory of Robert Graham, 1968. The second is, "follow me", in memory of Bartholomew Donnelly, 1956 and the third is the raising of Jairus' daughter. The east window has three lights and geometric tracery. It shows Jesus in the centre light, and it commemorates Caroline Beresford of Ashbrook who died in 1901. There are angels in the panels above.

Glendermott Church has some fine memorials. On the south wall of the nave, are memorials to Rose Virginie Knox of Prehen who died in 1904, to Sir John Hill, Bart., who died in 1872, and there is a fine classical monument to Lady Elizabeth Emma Hamilton Ash, sister of George Sholto Douglas, 17th Earl of Douglas. She died in 1857. Brass memorial plaques commemorate Raymond Baggley and his daughter Linda, both of whom were murdered in the course of their duties in the Reserve Police in 1974 and 1976. 2nd Lt. John McCurdy who was killed in 1916 in the Great War is commemorated, and there is a memorial to those who served in the second World War, 1939-1945.

On the north aisle wall, there is a fine brass memorial to those who fell and who served in the Great War, 1914-1918. There are also memorials to Alice McClintock of Ardmore who died in 1910, to Ross Acheson Smyth, J.P., D.L. of Ardmore who died in 1917, to John Acheson who died in 1874, and to 2nd Lt. John Ross Smyth who was killed in 1914 in the Great War. On the east wall, a monument commemorates the Rev. Anthony Grayson Cary, Perpetual Curate from 1821 until his death in 1848, and Susanna Stannus who died in 1819 is also commemorated. On the north wall of the sanctuary is a memorial to Canon Richard Babington who died in 1893, and on the right, the Rev. David Babington, Perpetual Curate, then Rector of Glendermott from 1848 until his death in 1889, and his wife, are commemorated. Also on the south wall, a memorial commemorates Capt. George Knox, D.L., of Prehen who died in 1893, and his wife, Maria. The Knoxes of Prehen, Londonderry, were a notable family in the parish. They were descended from Andrew Knox, (1559-1633), Bishop of Raphoe.

Outside the church, there is a monument, the Last Post, which was erected in memory of the men of the First Northern Battalion of the Ulster Volunteer Force who served in the Great War. Across the road, the Babington Hall was built in memory of Canon Richard Babington, 1893, and the Kelly Hall, 1973, adjacent to it, commemorates Canon David Kelly, Rector 1930 to 1969. The modern rectory was built in 1969.

*Church of Ireland Centre, New Buildings.*

The Church of Ireland Centre at New Buildings, five kilometres south of Londonderry, was built to meet the needs of that area of the parish. A dual purpose hall and church, it was consecrated in 1988. It is a hexagonal building with a porch and utility rooms to the right of the entrance. Inside, the main hall which is rectangular, is built within the hexagonal exterior, so as to form small triangular rooms adjacent. These have various uses. The main hall accommodates the congregation for worship, as well as being used during the week for parish activities. The sanctuary can be screened off. In it, there are two windows. One commemorates Julie Edgar who died aged two years in 1986, and the other, on the right, "I am the Bread of Life", is in memory of Wilhelmina Hempton who died in 1986. Mrs Hempton was the mother-in-law of Canon Noel Moore, Rector of Glendermott 1976 2000, during whose incumbency, the centre at New Buildings was built. The vestry room is to the right of the sanctuary.

The Holy Table was presented by Mr and Mrs Sam Mitchell, 1988. The prayer desk is in memory of Daphne McKeegan who died in 1985, the lectern is in memory of Wilhelmina Hempton, the sanctuary chairs commemorate two children, Leanne and Gemma Barnett, 1989, and the Communion rails are in memory of Sgt. Thomas Montgomery who died in 1987. The sanctuary chairs are also in his memory. The font commemorates Elizabeth Hayes who died in 1985. The War Memorial is in memory of Jim McClintock, 6th Co., U.D.R., who was murdered in 1981. One of the hymn boards was the gift of Mr and Mrs Samuel Devenny, and the other is in memory of Julie Edgar.

The Church of Ireland Centre at New Buildings has fulfilled a much-felt need for the people of the area.

## KILCRONAGHAN, TOBERMORE

KILCRONAGHAN, *"Cronaghan's Church"*, is a parish which is situated round the village of Tobermore, at the base of the Glenshane Pass in the Sperrin Mountains in County Londonderry. St. Cronaghan is supposed to have baptised St. Columba, and to have been his teacher.

***Kilcronaghan Church.***

As usual, Kilcronaghan Church was reported to be ruinous at the 1622 survey, and to have been in good repair in the 1768 survey. The ancient church was rebuilt in 1806, but was again in poor condition by 1856.

The present church, which stands at the upper end of Tobermore, was completed in 1858. It has a large nave with an entrance porch in the south-west corner, and a short north aisle. The vestry room is to the left of the chancel.

In the west wall are two windows, above which is a small window, which depicts the dove of the Holy Spirit. A plaque adjacent states that the top section of the window commemorates Henry and Elizabeth Averill, 1979, that the left section which depicts a hand, is in memory of William and Mary Richardson, 1979, and that the right section, which depicts the Lamb of God, is in memory of Henrietta Patterson, 1979. Below is the font, and there is a niche in the wall behind it. The clock on the west wall is in memory of Mary Jane Ross, 1999. There is a window in the south wall to the rear of the porch. There are four other windows in the south wall, four in the north wall, and two in the north aisle. All these windows have clear, lattice glass. The east window is a triple lancet which contains coloured, patterned glass. The left light has the words, "watch and pray". The middle section has the words, "the Lord is my light", and, "God is love", and the right section has, "praise ye the Lord". There is a little window with clear lattice glass in the south wall of the sanctuary.

The Holy Table is in memory of William and Mary Richardson, 1979, and the credence table commemorates Mr and Mrs William Thom and their family, 1959. There is a chair on the right side of the sanctuary, and the chair on the left is in memory of Robert Young, 1959. The Communion rails are in memory of Robert McLean, 1969, and the kneelers commemorate Ray Greene who died in 1997. The pulpit to the left of the chancel steps is in memory of Norman Clark, 1979, and the lectern was donated by Mrs Young, 1959. There is a prayer desk and chair to the right in the chancel.

The memorial to those who fell in the Great War is on the north wall, as is the memorial to Joseph Laverty of the Royal Irish Rifles who fell at Ypres in 1917. The Wilkinson family of Moneyshanere, Tobermore, is commemorated in the north aisle. On the aisle west wall, a monument commemorates the Rev. Thomas Wilkinson, Curate of St. Paul's Church, Belfast, who died in 1922. On the north wall of the aisle, Hiram Parker Wilkinson, KC, JP, is commemorated. He was a Crown Advocate for China, and a judge. He died in 1935. On the east wall of the aisle, there is a monument which commemorates Sir Hiram Shaw Wilkinson, LL.D. of the Consular Service in Japan, and Crown Advocate in Shanghai. He was Chief Justice of the Supreme Courts of China and Korea. He was High Sheriff for County Londonderry, and Pro-Chancellor of the Queen's University, Belfast. On the south wall of the chancel, there is a memorial to the Rev. Robert Hogg Faulkner, Rector of Kilcronaghan from 1945 until his death in 1966, and to his wife Rebecca, who died in 1959. There is also a memorial to his predecessor, the Rev. James Robert Kelly, Rector from 1906 until his death in 1945, and to his wife, Louise, who died in 1933. On the south wall, is a monument to Mary, wife of the Rev. Hugh Forde, LL.D, Rector 1874-1888. She died in 1880. The memorial to those who fell in the second World War is on the same wall.

## KILLELAGH

THE PARISH OF KILLELAGH, *"the church of the lake"*, is half way between Garvagh and Kilrea, both eight kilometres distant, in the village of Swatragh in east County Londonderry. A small lake in the area gives the parish its name. The church was ruinous in 1622. There was no church atall by 1806, but a new church and glebe house were built between 1808 and 1813.

***Killelagh Church.***

The present church was built by the Mercers' Company in 1855, and the older church, not being conveniently central, was abandoned. It is pleasantly situated amongst trees. The porch is adjacent to the tower and spire in the south-west corner. The tower base is square, and the upper section is octagonal with louvers. The spire is slated. The nave is supported by buttresses. There is a short transept on the north side, and a raised chancel and sanctuary with a vestry room to the left.

There are three windows in the west wall, two in the north wall with small circular windows above, two such windows in the north transept wall, and two in the south wall of the sanctuary. These, along with one of the two windows in the south wall, have lattice panes with pretty floral designs. The other window in the south wall has candles depicted on the right side, and the text, "faithful unto death", on the left. The north and south wall windows each have two lights. The east window is a triple lancet with three circular lights above. Above it, is a very small window in the roof eaves. The east window has coloured patterned glass. On the left side are the words, "hallow my Sabbath". In the middle, the words, "have faith in God", "watch and pray", and "take heed how ye hear", appear, and "reverence my sanctuary" is on the right side.

The font is in a baptistery in the south-west corner of the nave. The pulpit is on the left of the chancel, and the prayer desk is on the right, with the lectern adjacent below. The lectern commemorates Ina Kane, 1961.

To the left and right of the altar, the first four and the last six of the Ten Commandments are painted, and "Behold the Lamb of God" is on the reredos. Killelagh church has no monuments.

## KILLOWEN, COLERAINE, St. JOHN

THE PARISH OF Killowen is one of the smallest in geographical area in the Diocese of Derry, yet one of the largest in population. Its church, which is dedicated to St. John, is situated on the west bank of the River Bann in Coleraine, Co. Derry. The diocesan boundary with Connor Diocese is formed by the river, on the other side of which is the parish of St. Patrick's, Coleraine.

*Killowen Church.*

The name Killowen means, *"Owen (or Eugene's) Church"*. The dedication to St. John, which has lasted, is a mis-translation of the Irish. In ancient times, the parish was called *Drumtarsi*. In 1248, the English erected a castle and a bridge over the Bann. Stones for the castle came from the ancient abbey of St. Carbreus.

At the time of the Plantation, the Clothworkers' Company was established in the area, which then was a county, the County of Coleraine. The name Killowen was given to the parish at this time. In 1622, Killowen church was, "meanly repayred". In the 1768 survey, it was reported to be in very good repair. This church was converted into a schoolhouse in 1830, and in that year, a new church was built with financial assistance from the Clothworkers' Company, the Bishop, the Irish Society and the Board of First Fruits. In 1875, the church was practically rebuilt. The west wall was demolished and replaced, a porch was added, the east wall was partially replaced, and a chancel was added. The side walls were raised, and a new roof was built. The church was consecrated on 27th July 1875. The vestry room to the left of the chancel, was built in 1927 in memory of Henry Stewart O'Hara, Bishop of Cashel, at the expense of his widow. Bishop O'Hara was Rector of St. Patrick's, Coleraine from 1869 to 1894, and Bishop of Cashel, 1900-1919. He was largely responsible for the early building of St. Anne's Cathedral, Belfast, when Vicar of Belfast, 1894-1900. A plaque in the vestry room of Killowen Church was erected by Mrs O'Hara.

Killowen Church is entered by a small west porch. Inside, the nave is flanked by a south aisle, which on the outside, has two gables. The short aisle to the west is lower in height. This contains the baptistery. The font was presented by Robert McCandless. In June 2001, two new stained glass windows in the baptistery were dedicated by Edwin Whyte in memory of his wife Margaret and daughter Janet. Together, they depict the children coming to Jesus. At

*Baptistery and new windows.*

the other end of the aisle, to the east, is an extension which contains a porch and the organ chamber.

The west window has four lights and illustrates the four Evangelists. In the tracery, there is a crest with the Latin inscription, *Domine Dirige Nos*. In the baptistery in the south aisle, are two small windows with opaque lattice glass. The first window in the aisle also has opaque lattice glass. The other window has three lights. From left to right, the window illustrates, the Flight into Egypt, the Manger scene, and, our Lord as a boy in the Temple. This window anticipates the centenary of Killowen Branch of the Mothers Union in 2004. Each of the three windows in the north wall has two lights. The first, which was dedicated in 1998, commemorates Jim Oliver. A brass plaque adjacent acknowledges this window. The left side has the text, "He that hath ears to hear, let him hear", (St. Mark 4:9), and the right side illustrates the text of Revelation 3:20, "Behold I stand at the door and knock". The middle window commemorates, on the left, members of the 5th Battalion, Ulster Defence Regiment, who fell between 1970 and 1992, and on the right, members of the Royal Ulster Constabulary and Reserve members, 1996. The window on the right depicts Christ, the Resurrection and the Life, and it commemorates Rosemary, wife of the Rev. Alwyn Maconachie, Rector of Killowen, 1947-1964, who died in 1954. The east window depicts the Ascension of our Lord, and it commemorates those who fell in the first and second World Wars.

In the nave, the pulpit on the right below the chancel, commemorates Bishop O'Hara's wife, Hatton, 1937. There are two carved prayer desks on the left side, and there is a wooden eagle lectern adjacent which commemorates the Rev. W.H. Giles, Rector of Killowen, 1894 to 1923, and Mrs Giles. The Holy Table came from St. Augustine's Church in Londonderry in 1936. The Conacher organ has two manuals and pedals. It was built in 1894. It was transferred from the organ loft to the south side of the chancel in 1906. The organ chamber and a reading desk were presented by grandchildren of John Wilson and his wife, Catherine who emigrated to America in 1876. The organ stool commemorates Hugh Clements who died in 1998.

On the west wall, a monument commemorates Henry Kyle, JP, DL of Laurel Hill, who died in 1878. There is also a memorial to William Thompson Kyle, his youngest son, who died in 1913. On the south wall, his wife Elizabeth who died in 1865, and their son Henry who died in 1866, are commemorated. In the baptistery, a Latin memorial commemorates Elizabeth Todd who died in 1750. The Roll of Honour to those who fell in the Great War is on the east wall of the aisle, and on the south aisle wall, those who fell in the second World War are commemorated. On the east wall, left of the sanctuary, there is a memorial to the Rev. William Sillito, Curate of Killowen, 1824-1831, and Rector, 1831-1873. He died in 1875. On the east wall, to the right of the sanctuary, is a memorial to the Rev. Wilfrid Courtenay Abbott, Curate-in-charge, then Rector of Killowen, 1924-1947. On the north wall of the sanctuary, a brass memorial commemorates Hugh Clements, JP, a former Mayor of Coleraine, who died in 1954. On the north wall, there is a memorial to Margaret Emma, wife of the Rev. James Stewart, Rector of Killowen, 1873-1894, during whose incumbency the church was rebuilt. She died in 1884. There is also a memorial to Ann, wife of the Rt. Hon. Richard Jackson of Jackson Hall, Coleraine, daughter of Charles O'Neill of Shane's Castle, Antrim, who died in 1781.

## KILREA, St. PATRICK

KILREA, *"grey church"*, is a small town in east County Derry, 25 kilometres south of Coleraine. The Patron of the parish was St.Patrick. The ancient church is beside the present church at the top of the town. In the Royal Visitation, it was reported to have been repaired in 1613 by the Mercers' Company, which was allocated property in the Kilrea area at the time of the Plantation. The church remained in good repair, it seems, throughout the 17th century, but by 1768, it was not in good repair. It was burnt in 1780 and repaired in 1799.

Kilrea Parish Church was built in 1843, and consecrated on 18th April 1844. It is a lofty three bay hall with a two-storey classical square tower at the west end. This is surmounted by a smaller octagonal clock tower and an octagonal spire. The two shorter towers on each side of the central

# Derry and Raphoe Mothers' Union

In 1876, Mary Sumner, wife of the Rector of Old Alresford in Hampshire, founded the first branch of the Mothers' Union, because she felt that women needed training in, and support for their bringing up of children, the greatest of all careers.

The organisation spread rapidly. The first branch in Ireland was formed in 1887 in Raheny Parish in Dublin. The first branch to be formed in Derry and Raphoe was Glendermott in Londonderry in 1900. Killowen Branch dates from 1904. By 1905, Moville, Sion Mills, Muff, and Christ Church in Londonderry had branches. Many more branches have celebrated their fiftieth anniversary. Regrettably, some have ceased to exist.

The first General Council for Ireland was established in 1903. The first Council of all the branches of Derry and Raphoe met on 9th February 1905, and the first Executive met fifty years later, on 8th June 1955. The first annual Diocesan Festival Service was held in Derry Cathedral in 1911, attended by 400 members from ten branches. Numbers of branches and membership increased steadily over the years. In 2001, there are 38 branches in the United Dioceses, 29 in Derry and nine in Raphoe. The branches all have fine banners, which are paraded at the annual Mothers' Union festival service in St. Columb's Cathedral, Londonderry in May.

The Mothers' Union has had great influence in family life over the years, aiming to develop prayer and spiritual growth in families, and to help family life to be the basis of community life. Its Five Objects are,

1 To uphold Christ's teaching on the nature of marriage and to promote its wider understanding,
2 To encourage parents to bring up their children in the faith and life of the Church,
3 To maintain a worldwide fellowship of Christians united in prayer, worship and service,
4 To promote conditions in society which are favourable to family life and the protection of children, and,
5 To help those whose family life has met with adversity.

*Derry and Raphoe Mothers' Union Banner.*

*Mothers' Union Centenary Commemoration Window 1904-2004, Killowen Church, Coleraine.*

*Kilrea old church.*

*Kilrea Church.*

tower do not reach the height of the nave. Inside, these towers form a triple porch. The large gallery over the west end of the nave was built in 1862. The baptistery is at the west end below the gallery. The nave is divided into a central aisle of pews and a north and a south aisle. There are three triple round-headed lancets in both the north and south nave walls. In each, the central window is taller, and all of these windows have opaque and coloured glass. In the south aisle, the first window commemorates, on the left, Samuel Pinkerton, and in the middle, Edith Ablett who died in 1949, and the right lancet was presented by the Rev. Robert McKemey, Rector of Kilrea, 1969-1973, and his wife. The left lancet in the middle window commemorates Margaret Graham, and the right lancet, Matilda de Vere. The middle lancet was presented by T. Gardiner and family. The middle lancet in the third window was presented by the Youth Fellowship, and the left lancet commemorates Sarah Holden and Isabella McFadden.

In the north wall, the middle lancet of the first window was presented by the Youth Fellowship, and the right lancet is in memory of James Campbell. The middle window was presented in 1971 in memory of Thomas Proctor who died in 1996, and of his wife Rebecca, who died in 1964. The left lancet of the third window commemorates Kathleen Hutchinson who died in 1939, and the middle lancet commemorates John Garvin. The east window, which has three lights, the central one being taller, has coloured patterned glass. It was presented by the Girls' Friendly Society in 1947. In the central section are the texts, "I am the Good Shepherd", and, "I know my sheep".

The chancel extends into the nave. The pulpit is to the left of the chancel, in the nave. The prayer desk is on the first chancel step to the right. The brass eagle lectern on the second step to the left, is in memory of John Keenan. In the sanctuary, the altar commemorates Maria McFadden who died in 1908. The two prayer desks on either side are in memory of Elizabeth Long, 1966. The chair on the left commemorates the parents of Thomas Gardiner who presented it, and the chair on the right commemorates Richard McFadden and his wife Margaret, 1959. The aumbry in the south wall of the sanctuary commemorates Margaret Maria O'Fee who died in 1945. The vestry room is to the left of the sanctuary.

*Nave and Sanctuary.*

The organ in the gallery is said to have been played by George Frederick Handel. There is also a two manual Conacher organ with pedals in the south-east corner of the nave.

On the west wall, a plaque records the donation of floodlighting of the tower, and of the clock in memory of Margaret Hasson. Another plaque records the donation of the windows on either side of the main door in memory of Thomas Hasson, 1973. On the north wall there is a memorial to James Hunter who died in 1900, to his wife Marie Stinson who died in 1884, and to Nathaniel Ferguson who was killed in action in 1915 during the Great War. Reserve Constable Arthur McKay who was killed by terrorists in 1976 is also commemorated. On the east wall, to the left of the sanctuary, a plaque records the erection of the church in 1843 by the worshipful companies of Mercers, Masons, Cooks and Broderers, (embroiderers), of the City of London, who up to 1904 owned in association, property in the neighbourhood. Another plaque records the donation of the east window in 1947. On the east wall to the right of the sanctuary, there is a memorial to Edward Lennox who died in the Great War in 1917. A plaque records the donation of the amplifying system in memory of Margaret Proctor, Arthur McKay, Sandy Scott and Charles and Mary McCaw. On the south wall, there is a memorial to Robert Bradley who died in 1937, to Andrew Bradley who died in 1949, and to Margaret Bradley who died in 1961. John Johnston who died in 1890, and his wife Mary Ann who died in 1898, and members of the family are also commemorated.

## LANGFIELD LOWER, DRUMQUIN
## LANGFIELD UPPER, DRUMQUIN

THE NAME OF the parish of Langfield, near Drumquin, in west Tyrone, derives from the Irish *Leamcoill, "the elm wood"*. This is corrupted into Langfield. The village of Drumquin is mentioned as long ago as the 13th century in the reign of King John. The present village was founded during the Plantation about 1617 by Sir John Davies who was Attorney General for Ireland under James I. The ancient church was ruinous in 1622. Lackagh church nearby was replaced with Lower Langfield church which was built, according to a plaque over the door in 1842, one kilometre to the west of Drumquin. It was restored in 1865 and 1907. The chancel was built in 1867.

*Langfield Lower Church.*

The west porch and the west front of the church have pinnacles at the corners, and the structure is surmounted by a bellcote. There is a sundial in front of the porch. The porch was restored in 1983 in memory of George Thompson who died in 1969. The entrance door was presented in 1983 in memory of William Liggett who died in 1981. The staircase in the porch leads to a small landing above.

There is a window in the west porch wall, and two on each side of the entrance. There are four windows on each side of the nave. The first in the north wall is of opaque diamond glass. The second window depicts Jesus calming the storm, and is in memory of Sarah Johnston who died in 1909. It was restored in 1983 in memory of Robert Marshall who died in 1951. The third window depicts the Good Shepherd, and is in memory of Mary Johnston who died in 1899, and the fourth window, illustrating Mary and Martha, commemorates Mary Sproule. The Sproules of Kirlish House were an old established family in the parish who came over from Scotland in 1650. On the south side, the first window is of opaque diamond glass. The second window shows the Risen Christ, and is in memory of Alexander and Jane Bradley. It was restored in 1983 in memory of Joseph Fyffe who died in 1979. The third window illustrates the text, "I go to prepare a place for you", and is in memory of the Rev. Thomas Stack, Rector 1860-1876, who died in

1888. It was restored in 1983 in memory of the Rev. James Nethery who died in 1934. The fourth window illustrates the texts, "Consider the lilies of the field", and "Suffer the little children", and is in memory of Lillie Stack who died in 1867. The east window has three lights and tracery above. The middle section depicts Abraham about to sacrifice his son Isaac. It was restored in memory of Cassie Buchanan. The texts of the Lord's Prayer and of the Creed are painted to the left and right of the east window. The Ten Commandments are on the east wall to the right of the chancel.

The vestry room is to the left of the chancel. The pulpit is on the right, and is in memory of Hully Sproule, wife of Thomas Simpson, 1859. The font adjacent to it, is in memory of K.H.M. and M. Sproule, 1863. The prayer desk is in the chancel on the left side. It was given to the parish, along with the seat in the chancel, by the Rev. Charles Stack, son of the Rt.Rev.Charles Maurice Stack, Bishop of Clogher 1886-1903. Rev.Charles Maurice Stack (junior), married Anna Kathleen, daughter of the Rev. T. L. F. Stack, Rector of Lower Langfield from 1879 to 1923. The oak lectern was carved by Mrs Ann Olivia Stack, wife of the Rev. T. L. Stack, Rector 1860-1876, not to be confused with the Rev. T. L. F. Stack. The organ is also on the left. The carpeting is in memory of James Moffatt, 1983, the lighting is in memory of Ivan Boyd, and the public address system commemorates William Smyth, 1982.

On the north wall, there is a monument to James Sproule, Surgeon on H.M.S. *Scout,* who died in 1867, and one commemorating Ted Megahey who was killed while serving with the Ulster Defence Regiment in 1972. On the south wall is a monument to commemorate the Rev. Gilbert King, Rector of Lower Langfield from 1811 until his death in 1856.

*Langfield Upper Church.*

Upper Langfield Church is 2.5 kilometres to the east of Drumquin on the Omagh road. Built about 1803, it is a hall type church which is entered through a porch at the base of the tower. The three windows on each side of the nave have diamond opaque and coloured glass. The east window of two lights has tree patterns and coloured glass. The vestry room is to the left of the chancel. The pulpit on the left commemorates William Higgins. The prayer desk is on the right. A monument on the west wall was erected by the parishioners in 1904 to commemorate the jubilee of the ordination of the Rev. Henry Kennedy, Rector from 1860 to 1908.

The parishes of Upper and Lower Langfield were divided in 1795, and reunited in 1911.

## LEARMOUNT, PARK

LEARMOUNT, FORMERLY LEAROWEN, *"the little fork of the river",* was created as a perpetual curacy in the parish of Cumber Upper, with territory from that parish, Cumber Lower and Banagher in 1831. The church, in the village of Park near Claudy in Co. Derry, was consecrated on 13th December 1831. On 15th February 1847, Learmount was constituted as a separate parish.

The church is entered through a small porch at the west end, above which is a window with coloured diamond glass, and a bellcote. The nave has three windows on each side with clear diamond-paned glass and Y tracery. The east window illustrates the text, "Come unto me all ye that labour, (St. Matthew 11:28), and is in memory of John Barré Beresford, DL, VL of Learmount who died in 1895.

The baptistery is along the north wall, and contains a small prayer desk as well as the font. The one manual organ was built by the Positive Organ Company of London. The brass lectern adjacent to it is in memory of the Rev. James

*Learmount Church.*

Stevenson Hunter, Perpetual Curate from the time of the separation of Learmount district in 1831, then Rector of Learmount, 1847-1876. The pulpit is on the right, and the prayer desk nearby commemorates William Warnock. The vestry room is to the left of the nave.

On the south wall, there is a monument to Henry Barré Beresford of Learmount, son of the Rt. Hon. John Beresford, who died in 1837, and his wife Barbara, daughter of Sir William Montgomery, Bart. of Peeblesshire, Scotland. The Beresford crest is on the monument. On the west wall, a memorial commemorates John Claudius Beresford who died in 1846, and his son John who died in 1866. On the north wall, are monuments commemorating the Rev. James Hunter who died in 1876, Mervyn Dixon who died in 1991, the Rev. William Montgomery Beresford, son of Henry Barré Beresford, grandson of Marcus, 1st Earl of Tyrone, and Rector of Lower Badoney who died in 1868. Rosa his wife who died in 1908, is also commemorated on a memorial. On the east wall, left of the sanctuary, there is a monument to George de la Poer, son of Henry Barré Beresford, Captain, HM 16th Bedfordshire Regiment, who died in 1865. On the other side of the sanctuary, there is a memorial to Major J.C.M. de la Poer Beresford of the Royal Engineers who was killed in 1894.

## LECKPATRICK, ARTIGARVAN, St. PATRICK

LECKPATRICK PARISH is to the north of Strabane on the main Londonderry road. The parish church is in the village of Artigarvan, some seven kilometres from Strabane. The name means, *"the stone of Patrick"*. It was also anciently known as Magherynelec and Kylpatrick. The church was in good repair in 1679, but was dilapidated by 1692. It was reported to be in good repair again by 1768.

The present church was built in 1815-1816, and was consecrated in 1821. It was enlarged in 1824. It is T-shaped, with a nave and a very large transept half way along the north side of the building. The vestry room is to the right of the south wall. The church is entered through a porch in the west wall. The internal entrance door is in memory of John Donnell, 1984. All the windows are round-headed, and with the exception of one in the transept, all have clear square-paned glass, with etched figures in them. In the south wall, are four windows, as well as one in the vestry. The first window has St.Patrick etched upon it, with the words from St. John 6:28, "What shall we do that we might work the works of God?". It is in memory of Willie Kelly and his wife, Winnie, 1989. The second window has, "Let everything that hath breath, praise the Lord", from Psalm 150:6, and there are also figures and musical notation. It commemorates Robert and Isobel Dourish, 1986. The third window has, "Did not our hearts burn within us while he opened to us the Scriptures?", St. Luke 24:32. It is in memory of John and Sarah McMichael and their daughter Hilary, 1989. The

*Leckpatrick Church.*

fourth window, which was installed in 1989, illustrates the text, "He took them up in his arms and blessed them", St. Mark 10:16, and it commemorates Alana Robb who died aged two years in 1986. The window in the vestry room depicts the Good Shepherd, and was presented in 1989 by the Rev. Alan Tilson, Rector of Leckpatrick, 1979-1989, and his wife, Jenny. In the transept, there are two windows in the west wall. The first illustrates the parable of the Good Samaritan, St. Luke 10:33, and it commemorates Alfred and Ellen Milligan, 1993. The other window is clear. The east window has tracery, and it illustrates sheaves and grapes, which produce bread and wine, the food and drink of the Eucharist, and the words, "This do in remembrance of Me". A plaque adjacent records it as a memorial to Jackie Darragh, 1986.

The church has some unusual and interesting features. For example, the original box pews and two-decker pulpit have been retained. The pulpit, which incorporates the prayer desk, is mounted three steps above the nave, and is set out from the south wall, in front of the entrance to the vestry room, and facing the transept. The Communion rail is in the form of a large semi-circle, which encloses the sanctuary. On it, a plaque states that it is in memory of James Montgomery Sinclair who died in 1899, and of his wife, Mary who died in 1925. The altar was presented in memory of William Briggs who died in 1919. To the right is the baptistery. A plaque states that the carpet in it was presented in 1989 by Cecil and Susan Stevenson in memory of their son Mark, who died in 1982 aged twelve years, and of his brother Gareth who died in 1985 aged eleven years. The bowl in the font was presented in memory of Cecil Cunningham. There are two small prayer desks to the left of the sanctuary. The electronic organ, which has two manuals and pedals, and is near the south-west corner of the nave.

*Combined Pulpit and Lectern, Leckpatrick Church.*

Leckpatrick Church has some interesting monuments. Three of these are on the north wall, to the left of the transept. The first commemorates those who served and who fell in the Great War, and the second, below it, those who fell in the second World War. The third monument commemorates the Rev. Samuel McPherson, Curate of Leckpatrick, from 1854 until his death in 1865. On the same wall, to the right of the transept, there is a Latin monument to the Rev. John Sinclair, Rector of Leckpatrick from 1666 until his death in 1702. The monument also commemorates his wife Anna, and their eight children. There is also a memorial to Donald Brooke Sinclair, Indian Civil Service, who died in 1879. The other monument on the north wall also commemorates the Rev. John Sinclair, and has the family crest above. On the east wall to the left of the sanctuary, there is a memorial to James Sinclair who died in 1865, and to his widow, Dorothea, who died in 1864. The Sinclairs of Holy Hill near Strabane were an old and prosperous land-owning family in the parish.

On the east wall to the right of the sanctuary, a stone monument is inscribed, "under the Communion Table lyeth the body of the Reverd. and worthy Mr James Goodlatt who left this life on Saturday 10th June, anno 1727 in the sixtyeth year of his age. Incumbent of this parish". The stone obviously refers to his burial in the old church. James Goodlatt had been rector from 1703. Another memorial commemorates the Rev. William Macklin Edwards who was Rector of Leckpatrick from 1872 until his death in 1883. The wording on the monument which records Mr Edwards' abilities as a counsellor, preacher and pastor, is said to have been composed by Bishop Alexander. On the south wall, there is a memorial to Emily Augusta Grace, daughter of the Hon. Richard Ponsonby, Bishop of Derry, who was the wife of the Rev. Charleton Maxwell, Rector of Leckpatrick, 1853-1872. She died in 1856. On the north wall of the transept, a Roll of Honour commemorates members of the 6th Co. Tyrone Battalion, A Company, Ulster Defence Regiment, who were either killed in action, or who died of natural causes. On the east wall of the transept, James Porter White, Milltown, Artigarvan, who died in 1916, is commemorated.

*At the time of publication, Leckpatrick Church is undergoing major renovation, which may render some of the above obsolete*

## LISLIMNAGHAN, HOLY TRINITY

LISLIMNAGHAN, whose name may be translated, *"the fort of the little bare place"*, is a parish in mid-Tyrone. The church is six kilometres north-west of Omagh on the main Strabane road. It was built in 1862, and consecrated on 26th August that year, with the dedication, Holy Trinity. It is a five bay hall with a chancel and a porch in the second bay of the north side. The church is lit by five windows in the north wall, four in the south wall, three in the west wall with a circular light above, and two small windows in the porch. The east window has three sections, the central part being taller, with two lights. There is also a small window in the south wall of the sanctuary. All the windows have clear, lattice glass, giving the church a bright, airy feel inside. Furthermore, it is set in well kept, spacious grounds.

The font is situated beneath the west window. The lid is in memory of the parents and brother of Jack and Mary Elkin, 1987. The pulpit is below the chancel to the left, and the prayer desk is opposite, with a wooden eagle lectern adjacent. In the sanctuary, the Holy Table commemorates Elizabeth McQuade, and the credence table is in memory of Canon Robert Whelan, Rector of Lislimnaghan from 1931 to 1959. The vestry room is to the left of the sanctuary. The organ in the north-west corner of the nave has two manuals and pedals. It came from a church in Co. Westmeath. On the west wall, there is a memorial to Col. Robert Hawkes Ellis of Rash House who died in 1917, and to his wife Frances who was the daughter of William Knox of Clonleigh, Lifford,

*Lislimnaghan Church.*

and who died in 1926. On the north wall are both the Great War memorial, and a memorial to Canon Whelan. On the south wall, a plaque states that the carpeting is in memory of Canon Whelan. A plaque records the installation of electric light in the rectory in memory of Robert Hawkes Ellis of the Indian Civil Service, 1962. On the east wall, to the left of the sanctuary, there is a memorial to the Rev. Robert McQuade, Rector of Lislimnaghan, 1905-1930, and to his wife Elizabeth who died in 1921. To the right of the sanctuary, a memorial commemorates the Rev. Christopher Irvine, first Rector of Lislimnaghan, 1862-1898, who died in 1905. On the north wall of the sanctuary, there is a classical monument in memory of John Spiller who died in 1830, and of his wife Jane, and other members of the family. On the opposite wall, a memorial to George Thomas Spiller states that the church was erected by his mother in 1862.

## MAGHERA, St. LURAICH

THE TOWN OF Maghera in Co. Derry is at the foot of the Glenshane Pass through the Sperrin Mountains, just to the north of the main Londonderry to Belfast road. Anciently, the full name of the parish was, *Machaire ratha Luraich, "the plain of the fort of Luraich"*. Luraich was Patron Saint, about the sixth century. Maghera was the seat of the Bishops from about 1150, when the Bishop, Maurice O'Coffey transferred the See from Ardstraw in Co. Tyrone. It remained the seat of the Bishop until about 1280, when the See was transferred to Derry.

*The Maghera Lintel.*

To the east of Maghera town centre are the ruins of an old church. It is impossible to date these ruins, but parts of them could very well be eighth century. Most of the building could be 12th century.

*Maghera, old church ruins.*

*Maghera Church.*

The building, of which the tower and much of the nave and chancel remain, was in use until 1819. It was repaired in 1622, and burnt in the 1641 Rebellion. It was in good repair in 1768.

The present church in Maghera is across the road from the ruins of the old church. It was built in 1819. The tower at the west end is surmounted by battlements and tall corner finials. The inner porch at its base contains the stairs to the gallery. The outer porch which projects from the tower southwards. was built in 1975, and consecrated on 16th November that year in memory of Willie and Zelie Clark. A plaque records this. Also in the porch, an ancient stone lintel illustrates the Crucifixion of our Lord.

Inside, a spacious gallery over the west end of the nave contains the organ, which has one manual and pedals. The vestry room is to the left of the nave, half way along. There are two windows of three lights in the north nave wall. These have coloured glass with floral patterns. There are three windows with three lights of clear, lattice glass and tracery in the south wall. The east window is a triple lancet with cusped tracery. In the left side are the texts, "Thy Word is the truth", and, "the Lord is at hand". In the middle is the text, "God is Love", and the right side has the texts, "feed my flock", and, "have faith in God". The window contains both coloured and patterned glass.

In the sanctuary, the Holy Table and reredos commemorate Alexander Clark and Frances Clark,

1939. There is also a credence table. The prayer desk on the right of the sanctuary commemorates Thomas Clark, 1963, and that on the left, Hugh McKeown, 1962. The episcopal chair in the sanctuary, was placed there in 1961 to mark the

*Bishop's Chair.*

historic connection of the parish with the Bishopric in the 12th and 13th centuries. The sanctuary was tiled in memory of Jane Clark who died in 1935.

The pulpit is to the left of the chancel, and the font is adjacent below it. There are two prayer desks on the right side of the chancel. One of these commemorates Heather Sloan, 1993, and the other was presented by Maghera Branch of the Mothers' Union. The brass eagle lectern between commemorates William Clark who died in 1904.

Maghera Church contains the many monuments and memorials to the Clark family. On the west wall is a memorial to James Jackson Lenox-Conyngham Chichester Clark, Captain in the Royal Navy, DSO and Bar, DL and Member of Parliament for South Derry in the Northern Ireland Parliament, who died in 1933. There are memorials to Ensign Alexander Clark who died in 1863, and to Naval Commander Roland Clark, OBE, who died in 1926, as well as to the Rev. Francis Hall Clark, son of Colonel Clarke, President and Dean of Magdalen College, Cambridge. He died in 1953. A monument commemorates Elizabeth, wife of Colonel J.J.Clark, and eldest daughter of Sir William Lenox-Conyngham of Springhill, Moneymore, Co. Londonderry, who died in 1954, and there is a monument in memory of Col. James Jackson Clark, HML, who died in 1926.

On the south wall are the memorials to Dorothea Clark Hall who died in 1949, and to Flying Officer Robert, second son of Air Marshal Sir Robert and Lady Clark Hall, Christchurch, New Zealand, who was killed in action in 1944. There are memorials to John Hall, Registrar General of Shipping who died in 1902, to his wife Dorothea who died in 1936, to William Ovens Clark, Chief Justice of the Punjab who died in 1937, and to James Johnston Clark, DL, who died in 1891, and to his wife Frances.

On the north wall, memorials to Reserve Police Constable John Proctor who was killed in 1981, and to Elizabeth Bradley who died in 1922, and her sister-in-law, Annie Scott who died in 1923, can be seen. William, son of the Rev. James Spencer Knox, Rector of Maghera and Kilcronaghan, 1817-1862, and his wife Clara Beresford who died in 1837, her brother John Beresford de la Poer, and James and Henry who died in infancy, are commemorated. The Rev. James Knox was the eldest son of Bishop Knox, Bishop of Derry. There is a memorial to Maryanne Paul, wife of William Clark and daughter of Captain Newport of Suirville, Waterford. She died in 1891. Nora Tomb who died in 1917 and Pierce Noël Clark who died in 1933, are commemorated on memorial plaques. A monument commemorates Alexander William Maxwell Clark, JP, Ampertain House, Upperlands, High Sheriff, who died in 1973, and his wife Dorothy, daughter of Lt. Col. J. Lopdell, JP, Athenry. There are monuments to Henry Jackson Clark, MBE, DL, JP who died in 1956 and to his wife Alice who died in 1954, and to his son, Major Brian Clark, DL, who died in 1989, as well as to the Rev. Henry Barnard, LL.D., Rector of Maghera 1787-1792.

He was the second son of Dr. William Barnard, Bishop of Derry. His first wife was a daughter of Stratford Canning of Garvagh, a prominent family, and his second wife was Sarah, daughter of the Rev. John Robertson, Rector of Aughanunshin, Letterkenny, Co. Donegal. He died in 1793.

On the east wall, to the left of the sanctuary is a memorial to those who fell in the Great War. On the north wall of the sanctuary, the Rev. James Spencer Knox is commemorated, along with his wife, Clara. The Communion rails were presented in their memory in 1904.

# Flahertach O'Brolchain and the Origins of the Diocesan System

THE DIOCESAN SYSTEM which exists in Ireland today was established following the Synod of Rathbreasil in 1111. It was consolidated at the Synod of Kells in 1152, and the Synod of Cashel in 1172. These Synods were held to bring the Celtic Church into line with the Continental mainstream from which it had drifted considerably. Hitherto, there had not been dioceses and parishes as we now know them. The Celtic Church was structured around the many monasteries with their abbots as the head of the community. The bishops who ordained the clergy lived within the monasteries and were subject to the abbots. By 1100, the abbots of the monasteries had become powerful landlords, and the spiritual life of the monasteries was in decline. Reform was necessary.

In the north-west, St. Eugene founded the "Diocese" of Ardstraw about 540. This survived until about 1150 when Bishop Maurice O'Coffey transferred the See to his native *Rath Luairg,* Maghera. Maghera in turn survived until about 1280 when the See was transferred to Derry.

Though Maghera was the site of the See from c1150 to c1280, nevertheless, Derry during this period had an abbey which had originated in Columba's time. In 1164, the *Teampaill Mór,* or Large Church, was built to replace Columba's abbey. This abbey had bishops, and was a very important institution. By the twelfth century, bishops were emerging from the monasteries, and they were beginning to acquire jurisdiction over territory which usually coincided with the old *tuaths,* the ancient kingdoms.

A very important figure at this time was Flahertach O'Brolchain, who, it can be claimed, was the first Bishop of Derry, even though the See was still at Maghera. He was Abbot of Derry, and became bishop in 1158, shortly after Maurice O'Coffey became bishop in Maghera. His family had supplied many eminent ecclesiastics for the Abbey of Derry. They were sometimes known as *O'Brollaghan,* or Bradley in English, and they were a distinguished noble family. O'Brolchain was a very powerful character, whose influence was widely felt throughout Ireland.

The Four Masters relate the circumstances of O'Brolchain's election as bishop as follows, "An assembly was held by the Irish clergy at Brigh-mac-Taidhg in the territory of Hy-Laoghaire (in Co. Meath), at which were present, twenty-five bishops, together with the apostolic legate, for the purpose of establishing ecclesiastical discipline and the improvement of morals. In this assembly, the clergy of Ireland and the *coarb* of St. Patrick (Archbishop of Armagh), decreed by common consent that a bishop's chair *(cathaoir easpoicc),* and the supreme superintendence of all the abbeys in Ireland, (that is, of the Columban Order), should be given to the *coarb* of Saint Columbkille, Flahertach O'Brolchain. The bishops of Connaught set out on their way to this synod, but they were robbed and beaten, and two of their people were killed by the soldiers of Dermot O'Melaghlin, King of Meath at the wooden bridge at Clonmacnoise, after they had passed through the town; then they returned home."

Flahertach O'Brolchain owed his preferment to Gelasius, or *Gilla-mac-Liag,* who was a leading figure in the 12th century reformation of the Celtic Church. It was largely due to him that the present diocesan system was created, and that the Church at last emerged from the monasteries.

## MOUNTFIELD

MOUNTFIELD CHURCH in Mountfield village, ten kilometres from Omagh on the Cookstown road, was built in 1826. It was established in that year as a District Curacy out of Cappagh Parish. It became a perpetual Curacy in 1869, and it was amalgamated with Drumragh Parish, Omagh in 1918.

The church is a two-bay hall, with a tower and spire at the west end. The vestry room is left of the north side of the nave. Inside, the gallery is over the west end of the nave. The font is to the right beneath. The pulpit and lectern are to the right of the chancel, and the prayer desk is to the left.

There is a window in the west wall of the tower, one in the vestry room, and two on each of the side walls of the nave, all of which have rectangular, opaque panes. The east window has three lights, and commemorates David Monteith. The left light depicts the Bible, the midle one, the Lamb of God, and the right light, a lamp, and there is the text, "Behold the Lamb of God".

*Mountfield Church.*

On the west wall of the nave, a brass plaque records the donation of the lights in memory of Charles McCollum. These lights consist of two small candelabra in the nave, with rotary wheel designs in the centre. On the north wall, there is a plaque in memory of Andrew, Henrietta and Olive Jane Wasson, and of Caroline Allen.

## MUFF, CULMORE, LONDONDERRY, HOLY TRINITY, St. PETER'S, LONDONDERRY

THE THREE CHURCHES of Muff, Culmore and St. Peter's are grouped together as a parish. Culmore and St. Peter's are in the northern suburbs of Londonderry, and the village of Muff nearby, is just across the border in County Donegal. Indeed, the suburbs of Derry now reach out to Muff, which is ten kilometres from the city centre. The name Muff means *"a plain"*. The ancient church originated in an abbey which was founded by St. Columba at Ishkaheen about three kilometres away. In 1693, it was one of five chapels of ease attached to the Parish of Templemore.

The old church was in bad repair by the beginning of the 18th century. The present church in Muff village was built in 1737 by the Harts of Kilderry House, Muff. The tombstone of Col. Henry Hart, dated 1711, is in the floor of the aisle. In 1809, the parish became a perpetual curacy.

Muff church is a simple, three-bay hall which is entered by a porch at the west end. Inside is the staircase to a small landing and gallery. There are three plain glass windows in the south wall, and one below the gallery in the north wall. The east window, with three lights and tracery, has coloured glass and depictions of a cup and grapes, and the Lamb of God. It commemorates Commander George Vaughan Hart, RN of Kilderry and his wife, Jane Maria, both of whom died in 1895. The reredos in the sanctuary is finely carved. The vestry room is to the left.

The stone pulpit is on the left of the chancel, and there is a stone prayer desk to the right. This was given in memory of William Edward Hart of Kilderry who died in 1919, and of his wife, Bessie Louisa who died on 28th November 1892, three days after bearing a daughter. The daughter, Mrs

*Muff Church.*

Ada Foxlee, died on 4th January 1999, aged 106 years. She was a grand-aunt of the author! The brass eagle lectern is in memory of Officers of the Royal Inniskilling Fusiliers who fell in the Great War. The tiling in the aisle and porch was installed in 1921 in their memory as well.

On the north wall, there is a monument to John Hart of Ballynagard who died in 1816. Ballynagard House, just across the border at Culmore, was another residence of the Hart family. On the north wall of the chancel, a monument commemorates Lt.Andrew Chichester Hart, 11th Battalion, Royal Inniskilling Fusiliers, second son of William Hart, who was killed at the Somme in 1916, and on the south chancel wall, there is a monument to General George Vaughan Hart, military Governor of Londonderry and MP for Donegal, who died in 1832. On the south wall, his daughter Eliza who died in 1823 is commemorated. Diamond-shaped hatchments on each side of the east wall in the sanctuary bear Hart family shields and coats of arms. The one on the left states that Maryanne Hart, wife of George Hart died in 1725, and the one on the right states that Col. Henry Hart died in 1712, though his tombstone in the aisle gives the date 1711.

Muff Rectory, now a private dwelling, was built in 1879 with the aid of Commander George Vaughan Hart, who with William E. Hart, gave the site.

Holy Trinity Church, Culmore, is three kilometres from Muff, on the main road into Derry. The name Culmore means, *"the great corner"*. The church was originally one of the five chapels of ease in Templemore Parish, as was Muff. It was burnt by King James' army during the siege, and was not rebuilt.

In 1840, the Irish Society acquired land at Culmore from the Crown, and a new church with the dedication Holy Trinity was erected in 1867. It is a cruciform building, with nave, sanctuary and transepts. It is entered through a porch in the north-west corner, which is surmounted by a tower, which at the top is octagonal with louvers, and above this is a short spire. There is a window with four lights in the west wall, which has square opaque glass and tracery, with angels inset. There are two windows in the north nave wall, three in the south nave wall, and two in the south wall of the south transept with an oval light above. All these windows have square-paned opaque glass. The two windows in the north wall of the north transept illustrate St.Peter on the left, and St.Andrew on the right, and the oval light above shows the Heavenly Jerusalem. There are two windows in the north chancel and sanctuary wall, both of which have square-paned opaque glass. The east window has fine stained glass and tracery. The left light illustrates the text, "this is my beloved Son", the centre light illustrates the text, "I ascend unto my Father and your Father", and the right light, "do this in remembrance of me."

The font is at the west end of the church, below the west window. The cover commemorates Capt. Joseph Ballintine of the Royal Inniskilling Fusiliers who was killed in the Great War. It was presented in 1920 by his widow. There are choir pews in the transepts. The pulpit on the left was erected in 1920 in memory of David McCorkell of Ballyarnett who died in 1897, and of his daughters, and it was

*Culmore Church.*

presented by his wife, Eva. The prayer desk in the chancel, was presented by the Irish Society in 1920. The wooden eagle lectern is in memory of Violet and Andrew Watt, 1933. The marble steps into the sanctuary commemorate the Rev. J. S. Wylie, 1933, and his sister, Annie Wylie, as does the Holy Table, 1934. The hand rail at the steps was presented in memory of James Cochrane. The oak panelling in the sanctuary commemorates those who fell in the Great War. It was erected in 1920. The organ by Telford and Telford is in the south transept. It has one manual and pedals. The organ stool and chancel carpet commemorate Audrey Fleck.

On the west wall, a plaque states that the tiling in the church was replaced by Commander G. F. Gilliland of Brooke Hall in 1933 in memory of members of his family. On the north nave wall, a plaque records the installation of the sanctuary panelling, and of the electric light in memory of those who fell in the second World War. On the north wall of the north transept, there is a memorial to Marjorie Watt who died aged fourteen years in 1914, and to Jocelyn, her sister who died aged five months in 1904. It was erected by their parents Samuel and Blanche Watt. The tiles below record the erection of the window illustrating St.Peter above, in memory of Thomas Calvert Wylie who died in 1942, and on the other side of the window, is St.Andrew, in memory of Roy Wylie his brother of Natal, South Africa, who died in 1944. On the east wall of the north transept, is a memorial to Helen McCorkell of Ballyarnett who died in 1970. There is also a memorial to her husband Dudley McCorkell, Knight of the Order of St. John of Jerusalem, and their son, Lt. Francis McCorkell of the Irish Guards who was killed in 1944. On the south wall of the south transept, Valentine Gilliland of the Royal Inniskilling Fusiliers who was killed at Ypres in 1915, is commemorated. On the south wall of the nave, a brass plaque commemorates Bishop Cuthbert Irvine Peacocke, Bishop of Derry and Raphoe, 1970-1975, who died in 1994, and his wife Helen who died in 1988. A plaque adjacent records the replacing of the windows in 1960 in memory of Mrs Myra Wylie who died in 1957.

Due to the growth of the City of Londonderry in the mid-1960s, it was considered necessary to build a new church, St. Peter's, at Belmont in the northern suburbs of the west bank of the Foyle. This was made a daughter church of Christ Church, until 1976, when the curate-in-charge, at that time the Rev. (later Canon) Leslie Maconachie, under the Rector of Christ Church, the Rev. (later Bishop) Brian Hannon, became Vicar. In 1978, St. Peter's was amalgamated with the adjoining parish of Muff and Culmore, and, with two Select Vestries, they are administered together as a parish. With the civil unrest of the 1970s and 1980s, much of the parish population left the area, and the numbers went down. The opening of the new Foyle Bridge in 1984 has been of great help in stabilising the parish.

*St. Peter's Church, Belmont, Londonderry.*

St. Peter's Church was consecrated by the Right Rev. Charles John Tyndall, Bishop of Derry and Raphoe, on 8th October 1966, during the Incumbency of Canon Victor Griffin, then Rector of Christ Church, Londonderry, later Dean of St. Patrick's Cathedral, Dublin. The Rev. James Miller, Curate of Christ Church, became first curate-in-charge of St. Peter's. The church is entered through a porch in the north-west corner of the building. The font is in the middle of the west wall. The vestry room and choir robing rooms are to the left of the sanctuary. The east wall has three sides which form a very shallow apse, and in it is set a large illuminated wooden cross. The altar was presented by the Poyntz family. The sanctuary chairs and Communion rails were presented by Christ Church Bowling Club in memory of Matilda McKeane. The pulpit on the left was the gift of St. Peter's Fellowship and of Miss Reynolds. There are two prayer desks, one of which, on the right, commemorates John Kenwell who died in 1971. The organ is a large instrument with two manuals and pedals. It came from St.Barnabas' Church in Belfast, and was dedicated on Easter Sunday, 7th

April 1996 in memory of James and Phyllis Payne. The flags of the Royal British Legion, Messines Park Branch, are placed over the entrance door. The original standard was dedicated in 1928, and laid up in 1970. The other two flags were laid up in 1976.

The west window has three lights. It depicts the River of Life flowing from the Throne of God in Revelation. There are seven windows in the south wall. The first of these depicts St.Luke the Physician. St. Peter's Church is the Diocesan centre for the Church's Ministry of Healing. The next two windows have opaque rectangular glass. The fourth window commemorates those who fell in the second World War, and was presented by Messines Park Branch of the Royal British Legion. It depicts St. Andrew, and also contains the insignia of the Legion. The next two windows have rectangular-paned opaque glass. The seventh window, which is in the sanctuary, has two lights, and is built round a large cross in the wall. It depicts St.Patrick on the left with a bell above, and St.Columba on the right with a dove above. Of the three windows in the north wall, two have rectangular-paned opaque glass, and the middle one depicts St. Peter.

*St. Luke, Ministry of Healing Window (left) and St. Peter Window (right).*

*Ministry of Healing Chapel.*

The fine suite of parish halls, which are at right angles to the church, were built in 1969. Upstairs is a little chapel, dedicated to St.Luke, where healing services and daily worship take place.

## St. AUGUSTINE'S, LONDONDERRY

St. Augustine's Church is situated on the historic walls of Derry. It stands upon the site of an ancient Augustinian abbey which dated from the end of the 13th century. This abbey was used by the planters at the beginning of the 17th century until the completion of the cathedral in 1633. The church was rebuilt by Bishop Barnard about 1768, and named, "ye chapel of ease".

The present church was consecrated on 11th June 1872. It is a benefice in the Parish of Templemore. At the west end, there is a lean-to porch with a gabled door and a bellcote. The window above the entrance contains four circular lights and geometric tracery. Inside the porch are the steps to the gallery, beneath which is the baptistery. A plaque in it states that the font was

*St. Augustine's Church.*

presented by the Mothers' Union, and that it was dedicated on the Ascension Day, 6th May 1948. A lectern in the baptistery was presented by Samuel Heatley in memory of his wife, Margaret, who died in 1996. The choir stalls are on either side of the chancel. They were presented in 1961 by members of the junior Girls' Friendly Society in memory of Scott Gallagher who died in 1955. The prayer desk on the left was presented by the G.F.S. in 1935, and the prayer desk on the right was presented by the family of Cecil Allen who died in 1996. The brass eagle lectern and the Holy Table were presented in 1931, and the pulpit was dedicated in 1934. These furnishings were provided at the time of the renovations which were carried out from 1931 to 1934. The original Holy Table was presented to Killowen Church, Coleraine. There are three chairs in the sanctuary, one of which was given in memory of Meta Armstrong who died in 1967. There are also two small prayer desks in the sanctuary. The organ by Conacher, has two manuals and pedals. The organ chamber is to the left of the chancel, and the vestry room is to the right of the sanctuary. The sanctuary walls are lined with lovely Minton tiles which depict wheat sheaves, and above them, running round the three sides, the tiled frieze depicts grapes.

St. Augustine's has some very fine windows. The two in the porch, as well as the first window in the south wall, have opaque lattice glass. The nave windows each have two lights and small sections above. The second window in the south wall shows Jesus calling the little children, with a Bible in the tracery, and it commemorates Violet Roulston, her husband Christopher and their son Maurice, 1999. The third window contains the War Memorial, and the names of those who fell in the second World War. It depicts Elisha encouraging his servant on the walls of Dothan, (2 Kings 6:17). The fourth window was dedicated in 1989, and it commemorates Canon Herbert McKegney, Rector of St. Augustine's, 1930-1972. Canon McKegney was a keen Scouter, so the window shows the world badge of Scouting in the tracery, and it also illustrates the Lamb in the midst of the Throne and the multitudes in white, from the Book of Revelation.

In the north wall of the nave, the window by the baptistery depicts the Baptism of Jesus in its two lights. The Lamb of God appears in the tracery above. The window was dedicated in 2001 in memory of Mrs Annie (Nan) Heatley and her daughter, Joy. It also commemorates Samuel and Margaret Heatley, and was donated by the family. The second window has opaque lattice glass. The third window depicts Ruth and Naomi, and commemorates Elizabeth Frances Algeo who died

*St. Augustine's Church, Nave looking east.*

in 1944. The east window has three lights and geometric tracery. The upper sections depict the Good Shepherd, and the lower sections depict the Prodigal Son. Noah's Ark appears in the tracery above. The window commemorates Thomas Scott of Willsborough who died in 1872. There is a small window in the north wall of the sanctuary, the gift of the Rev. Thomas Scott, Incumbent, 1870-1877, during whose incumbency, the present church was built. It depicts Simeon receiving the Child Jesus in the Temple (the Nunc Dimittis).

In the porch, a monument commemorates Lt. Robert Boyd of the Bengal Army who was killed at Malaga in Spain in 1831. Robert Boyd's sister married Lt.Col. Colby who was involved in the production of the first Ordnance Survey of Ireland in 1836. There is also a stone with the Red Hand of Ulster, which has the inscription, "to the memory of John McCombe who departed 1689". The Roll of Honour commemorates those who served and fell in the two world wars. There is an old stone tablet of unknown origin on the window sill in the porch.

On the north nave wall is a monument to William Algeo, ship's surgeon on S.S. *California*, who died when the ship was torpedoed in 1917. There is a memorial to Charles Algeo who died in 1926, and on the arch adjacent to the organ, a brass plaque commemorates David and Ruby Holmes, by whose bequest the organ was rebuilt in 1983. The Great War memorial is on the south wall, and there is a memorial to Mary Caroline Maguinness, who died in 1986, on the west wall.

## TAMLAGHTARD, St. CADAN

Tamlaghtard, *"the high plague monument"*, is situated on an exposed, windswept site, on the slopes of Benevenagh Mountain, overlooking the Magilligan peninsula at the north-eastern tip of Lough Foyle. The church is said to have been founded by St. Patrick. Patrick's work was continued by the patron saint of the parish, Cadan, who lived around the beginning of the sixth century, and whose tomb is supposed to lie close to the old church. The ruins of this church are adjacent to St. Aidan's Roman Catholic Church nearby, the site of which was given to their congregation by the Earl Bishop when Tamlaghtard church was built.

The exact date of the present church is uncertain, but it was built between 1778 and 1787, with assistance from the Earl Bishop. It is a simple, three bay hall church with a tower, through which the church is entered . At its base is a flight of steps, and on both sides, there are two smaller towers which are, in fact, extensions to the nave, and of the same height.

On the north wall, and on each side of the tower entrance, are blind windows. There is a window in both of the miniature towers at the west end, and three windows of two lights and Y tracery in the south wall of the nave. The east window has three lights and tracery.

*Tamlaghtard Church.*

Inside the porch are the stairs to the gallery. In the nave, the baptistery is in the south-west corner beneath the gallery. The chancel and vestry room to the left, were built in 1854. The stone pulpit is to the left. The prayer desk on the right is in memory of Sir Frederick William Heygate, DL who died in 1894, and the wooden eagle lectern adjacent commemorates the Rev. John McAdams, Rector of Tamlaghtard, 1870-1899. In the sanctuary, the reading lights commemorate Sir Henry McDonald Tyler and his daughter, 1980, and the prayer desk was presented by the Rev. Robert Stanley, Rector, 1954-1960, and Mrs Stanley.

Tamlaghtard Church has some fine monuments and memorials commemorating the Heygate, McCausland, Gage and Tyler families. On the north wall is a monument to Sir John Heygate, 4th Baronet, of Bellarena, and second son of Arthur Conolly Gage. There is a memorial to Connolly McCausland of Drenagh who died in 1827. The section below commemorates Marcus McCausland who died in 1862, and below again, a part of the memorial commemorates Marianne McCausland who died in 1864. There are memorials to Ann Gage who died in 1868, and to her husband Marcus Gage who died in 1890. Henry Tyler who died in 1897, and his daughter who was the wife of Canon Henry Francis McDonald Tyler, Rector of Tullyaughnish (Ramelton), and Conolly Gage of Bellarena, and his wife Henrietta, who died in 1869 are all commemorated. Monuments commemorate Col. Robert Henry Gage Heygate, DSO who died in 1923, and Sir Frederick William Heygate, 2nd Baronet, DL, who died in 1894, and Marianne, daughter of Conolly Gage of Bellarena, wife of Sir Frederick Heygate, and the Rev. Thomas Thomson, LL.D., Rector 1921-1928.

On the east wall are the memorials to Eliza Dysart who died in 1871, and to her husband, the Rev. William Dysart, Rector of Tamlaghtard, 1856-1874, and who died in 1881. On the south wall, there is a memorial to Christopher Gage Heygate who died in 1905, aged twelve years, and Conolly McCausland of Fruithill (the old name of Drenagh), who died in 1794, and his wife, are commemorated.

## TAMLAGHTFINLAGAN, BALLYKELLY, St. FINDLUGANUS
## MYROE CHAPEL OF EASE, St. JOHN THE BAPTIST

TAMLAGHTFINLAGAN PARISH CHURCH is in Ballykelly, Co. Londonderry, five kilometres west of Limavady on the Londonderry road. The name means, *"the plague monument of Findluganus"*. Findluganus, or Finlagan, Patron Saint of the parish, was a contemporary and friend of Columba. Columba is supposed to have founded an abbey in the district about 585.

In 1622, the church was in ruins. The Fishmongers' Company which had settled in the area after the Plantation, repaired and enlarged the old church, which was dedicated to St. Peter. It was also known as the Garrison Church. This church was destroyed and restored twice during the 17th century. It was kept in good repair in the 18th century, with a chancel being built in 1719.

*Tamlaghtfinlagan Church.*

The Fishmongers also erected a castle at Walworth, west of Ballykelly. Walworth was named after Sir William Walworth who was Mayor of London at the time of Wat Tyler's revolt in 1381.

The present church in Ballykelly was built in 1795 by the Earl of Bristol, Bishop Hervey. The chancel, vestry and gallery were added in 1851, and the north aisle, by Joseph Welland, was built in 1859. Set amongst trees in spacious grounds at the edge of the village, Tamlaghtfinlagan church is an impressive sight. It is a three bay hall with a tower and a tall, elegant ashlar spire. There are crenellations along the external nave walls. The nave walls are supported by buttresses.

The window in the west wall of the porch is in memory of Private Michael Boxall, 5th Co. Londonderry Battalion, Ulster Defence Regiment. Two Rolls of Honour in the porch commemorate those who fell in the Great War. The gallery is over the west end of the nave. The nave ceiling has a flat, classical design, and the ceiling in the sanctuary is vaulted. There are three windows in the south wall. Each has two lights and diamond panes with rectangular edges, and Y tracery and various crest insets. The middle window was installed in 1995 to

*Interior of Ballykelly Church.*

mark the bicentenary of the church. On the left are inset illustrations of the church, 1795, of the rectory which was built in 1863, and of Jesus calling the children. On the right, are illustrations of the texts, "go into all the world" and "do all to the glory of God", and St. John's chapel at Myroe, 1863, is depicted. The arms of the Beresford family also appear. The Hon. John Beresford was a son of Marcus, Earl of Tyrone, who became Marquis of Waterford. At the end of the 18th century, he was a member of the Privy Councils of England and Ireland, and First Commissioner of the Revenue. The third window in the south wall, nearest the chancel, displays the arms of the Earl of Bristol and the Diocesan crest, combined with the Bristol arms. There are similarly three windows of two lights each in the north aisle wall, which also contain crests. The middle window depicts on the left, the Empty Tomb, and on the right, the loaves and fishes for the feeding of the five thousand. It commemorates Arthur Sampson, JP, 1860. The east window has three lights of diamond coloured glass and double Y tracery. The tracery displays the arms of the Marquis of Waterford, head of the Beresford family. There are also the arms of the Sampson family, and of the Fishmongers' Company and of the Hon. the Irish Society.

The aisle and nave are separated by one small arch under the gallery, and three large arches. The baptistery is in the west end of the aisle. The altar was purchased in 1947 to mark the 150th anniversary of the church two years earlier. The old altar was then given to St. John's, Myroe. The reredos and Communion rails commemorate those who fell in the second World War. There are two chairs in the sanctuary. That on the left is in memory of William and Margaret Quigg. The credence table was presented by the Brown family in memory of their parents. The vestry room is to

*Bicentenary Window, 1795-1995.*

the left of the chancel. The vestry table is in memory of Robert, John and James McMichael, 1968. The pulpit on the left, which was presented in 1923, is in memory of Conolly Gage of Drummond, who was the last Irish agent to the Fishmongers' Company. He died in 1922. The lectern on the right commemorates Maria Hester Sampson who died in 1895. The prayer desk on the right is in memory of William Charles Gage and his sisters. The electronic organ is on the right side of the nave near the chancel. Ballykelly has had long associations with the Royal Air Force. Two RAF flags are placed at each corner of the gallery.

There are numerous monuments in the church. On the west wall, there are memorials to James Beresford, a midshipman aboard HM Frigate *Phenix* who was drowned in 1807, and to John McCausland who died in 1844. On the north wall are memorials to those who fell in the two World Wars. On the south wall are monuments commemorating Capt. George Stirling of the Queen's Royal Regiment who died in 1863, David Cather who died in 1846, Thomas Sampson who died in 1863, and the Rev. George Sampson, Rector of Errigal (Garvagh), who died in 1827. A memorial commemorates Arthur Sampson who died in 1859. It was erected by the Fishmongers' Company. Another monument commemorates Maud Ingram, daughter of Sir Frederick Heygate, who died in 1931. There are also memorials on the south wall to Geoffrey Brown who died in 1987, to Canon Ernest Crawcour, Rector 1933-1964, who died in a car accident in 1975, and to the Rev. George Sampson, son of Rev. George Sampson above, Rector of Tamlaghtfinlagan from 1846 until his death in 1860. A monument in the chancel north wall records the erection of the chancel, vestry and gallery by the Fishmongers in 1851. In the north aisle wall is a memorial to Mary Victoria, wife of Conolly Gage of Drummond House, who died in 1920. There are memorials to Theodosia Scott who died in 1892, and to William Charles Gage of Drummond House, Ballykelly, which was erected by the Wardens of the Fishmongers' Company in 1882. A very fine classical monument on the east aisle wall commemorates Jane Hamilton (1672-1756), wife of the Hon. Sir Randel Beresford, Bart. It is one of the finest monuments of its kind in the north-west, and is based on Grinling Gibbon's monument to Mary Beaufoy (1705) in Westminster Abbey.

*Jane Hamilton Monument.*

Myroe chapel of ease is situated seven kilometres to the north-east of Ballykelly. It was built in 1863, and consecrated on 1st September

*Myroe Church.*

1864 and given the dedication St. John the Baptist. It is entered through a porch in the north-west corner. Inside are two windows in the west wall with a small window above. There is one window with a single light in the south wall, and one other of two lights. Opposite in the north wall, is a window with two lights. In the chancel north wall is another single-light window. All of these have clear lattice glass. The east window has three lights of diamond panes and tracery.

The vestry room is to the right of the chancel and sanctuary. The altar came from Ballykelly in 1947. The credence table is in memory of James and Isabella Devlin. The font, just inside the door, bears the inscription, AWE and CSE DD 1863. The pulpit is on the left side of the chancel. A monument on the north wall records the donation of the prayer desk and lectern in memory of those who fell in the second World War, and the memorial to those who fell in the Great War is on the south wall.

In 1896, a parishioner, Thomas Nicholl, was ploughing a field close to Tamlaghtfinlagan Church, when his plough hit an object below the ground. This turned out to be what became known as the Broighter Hoard. It consists of a model boat including oars, a small, shallow bowl, two gold chains, a gold collar, and part of a second gold collar, of unknown date. They are in the National Museum in Dublin.

## TAMLAGHT O'CRILLY UPPER, TAMLAGHT O'CRILLY TAMLAGHT O'CRILLY LOWER, INISHRUSH

TAMLAGHT O'CRILLY, *"the plague monument of the O'Crillys"*, is a parish in east County Derry, close to Portglenone. The O'Crillys were herenachs, (agents or stewards), of the church lands in the area in the late Middle Ages. The monument is supposed to be the burial cave on rising ground above Tamlaght village. There was a church in ancient times.

The church was roofless in 1622, though otherwise, in good repair. It was ruined in the 1641 rebellion, and remained so throughout the remainder of the 17th century. By the 1768 survey, the church was in good repair. In 1775, the parish was divided into Tamlaght O'Crilly Upper and Lower.

Tamlaght O'Crilly Upper Church is in Tamlaght O'Crilly village in Co. Londonderry, sixteen kilometres east of Maghera. The church was rebuilt in 1815, and the chancel dates from 1859. It is entered through the porch which is at the base of a louvered tower. The interior entrance door is in memory of Arthur McCay, and James and Sarah Michael, 1980, and there is a window with coloured lattice glass in the tower. There are three windows in the south wall, each of which has coloured lattice glass and Y tracery, and no windows in the north wall. The east window has three lights and tracery. Our Lord is in the centre, with praying figures on either side. The window commemorates Katherine Frances, wife of Canon Robert McQuaide, Rector of Tamlaght O'Crilly Upper, 1909-1956. She died in 1935. There is also a small window in the south wall of the chancel.

*Tamlaght O'Crilly Upper Church.*

In the sanctuary, the stone reredos behind the Holy Table commemorates Godfrey Samuel, Alicia Greene and Godfrey Greene. The east wall is panelled in stone, which extends both sides of the reredos. The first of three sections on the left commemorates Thomas McKay, the second, those who fell in the Great War, and the third, L.Cpl. Alston Neely who was killed in action in 1918. Similarly, the three sections to the right of the Holy Table commemorate, first, William and Margery Kernaghan, second, Alice Crockett, and third, James and Elizabeth Crockett. Over the whole reredos are carved the words, "Blessing and Honour and Glory and Power be unto the Lamb". The vestry room is to the left of the chancel.

The baptistery and font are in the north-east corner of the nave. They commemorate the Rev. Henry Innes Law, Rector 1957-1963. The pulpit on the left commemorates both Canon MacQuaide and the Rev. H. I. Law. The lectern is in memory of James Lennox and his son John, 1964. The prayer desk and chair in the chancel were presented by past and present parishioners, 1960. There are some chairs in the sanctuary. One of these commemorates the Rev. Maiben Cunningham Motherwell, Curate from 1826 to 1854. Another chair is in memory of Thomas and Sarah Crockett, 1960. The credence table is in memory of William and Margaret Neely, 1971. A plaque states that the Communion kneelers are in memory of Samuel and May McClintock and Bessie Nelson, 1995. There is a one manual Telford and Telford organ with pedals. One hymn board was presented by St. James' Church, Belfast, in 1958, and the other is in memory of Bobby McClintock.

On the north wall, a plaque states that the electric lighting was installed in memory of the Rev. H. I. Law and others. There is also a memorial to Mr Law. On the south wall, there is a brass memorial to those who fell in the first and second World Wars.

Tamlaght O'Crilly Lower Church is five kilometres to the east of the Upper Church, in the village of Inishrush. Upon the division of the parish of Tamlaght O'Crilly in 1775, it was constituted a Perpetual Curacy. In that year, the Earl Bishop built a small church at his own expense. This was rebuilt in 1815. Tamlaght O'Crilly Lower became a parish in 1883.

*Tamlaght O'Crilly Lower Church.*

The church is entered through the porch at the base of a louvered tower. There are two blind windows in the west wall, and a window with coloured glass in the west wall of the tower. Inside, the church is a three bay hall, with three windows in the south wall and none in the north wall. These windows all have square-paned coloured and opaque glass. The east window depicts the Good Shepherd. It commemorates the Rev. Samuel Scott Frackelton, Rector of Tamlaght O'Crilly Lower from 1883 until his death in 1911.

The chancel step extends westwards on both sides of the nave, to form a podium for the baptistery adjacent to the north wall. The pulpit and prayer desk are on the left side of the chancel. The prayer desk and chair are in memory of William Greer who died in 1977. The Holy Table and the chair on the left side of the sanctuary are both in memory of James and Elizabeth Kissick, 1992. The lectern on the right commemorates Robert McCullough, 1968. There are two chairs and a credence table on the right side of the sanctuary. The organ is on the right of the chancel.

A monument on the north wall commemorates Reserve Constable William James Greer who was killed in 1977, and another, Trooper John Smyth of the Royal Inniskilling Fusiliers who was killed in 1917 during the Great War. On the south wall are memorials to James Courtenay and his wife, Martha, 1899, and to John Patton who died in 1927, his wife Sarah who died in the same year, and Archibald Patton who died in France in action in 1917. On the east wall of the sanctuary, there is a memorial to Elizabeth, wife of the Rev. Samuel Frackelton, who died in 1914, and on the south wall of the sanctuary is a memorial to those who fell in the first and second World Wars.

Tamlaght O'Crilly Upper and Lower were reunited in 1963.

## TERMONAMONGAN, KILLETER, St. BESTIUS

TERMONAMONGAN MEANS, *"O'Mongan's termon, or church land"*. In ancient times, it was known as Kylchyrll, or O'Caireall's Church, which was either founded by or dedicated to St. Caireall. The church is dedicated to St. Bestius, and is situated in the village of Killeter, seven kilometres from Castlederg in west Tyrone, on the banks of the Derg River.

The present church was built in 1822 and consecrated in 1827. Entry is through a porch in the west end. The coloured glass window and panelling and floor commemorate Hugh and Margaret Sproule, 1977, and the ventilation system is in memory of Joseph and Elizabeth Livingstone. Inside, the church is a large hall of four bays. On the north side is an aisle which is nearly as large as the nave. It was added in 1870. From the outside, the nave and aisle appear almost like two churches which are joined, the nave being plastered externally, and the aisle being of undressed stone.

The four windows in the south nave wall were all dedicated following major renovations in 1977. They each have two lights of clear glass, with small circular lights above. The first has insets of coloured glass depicting a boat on a lake on the left, and Jesus on the right, and was donated by Herbert and Mary Speer. The second is in memory of James Speer who died in 1929, and of his wife Eunice. The third commemorates the three daughters of William and Mary Clarke, and the fourth commemorates William and Mary Clarke themselves. In the north wall of the aisle, there are three groups of windows, each with three lights. The first set commemorates Andrew Crawford who died in 1954, and the second set commemorates William Scott who died in 1948, Charles Cooper who died in 1937, and Samuel Robb who died in 1977. The third set behind the organ is unmarked. There is a set of three windows in the east aisle wall. The east window, also of three lights, is in memory of Robert Hamilton who died in 1909, and of his wife, Martha. All the windows have coloured glass with patterned insets.

*Termonamongan Church.*

There is a small room at the west end of the aisle. The vestry room is behind the sanctuary. The baptistery is in the south-west corner of the nave. A plaque states that the panelling and furnishings, consisting of a table and lectern in the north-west corner of the nave, are in memory of Joseph and Matilda Monteith, 1977. Another plaque records the donation of the carpeting by Charles and Ruby Clarke, 1977, and another, the panelling in the baptistery in memory of Andrew Cooper and his sister Fanny, 1977.

A plaque in the porch states that the chancel furnishings, the pulpit on the left side of the nave, and the pews came from St. Paul's Church in Bray, Co. Wicklow, and were installed during the renovations in 1977. The lectern and prayer desk are on the right of the nave, and the electric bell was presented in memory of Jennie Crawford, 1985. The Conacher organ of two manuals and pedals is at the east end of the aisle.

On the south wall, a monument commemorates Robert Mowbray, MD, who died in 1935, and there is a memorial to Mary and Florence Verner, daughters of the Rev. William Verner, Rector 1883-1921, who were drowned at Bundoran, Co.Donegal in 1904.

Bishop William Alexander, husband of Cecil Frances, was Rector of Termonamongan from 1850 to 1855.

## TERMONEENY, KNOCKLOUGHRIM

TERMONEENY PARISH is between Maghera and Castledawson in Co. Derry. The church, which was built in 1801, is in Knockloughrim village. The name means, *"the termon or sanctuary of Heaney"*.

Termoneeny Church has a pinnacled tower at the west end, through which the building is entered. On the south side of the nave are three windows. Each has two lights and Y tracery. The first window depicts, on the left, Jesus, and on the right, his first miracle at Cana in Galillee, and it commemorates Minnie Pallett who died in 1956. The other two windows, as well as the two on the north wall have opaque lattice glass with crosses inset on each side. The east window has three lights and tracery, with coloured and opaque lattice glass. The vestry room is to the left of the sanctuary.

The baptistery is to the left of the entrance. The font commemorates John Victor Bates who died in 1862, and on it is the verse, "My mouth shall speak the praise of the Lord, and let all flesh bless his holy Name for ever and ever", Psalm 145:21. The prayer desk is on the right, and the pulpit and lectern are on the left. The lectern is in memory of John Morrow, 1983. In the sanctuary, the credence table commemorates Robert Henry Lennox, 1977. There is a two manual electronic organ with pedals.

*Termoneeny Church.*

On the north wall, there is a memorial to Joseph Bradley and his wife, of Bank House, Drumard, Knockloughrim. Memorials have also been erected to John Bates, Solicitor who died in 1855, and to those who fell in the Great War. On the south wall, there is a memorial to Staff Sergeant Robert Lennox of the Ulster Defence Regiment who was killed in 1976 in the course of his duty.

## URNEY, CHRIST CHURCH
## SION MILLS, THE CHURCH OF THE GOOD SHEPHERD

URNEY, *"an oratory"*, is a parish in west Tyrone on the banks of the River Finn. The parish church is beautifully set among beech trees near the village of Clady, seven kilometres south of Strabane. It was built in 1865 to replace a church of 1734. There is a porch at the west end and another on the south side. On the north side is a tower which is surmounted by a spire. The tower is at the west end of the north aisle. There is a five-sided apsidal chancel.

The rose window in the west wall over the entrance, is a feature of the church. In the south wall are three windows of two lights. Two of these are of clear glass, and the third which depicts, "Blessed are the pure in heart" from the Beatitudes, (St. Matthew 5:8), is in memory of James Baird, J.P., 1894. Part of the south wall is recessed behind two arches, to the right of which is the vestry room. The north aisle wall has two clear windows of two lights, and there are five stained glass windows in the sanctuary. From left to right, the first two, depicting "On earth peace, good will towards men", and "Truly, this was the Son of God", commemorate those who fell in the Great War. The middle window depicts the text, "I will not leave you comfortless", and the two on the right depict the texts, "I ascend unto my Father and your Father", and, "I am he that liveth and was dead". Both are in memory of John Colquhoun of Castletown House, Strabane who died in 1901, and of his wife.

The baptistery is at the east end of the aisle. The window in it depicts a dove and a cross, and is in

*Urney Church.*

memory of John Herdman who died in 1987. The pulpit on the left is in memory of Thomas Olphert, Dean of Derry, and Rector of Urney, 1872-1898. The two prayer desks, one on either side, commemorate John Herdman who died in 1903. The Herdmans were the owners of the mills at Sion Mills. There is a fine brass eagle lectern. The tiling in the chancel is in memory of Andrew Ferguson Knox, 1878. The panelling round the sanctuary is in memory of John Herdman, D.L., 1906. The two manual Conacher organ with pedals was given by Joseph Keterson of Toronto in 1889. It is situated in the north-west corner of the nave.

On the west wall is a monument to Sir James Galbraith who died in 1827. On the north wall is a memorial to William Stewart, M.D. who died in 1851, and to his wife and sons. A brass memorial commemorates Lilla Ferrier, and another one, Brigadier General Tom Pearse who died in 1947. On the north aisle wall are memorials to Olive Colquhoun, to James Jones, Rector of Urney, 1814-1835, to Benjamin Fenton who died in 1804, and to William Maxwell who died in 1789. On the south wall, John Olphert, Rector 1899-1921, is commemorated. He died in 1923. There is also a brass memorial to Kenneth Smyth who died in 1971.

The Church of the Good Shepherd in the village of Sion Mills in the parish of Urney, was built in 1909. It is a splendid church, built in Italian Renaissance style, and modelled on a church at

*Sion Mills Church.*

Pistoia near Florence. The architect, W.F.Unsworth, designed the first Shakespeare Memorial Theatre at Stratford-upon-Avon.

The west end consists of two low, lean-to porches, with a semi-circular projection, balustraded at the top, between. This houses the spiral staircase to the gallery. In the north-east corner, a tall square campanile is capped by a pyramid. There is a shorter tower opposite on the south-east side. Inside the church is a narrow

*Church of the Good Shepherd, Sion Mills, the Sanctuary.*

porch, with three doors into the nave. The two manual Conacher organ is in the gallery above.

There are two semicircular windows in the west wall of the gallery, with a circular window above. Beneath the gallery at the west end is the baptistery. The nave is a five bay hall with semi-circular clerestory windows of clear glass on each side. Below these are smaller windows of clear glass in the three middle bays, and at the base are four semi-circular niches. Beneath the gallery in the first bay on each side, are three small windows. In the easternmost bay on each side are two openings, behind which are semi-circular recesses, each with three windows.

The chancel is impressively raised seven steps above the nave. On each side there is a large pulpit and lectern of green and grey Connemara marble. The chancel is a spacious semi-circular area, with eleven windows round its circumference at clerestory level, and two windows beneath on each side.

On the north wall is a marble monument to Emerson Tennent Herdman who died in 1918 and to his wife Fanny who died in the same year. On the south wall there is a marble memorial to Brigadier General Ambrose St.Quintin Ricardo, CMG, CBE, DSO, of the Royal Inniskilling Fusiliers who died in 1923. There is also a memorial to him outside the church, before the main entrance. The plaque listing the Rectors of Urney and Sion Mills in the porch commemorates Commander Claudius Herdman, DL, RN, who died in 1993, and his wife, Barbara who died in 1984.

The earlier church of St.Saviour adjacent, is now in use as a parish hall. It was built in 1889.

# The Diocese of Raphoe

## THE CATHEDRAL CHURCH OF St. EUNAN, RAPHOE
## PARISH OF RAPHOE

RAPHOE, WHICH MEANS, *"the fort, or enclosure of the huts"*, is the site of a monastery which was founded by St. Columba in the sixth century. This was restored by St. Eunan, or Adamnan, who died c.703. The earliest record of a bishop of Raphoe is Oengus O'Lappin in 959.

Like many buildings which occupy an ancient site, Raphoe Cathedral has undergone much alteration over the years, so that most of the present building is 17th to 19th century. The earliest remains of any original building are part of a 9th century door lintel in the porch with scenes carved on it depicting the Arrest in the Garden. Some other remains of this are embedded in the outside north wall. There are also mediaeval lancets in the south choir wall with unusual shamrock carvings containing 12th century triple stone sedilia. These were discovered during restoration work in 1893, concealed behind plaster.

*9th Century Lintel Stone showing the Crucifixion.*

*St. Eunan's Cathedral, Raphoe.*

Bishop Andrew Knox, Bishop of Raphoe 1611-1633, found the cathedral, "ruynated and all decayed saving the walls unto which hath been two years past reparing a roofe which, God willing, will be got up at the Bishop's and Parishioners' charges". Bishop John Pooley, Bishop 1702-1713, in 1704, declared that he intended to repair and beautify the church by adding two aisles. This work was completed under his successor, Nicholas Forster, Bishop 1716-1743. Bishop Forster also built the tower in 1738, and the Galilee Porch, and he provided the Volt (folk) House as a residence for widows of diocesan clergy. He founded the Diocesan Library, and he built much of the Royal School, which had been founded in 1618. A tablet in the sanctuary informs us that Bishop Forster's remains were buried beneath the altar.

Further substantial restoration work was carried out in 1893 by the Knox family of Prehen, Londonderry, descendants of Bishop Knox. The two aisles were removed, as was the gallery at the west end.

*Raphoe Cathedral before the removal of the Transepts in 1893.*

Raphoe Cathedral is a two-chamber building, the two parts being connected by an arch. At the west end is the massive four storey tower. The clock in it was constructed and installed by Canon Fred Carre, Rector of Inver, in 1897. The west door has a series of representations of the four evangelists which were carved in 1907 by Mrs McQuaide, wife of Canon J. W. McQuaide, Rector of Raphoe, 1905-1914. Mrs McQuaide was the daughter of Dean Potter, Dean of Raphoe 1903-1905.

*West Door.*

Beyond the porch is the Consistory Court. This was originally where the Bishop held court, but in time, it was used for granting probate and for

*Consistory Court and Font of 1706.*

issuing marriage licences. It is now the baptistery. The font was presented by Bishop Pooley in 1706. The font cover was carved by Mrs McQuaide. On the south side is the vestry room.

Inside, to the right, is the original entrance to the cathedral, the Galilee Porch. The nave of the cathedral continues past the arch, beyond which are the pulpit to the left, and the brass lectern, which commemorates the Rev. James Weir, LL.D., on the right. The choir stalls, which date from 1908, and the prayer desk are raised one step above the nave. The Dean's, and two canons' stalls are in the

*13th Century Sedilia.*

*Wells Kennedy Organ, 1997.*

*The Bishop's Throne, 1665.*

13th century sedilia. The Archdeacon's and the other two canons' stalls on the north side of the choir, date from 1740. The Bishop's throne, which was placed in the north side of the sanctuary in 1962, dates from 1665. There is a prayer desk and chair on the right side of the sanctuary. There is a mediaeval piscina in the south wall of the sanctuary, and an aumbry in the north wall. The organ, on the north side of the choir was brought over from England and installed in 1997. It is a fine two manual instrument with pedals, which replaced an old Hammond organ of 1951.

Raphoe Cathedral has some interesting windows. The west end of the nave is lit by one window in each side wall. Each has two lights and square-paned coloured glass. In the south there are four windows together which depict the four Evangelists, in the order from left to right, St. Mark, St. Matthew, St. John and St. Luke. Also in the chancel, a window depicts St.Eunan writing the life of St.Columba. Below it are two niches. On the north wall is a stained glass window in memory of Sarah Thompson who died in 1911. It depicts the Good Shepherd. Beside it, there is a window which illustrates the text, "Mary has chosen the good part". It commemorates Mary Smith who died in 1906. Behind the throne, in the north wall of the sanctuary, there is a coloured glass window with an inset projecting from it in glass containing the arms of the diocese. The east window is a triple lancet which depicts the Ascension. It is particularly fine and colourful. It is in memory of Michael Bell Cox, Archdeacon of Raphoe 1880-1897. Archdeacon Cox was made Dean of Raphoe in 1897, but he died a few weeks later, before he was installed. The east window also commemorates the Rev. Dr. J. A. Weir.

The oldest monument in the cathedral, which is beside the Galilee Porch, on the south wall of the nave, is in memory of Mrs Jeneta Adair, whose husband was Dean to 1630. Jeneta, who died in 1618 aged 20 years, bore two sets of twins! Also on the south wall is a memorial to Dean Potter by the window which depicts St. Mark, and there is a brass memorial to Ethel Mary, wife of Capt. F. S. Merrick and daughter of Capt. Stoney, who died in Nigeria in 1911. On the north wall of the nave, there is a memorial to those who fell in the two World Wars. A memorial to the Sheldon family, benefactors of the Cathedral over many years, was erected in 1978 and also, John Moffatt who died in 1971 is commemorated. A monument commemorates Thomas Butler Stoney, D.L., of Oakfield Park, Raphoe, who died in 1912, and another adjacent commemorates Annie Butler Stoney who died in 1923. On the north choir wall is the monument to William Bissett, the last Bishop of Raphoe before the See was united with Derry in 1834. The Latin inscription was composed by Archer Butler. On the north wall of the sanctuary, a monument commemorates James Hawkins, Bishop of Raphoe, 1780-1807, and Catherine, his wife. On the east wall is a large Latin monument to William Archer Butler, first Professor of Moral Philosophy in Trinity College, Dublin, and Rector of Raymochy, who died of famine fever in 1848 at the age of 36 years. Archer Butler possessed one of the most brilliant minds of his day. He was a great thinker, preacher and writer. Legend has it that there is a relic of the True Cross in the east wall! On the south wall of the sanctuary, a monument commemorates Alicia, wife of Bishop Ezekiel Hopkins, Bishop of Raphoe 1671-1681. Below it, a tablet records the burial of Bishop Nicholas Forster under the altar of the

*St. Eunan's Cathedral, the Choir and Sanctuary.*

*Raphoe Castle.*

cathedral. The Bishop's Palace in Raphoe was built by Bishop John Leslie upon his translation from the Diocese of the Isles in 1633. It was burned down shortly after the death of Bishop William Bissett in 1834, and is an imposing ruin. The present rectory was built in 1904, and the Cathedral parochial hall was built in 1963.

The Royal School, Raphoe, was founded by King James I in 1618. Bishop Forster built new buildings for the school in 1737. The Royal School was amalgamated with the Prior School, Lifford in 1971, to form the Royal and Prior Comprehensive School. The old buildings are now used for boarding accommodation.

# Saints of Derry and Raphoe

THE NORTH-WEST produced a remarkable number of remarkable men, chief of whom was, of course, St. Columba.

**Saint Baithin** was a cousin of Columba. He was born in the Laggan Valley of east Donegal about 536. In 560, he founded a monastery at St. Johnston on a site which was given to him by the ruling chieftan of Aileach. This became known as *Tigh Baithin,* the House of Baithin, hence the name of the Parish of Taughboyne. Baithin became Abbot of Tiree in the Hebrides, and he eventually succeeded Columba as Abbot of Iona. He died on 9th June 600.

**Saint Canice** was born about 516 near Limavady. He was educated at Clonard under St. Finian, and at Glasnevin under St. Mobhí. After a period in Rome, Canice returned to Limavady about 550, where he founded a monastery. He accompanied Columba to Iona in 563, and in subsequent years, he founded several churches. He came back to Ireland with Columba for the Convention of Drumceatt in 575. After that, Canice remained in Ireland. He went south, where he founded the great monastery of Aghaboe in Co. Laois. His most notable foundation was at Kilkenny, which bears his name. He spent the remaining years of his life at Aghaboe, and died about 598.

**Saint Eunan,** or **Adamnan** was born about 625. His church at Raphoe took the place of Columba's foundation there some time late in the seventh century. He became Abbot of Iona in 679. The Venerable Bede described him as, "a wise and good man and most eminently learned in the science of the Holy Scriptures." Eunan wrote a biography of St. Columba. He died about 703.

**Saint Fiacra** lived at some time in the seventh century. He came from Conwall, near Letterkenny. He went to Paris, where he set up hospices for the sick and poor. He used to gather them up in the streets and take them to his hospices in a rickshaw-like vehicle. Thus, to this day, one French word for taxi is *Fiacre!*

*St. Eunan Window, Raphoe Cathedral.*

Two other prominent figures were **Saint Eugene** of Ardstraw in the mid sixth century, and **St. Luraich** of Maghera. As well as these well known luminaries of the Celtic Church in the north-west, there are others whose names survive in the dedication of churches. They would have been local evangelists, but otherwise, little or nothing is known of them. Examples are **St. Lugha** at Aghanloo, **St. Toit** at Ballyscullion, and **St. Fiach** at Killea.

## ALL SAINTS, NEWTOWNCUNNINGHAM

THE PARISH OF All Saints, Newtowncunningham, Co. Donegal, lies along the east shore of Lough Swilly, south of Inch Island. Newtowncunningham is half way between Letterkenny and Derry. At the time of the Plantation of Ulster in the 17th century, the area was planted by the Cunningham family, hence the names of the villages of Manorcunningham and Newtowncunningham.

*All Saints Church.*

All Saints Church was built in 1722 as a private chapel for the Forward Family of Castleforward, and was consecrated on All Saints' Day, 1st November that year. On 9th December 1728, it became a chapel of ease in the Parish of Taughboyne. At the Disestablishment of the Church of Ireland in 1870, All Saints district was separated from the Parish of Taughboyne, and it became a parish in its own right.

All Saints Church possesses one of the two lych gates in the Dioceses of Derry and Raphoe, the other being at Baronscourt Church in Co. Tyrone. It was erected in 1920 to commemorate the Rev. Alexander George Stuart and his wife, Christine Emma of Bogay House, Newtowncunningham. Bogay House was given to the Rev. Thomas Pemberton, Rector of Taughboyne for use as a rectory about 1800. Mrs Stuart was a sister of the Very Rev. Edward Bowen, Rector of All Saints, 1868-1886, and Dean of Raphoe, 1882 until his death in 1897.

There is a three storey tower at the west end of the church which is surmounted by corner finials. It was built in 1808. A stone in the interior west wall records the presentation of the clock in the tower by the Rev. Robert Blackmore Rankin, Rector of All Saints, 1885-1917. Also in the porch are two crosses which came from the grave of Lt. Col. A.G.Stuart who was killed at Westoutre in Flanders in 1916 during the Great War.

The nave is lit by four windows in the south wall and three in the north wall. Each has two lights with clear lattice panes and Y tracery. There are five windows with coloured patterned glass in the sanctuary. The central window has two lights and cusped tracery.

The baptistery is in the south-west corner of the nave. It was erected in 1992 in memory of nine-year old Audrey Christine West who was killed in a car accident in 1991. The vestry room is to the left of the nave. The stone pulpit has marble columns, and inscribed upon it are the names of the four Evangelists. It is on the left side of the nave, outside the chancel. The prayer desk is on the right side opposite. The wooden eagle lectern commemorates Dean Bowen. There is a two manual electronic organ with pedals.

*Lych Gate, All Saints' Church.*

The chancel was built in 1896. The two marble steps into it were erected in 1905 in memory of Isabella Kerr. The reredos commemorates those who served and those who fell in the Great War. The names of the former are inscribed on the left side of the altar, and those of the latter, on the right. The prayer desk in the sanctuary was given in thanksgiving for the survival of a serious illness in infancy of Stephen Devenny in 1991.

The three classical monuments on the north wall commemorate the Forward family. The Rt. Hon. Ralph Howard of Shelton House, Arklow, Co. Wicklow, 1st Viscount Wicklow, M.P. for the County of Wicklow, married Alicia, daughter of William Forward of Castleforward in 1755. William Forward, who built the church, is commemorated on a monument over the vestry door. He died in 1770. Alicia is commemorated in the middle monument. William, son of Ralph and Alicia Howard became the third Earl of Wicklow, and in 1780, he assumed the surname and arms of the Forward family. The other monument on the north wall commemorates his wife Eleanor, who died in 1807.

On the south wall is a memorial in the baptistery to Audrey West. John Gordon Bowen, brother of Dean Bowen, who died in 1891, and his wife Harriet who died in 1885 are commemorated on a brass plaque. There is a memorial to Dean Bowen, and above it, his Father, the Rev. Edward Bowen, Rector of Taughboyne, 1819-1867, is commemorated. Another memorial commemorates the Rev. A. G. Stuart and his wife Christine and the family. Their son Lt. Col. Alexander Stuart who was killed in Flanders in 1916 is commemorated. There is also a memorial to the Rev. R. B. Rankin. William Forward's gravestone is set into the south wall.

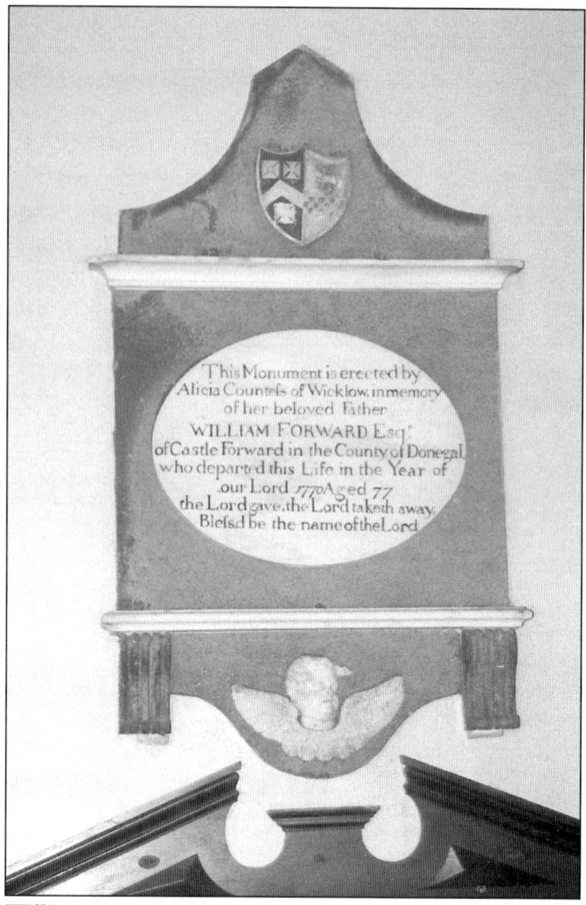

*William Forward Monument.*

## ARDARA, St. CONALL

ARDARA, *"the hill of the fortress"*, is a village in south-west Donegal. The parish was created out of townlands from Killybegs and Inniskeel parishes, for both of which the church was built as a chapel of ease, and consecrated on 11th June 1820. A new church was built shortly afterwards, in 1833. During extensive renovations in 1906, the nave was restored, and in 1908, the chancel was added.

There is a large bellcote over the west wall. The door in the south side of the porch is in memory of Jack Baskin, and the door opposite commemorates James and Elizabeth Baskin. The window in the porch depicts "the Word of God", and is in memory of Thomas and Annabella Deane, 1978.

The interior entrance doors are in memory of John and Isobel Freeborn, 1994. There is a lattice window in the west wall over the entrance. The three windows on each side of the nave are of patterned, coloured glass, and some depict Biblical scenes. On the south side, the first window is in memory of Alexander Morrow who died in 1906, and of his wife. The second window depicts the Transfiguration, and is in memory of Robert Porter and his son, and the third window, "the Good

Shepherd", is in memory of John and Frances Baskin. On the north wall, the second window commemorates John Baskin, 1924, and the third window, depicting Jesus the Carpenter, commemorates David and Ellen Baskin, 1978. There is a small window in the south sanctuary wall, and the east window, of three lights, has square panes and coloured glass.

The vestry room is north of the sanctuary. The altar was presented by General J. R. Tredennick, D.L. in 1906. The chair on the right was given by George Cunningham, and the chair on the left is in memory of James Baskin who died in 1905, and of Margaret, his wife. Both date from 1906. There is fine wood panelling in the sanctuary.

The font is left of the entrance. The cover on it was presented in 1906 by the Rev. A. G. Stuart, brother-in-law of Dean Bowen and Rector of Leckpatrick, 1883-1886. The pulpit on the left was renovated in 1955 by Ellen Hanlon, and the lectern adjacent to it was presented by the Rev. A. McQuade, Mrs Knight and Mrs Mahon in 1906. The prayer desk is to the right.

A monument on the east wall to the right of the sanctuary entrance commemorates the Rev. John Barrett, Rector and Vicar of Inniskeel, 1802-1844, and his wife Mary who died in 1858. Their daughter, and their son, the Rev. Knox Barrett, Rector of Ardara from 1836 until his death in 1867, are also commemorated on the monument.

*Ardara Church.*

## AUGHANUNSHIN

THE REMAINS OF old Aughanunshin abbey church can still be seen about 4 kilometres north of Letterkenny. The name Aughanunshin means *"the field of the little ash tree"*. This church seems to have been abandoned, being in bad repair about 1837. It was replaced with a simple hall church of three bays in 1838.

Aughanunshin and Leck parishes were amalgamated in 1872, and both were amalgamated with Conwall in 1900 to form Conwall Union. Aughanunshin church was closed in 1985.

*Aughanunshin Church.*

*Aughanunshin Abbey.*

# Francis Robertson, 1737/38 -1791 and the Robertson Board

Francis Robertson was born in 1737 or 1738, the son of the Rev. John Robertson, who was Rector of Donegal, Gartan, then Aughanunshin in Co. Donegal. In 1764, he sailed for India, where he had a distinguished military career in the Bengal Army. The Bengal Army was maintained by the East India Company. In his early days in the Army, Robertson became involved in a dispute over the award of a special allowance to soldiers, which almost amounted to mutiny. For this, he was stripped of rank. In due course, he was reinstated, and he eventually rose to the rank of Colonel. In the course of his career with the Bengal Army and the East India Company, Robertson became a very wealthy man.

Francis Robertson in his will, which is dated September 1790, made a number of bequests to close relatives, as well as to the poor of his Father's parish of Aughanunshin. The main part of his will was a bequest, "to the parishes of the Diocese of Raphoe, a sum of money, which by its interest at the rate of five percent shall be found sufficient to produce fifteen pounds sterling annually to each parish for or towards establishing a school therein, and purchasing books as well as entertainment and instruction in every parish of said diocese, and it is to be understood that such as in said parishes may not be of the Established Religion are notwithstanding to share equally in this Legacy which it is to be hoped will contribute to their conformation to the English Church by enlightening their understanding".

The total sum bequeathed was £9,300. Thus, each of the thirty-one parishes would receive £300, which, when invested, would produce enough interest to build and run the school, and provide books and the master's salary. The Trustees whom Robertson appointed to administer the will were the Archbishops of Armagh and Dublin, the Bishop of Raphoe, the Archdeacon and the rectors of the parishes of Raphoe Diocese.

Robertson died in 1791, and so did not live to see his incredible will carried out. In 1803, the High Court in Dublin allocated the sum of £30 Sterling for the building of a school in each of the 31 parishes. £3 were allocated for books, and £15 for masters' salaries. Inflation, which was high at the beginning of the 19th century, drove the cost of each school up to £45, so masters' salaries had to be scaled according to the number of pupils at each school.

It was to be some time before the first schools were built, but once building began, progress was steady, if slow. The first schools to be built, were, it seems, Raphoe and Killygarvan (Rathmullan) in 1810. Building continued throughout the 1810s, with Donegal, Clondehorkey and Taughboyne schools being built in 1824. It was agreed that the Robertson Board should support schools in parishes such as Convoy and Ardara which came into being after the bequest was set up.

In the fullness of time, the Irish State took over control of Education, and gradually, many of the Robertson Schools closed. Most of them have been sold to the parishes. Nowadays, the Governors of the Robertson Endowments, who administer Francis Robertson's fortune, award grants to students who are at third level educational institutions. Many thousands of young people for over two hundred years, have much for which to be grateful to Colonel Francis Robertson.

## BURT, CHRIST CHURCH

Burt, *"Druim Bearta" - the height of Bearta,* is between Derry and Newtowncunningham. The ancient church belonged to the Abbey of Macosquin, and later became one of the five chapels of ease of Templemore Parish. There have been several churches on different sites, built about 1620, 1737, and around 1805. The present church was built about 1860 to a design by John G. Ferguson. It is a rectangular hall with a porch and a tower on the north-west corner, and a porch to the side of the sanctuary. The tower is surmounted by a cream brick turret and short spire.

There is a lattice window of three lights in the west wall, and a stained glass window of three lights in the east wall. There are four lattice windows in the south wall, and three in the north wall, the middle one of which is lattice. The first window is in memory of the Rev. Connolly Cheevers, perpetual curate 1820-1871, and the other window is in memory of Frances Crookshank who died in 1880.

Burt Church was closed in 1973. It has since been sold and is now a local heritage centre. It is to be regretted that the restaurant within contains a pub, with the old church furnishings and fittings, including the pulpit, adjacent to the bar, which to say the least, is in very bad taste.

*Burt Church.*

## CLONCHA, MALIN

THE NAME Cloncha means *"battlefield"*. The parish, which is around the beautiful little village of Malin in Inishowen, is the most northerly in Ireland. The old parish church marks the site of an abbey, and there is an ancient cross there.

The present parish church was built in 1827, the first stone being laid by Mrs Harvey of Malin Hall on July 27th that year. The Harveys of Malin Hall were one of the prominent families of the parish in days gone by.

Cloncha Church, on the green in Malin village, is a simple, rectangular building, with a tower at the west end. The tower has battlements and finials. The church is entered through a porch on the north wall. On the south wall are three diamond pane windows. The east window has two diamond pane lights and Y tracery. The north wall is windowless, but has the doorway into the vestry room and porch. The pulpit is on the north side, and the lectern is in memory of George Miller Harvey of Malin Hall. The harmonium was restored and given in memory of Caroline Lynam who died in 1991.

In the porch beneath the tower is a monument to Florinda Lyne who died in 1886, and to her sister, Elizabeth. Florinda's daughter gave the bell in their memory. On the north wall are memorials to Lily Ann McCandless Bree who died in 1986, and to her husband, David who died in 1991. A memorial to

*Cloncha Church.*

Neil and Ellen Devenny was erected in 1991. John Harvey of Malin Hall who died in 1940, and his wife Florita Ann who died in 1943, and their son George Miller Harvey who died in 1973 are commemorated. On the same wall, monuments commemorate Flora Lilian Ham, daughter of John and Florita Harvey, and the Rev. William Smyth Willcocks, Curate of Cloncha from 1841 until his death a year later, and also, Julia Mary Harvey who died in 1912. On the south wall is a memorial to Ellen, wife of the Rev. Gregory Cuff, Rector of Cloncha, 1872-1874. She died in 1873. Dora Luz O'Donohue who died in 1926, and her son Griff, who died in 1978, are also commemorated.

## CLONDEHORKEY, BALLYMORE, St. JOHN, CASHEL, St.COLUMBA'S CHAPEL OF EASE

The ancient parish church of Clondehorkey, *"the Meadow of Horkey"*, was near Dunfanaghy. In 1729, there was both a church and a chapel in good repair. The present church, at Ballymore, between Creeslough and Dunfanaghy, on the north coast of Donegal, was built in 1752. It is considered to be one of the finest Georgian churches in Ulster. It is entered by a large porch. There is a bellcote over the west end of the nave, above the porch. Under the spacious gallery, to the right of the entrance, is the baptistery, in memory of Sergeant Charles Stewart Campbell, Northants Regiment, who died in Teheran in 1943, and of Lt. Ion Butler Westropp George, M.C., Royal Engineers, who was killed in action in Sicily in 1943. A brass plaque on the north wall commemorates him.

*Clondehorkey Church.*

The entire interior of the church is beautifully panelled in wood to a height of nearly two metres. This culminates in a fine reredos behind the altar. The Communion rails are in memory of Thomas Henry Staunton, Dean of Raphoe, and Rector of Clondehorkey, 1901-1947. To the left of the sanctuary is the vestry room which was added in 1853. The lectern is in memory of the Rev. Edward D'Arcy Staunton, Assistant Chaplain General to the Forces, who died in 1952. The altar, pulpit, prayer desk and seat, all came from Kirwan House Orphanage in Dublin, and were given in memory of Captain Richard Westropp George, M.B.E., who died in 1959. On a brass plaque on the south wall are listed the several names of those who gave the organ. The brass light on the organ is in memory of Canon David Stewart-Maunder, Rector of Clondehorkey, 1970-1988.

The church is well lit by four large, multi-paned, segment-headed windows on the south wall, as well as by a large window of three lights in the east wall over the sanctuary. These windows, which are a striking feature of the church, have Gibbs surrounds, an architectural characteristic of the work of James Gibbs (1682-1754). There is a smaller window of similar design in the west wall of the porch. There are four blank window spaces in the north wall.

As well as those plaques already mentioned, there are on the south wall, memorials to Margaret Pennell who died in 1965, and to Charles and Catherine McBride, 1985. On the north wall is a brass plaque in memory of F. and E. Stewart, parents of Thomas and Sophie Stewart. There is a momument to four men of the parish who fell in the Second World War. Ion George, already mentioned, is commemorated, and there is a memorial to Lt. Commander Denis Westropp George, O.B.E., R.N.R., who died as a result of injuries in Tasmania in 1947, as well as a monument to Captain William Stewart, who served in the Crimean War, and who died in 1864.

The old Robertson school is now used as a parish hall, and the present school was opened in 1958. There is a fine old Rectory.

When Dunfanaghy parish was carved out of Clondehorkey in 1872, a portion of Kilmacrennan parish containing Cashel chapel of ease was transferred to Clondehorkey. Cashel Church, dedicated to St. Columba, was built in 1847. It is near Doe Castle on Sheephaven Bay, the ancestral seat of the McSwyne Family, and later of the Hart family.

Cashel church is rectangular with a small porch in the north wall. There is an empty bellcote over the west wall. Outside the church is the old bell from Dunlewey Church. It has the date 11th October 1860, and the name of the Rev. J. H. Bor, Rector of Dunlewey.

*Cashel Church.*

Inside, the area at the west end of the church is partitioned off into two rooms, one, a vestry room, and the other, a Sunday School room which has been refurbished in memory of Alexander and George Wilkin, 1992. There is a hexagonal stone font with the date 1684. The brass lectern is in memory of the Rev. H. Smyth, Chancellor of Cashel, who died in 1892. The harmonium commemorates Dean Staunton, and the chairs in the sanctuary are in memory of Samuel Moore who died in 1966. The pulpit is to the left of the sanctuary which is separated from the nave by three-sided communion rails, and there is a spacious prayer desk to the right.

On the north wall, a brass plaque states that a burse, veil and pulpit falls were given in memory of Canon Stewart-Maunder. On the south wall, a brass plaque records the donation of the chancel carpet and lights in memory of Samuel Moore who died in 1998.

All the windows, which date from the late 1980s and early 1990s, are of clear glass, lattice pattern, and are in memory of various parishioners. There are three windows in the west wall. The first is in memory of John and Jane Moore and family, the second was presented by George and Elizabeth Hay, and the third is in memory of James and Mary Moore and family. Starting from the rear, on the north wall, the first window is the gift of the Rev. David Griscome, presently Dean of Elphin, and Rector of Clondehorkey 1991-1995, in memory of all past rectors. The second window is in memory of Gideon and Cassie Moore, the third is in memory of Robert Moore, the fourth is in memory of Mary and Samuel Moore, and the fifth was presented by Frank and May Whoriskey. The three windows in the east wall commemorate William and Annie Gallagher, Robert and Alexander Wilkin, and Richard and Annie Wilkin. Continuing round the church, on the south wall, the first window was presented by James and Elizabeth Kearney, the second is in memory of Elizabeth, David and John Wilkinson, the third commemorates George and Mary Wilkin, and the fourth, on the other side of the entrance, is in memory of Samuel Moore.

## CLONDEVADDOCK; ROSSNAKILL, CHRIST THE REDEEMER, PORTSALON, ALL SAINTS CHAPEL OF EASE LEATBEG CHAPEL OF EASE

THE PARISH OF Clondevaddock is located in the northern part of the Fanad Peninsula, between Mulroy Bay and Lough Swilly. The whole area is spectacularly scenic. The ancient parish of Clondevaddock, *"the Meadow of Baithin"*, had a church as long ago as the sixth century. Baithin was Columba's cousin, and his successor as Abbot of Iona. He died in 600. The present parish church is Christ the Redeemer in the village of Rossnakill. All Saints, Portsalon and Leatbeg are chapels of ease.

Clondevaddock church is very old, dating back to at least the 17th century. Some even think that it might date from the 14th century. It was reported to be in good repair in 1729. It was restored in 1830, and further repairs were carried out in 1868. The

*Clondevaddock/Rosnakill Church.*

building is entered through a porch in the south-west corner, which also contains the vestry room. The entrance door is in memory of Robert and Mary Gallagher, and the window commemorates Thomas and Sarah Kyle. Two brass plaques in the porch record the gift of the carpet by William Gallagher in 1993, and the donation of the sound system by Albert Thompson the same year.

Inside is a large gallery, with a window in the rear wall. Underneath is a font and a small lectern. The south wall is lit by one small window, and three larger ones of two lights. Each has clear lattice glass and Y tracery. Two of these windows are in memory of the Gallagher family, 1991, and the middle one commemorates Valerie Griffith who died in 1990. On the north wall, there are two similar windows, each of two lights, the first of which is in memory of Daniel and William Carre and James Carre, 1992, and the second of which is the gift of the Rev. Dr. Arthur Kerr, incumbent since 1990, and Mrs Kerr. The interior part of the double east window in the sanctuary is of coloured glass, and the exterior part is in memory of Benjamin and Agnes Carr, 1990.

To the left of the sanctuary is the wooden pulpit. Under the altar is a stone on which is written the name of the Rev. John Johnston, who was rector of Clondevaddock from 1702 until his death in 1730. The Holy Table has a carved anchor on the front, and a finely carved reredos behind. Outside the sanctuary, to the right, there are choir pews, and a two manual electronic organ with pedals. The lectern is in memory of the Rev. Henry Maturin, who was rector from 1797 until his death in 1842. His son was rector of Gartan.

There are two monuments in the sanctuary, on the east wall. The one on the left is in memory of Lt. Ralph Edward Barton who died in India in 1906, and the one on the right commemorates the Rev. Henry Maturin. On the north wall, a monument commemorates the Rev. William Baillie, LL.D., who was rector 1842-1859. Previously, he had been Headmaster of Kilkenny College. There is a brass memorial to the Rev. Thomas Irwin who had been Rector of Charlynch in Somerset, and who died in 1883. A circular stone monument was erected by the parishioners of all three churches in the parish to mark the Millennium Year A.D. 2000.

All Saints Church, Portsalon, was consecrated by Bishop Charles John Tyndall on Easter Monday,

*Millennium Monument, Rossnakill Church.*

15th April 1963. It replaces the old iron church which had been built in 1912, and which was blown down by "Hurricane Debbie" in September 1961. It is a very small, but beautiful church. In the porch at the west end, a brass plaque records the demise of the old church and the building of the new one. Another records the fact that the bell in the belfry on the roof, came from the RMS Laurentic, which was sunk by German submarines at the entrance to Lough Swilly in January 1917. The bell was recovered from the sea bed in 1924, and was presented by Lords Commissioners of the

***All Saint's Church, Portsalon.***

*Sanctuary Window, All Saints, Portsalon.*

Admiralty. In the porch, there is a window over the exterior and interior entrance doors.

There are four windows in the north wall, three in the south wall, and two in the west wall. All of these contain superb and beautifully coloured stained glass, depicting various biblical and nautical themes. The east window is the finest, and is brilliantly coloured. It depicts the Risen Christ. There are also two little stained glass windows on each side of the sanctuary.

The pulpit and the lectern are on the left of the nave, and the vestry room is opposite, to the right of the nave. The organ has two manuals and pedals, and is by Thomas Hughes of Huddersfield. A plaque records that Ann Barton was organist for fifty years. The organ was restored in 1996. There is a small baptistery at the west end of the church, to the left of the entrance.

On the east wall is a memorial to Col. Baptist Johnston Barton, D.L., who was responsible for the erection of All Saints chapel of ease. He was the last colonel of the 5th Battalion of the Royal Inniskilling Fusiliers. He died in 1914. A brass plaque on the south wall commemorates his wife Isabel who died in 1936. There is also a brass plaque on the south wall in memory of Capt. Charles Geoffrey Barton, M.C., 6th Battalion, Royal Inniskilling Fusiliers. He was killed in the Great War in 1918.

*Clondevaddock/Leatbeg Church.*

Leatbeg chapel of ease is in the north-west corner of the Fanad peninsula. It was built in 1843 as a combined church and school. The entrance porch at the west end of the building also contains the vestry room. There is also a miniature font in the porch. The interior is lit by three square windows of clear glass on each side wall, and a stained glass east window, depicting a chalice and grapes and wheat, symbolising the Holy Eucharist. It is in memory of David and Elizabeth McNutt and their son, Robert, 1988. There is a little niche on each side of the window, and the pulpit is on the left side of the sanctuary.The altar commemorates Frank McKemey, 1988, and the chair in the sanctuary is in memory of James and Margaret McElhinney.

# The Churches and their Architects

IT IS POSSIBLE that Clondevaddock Parish Church at Rosnakill in the Fanad peninsula in Co. Donegal is the oldest church in use in Derry and Raphoe, as it is thought by some to have been built in the 14th century. Several churches such as Raphoe Cathedral have very old fragments, and adjacent to or near many of them, are the ruins of mediaeval and earlier churches.

More or less all the churches in Derry and Raphoe in their present form date from the post Reformation period. The oldest ones include Derry Cathedral, Clonleigh, Taughboyne and Dunboe from the seventeenth century. Eighteenth century churches include Castlederg, Conwall at Letterkenny and Culdaff. Most of the churches in the Dioceses were built in the nineteenth century. In Derry Diocese, Sion Mills, St. Peter's in Derry, the Church of Ireland Centre at New Buildings, and Strathfoyle, Londonderry, and Clare chapel of ease at Drumquin are twentieth century buildings, as are All Saints, Portsalon and Meenglass in Raphoe Diocese.

At the Royal Visitation in 1622, almost all of the churches were found to be in ruins. Whatever rebuilding may have been done after that was destroyed again in the 1641 Rebellion. There were surveys at various intervals in the 18th century, notably in 1729, 1733 and 1768. In this period, the churches were generally reported to be in reasonable repair. Many of them were abandoned and replaced in the first half of the 19th century, with generous financial assistance from the Board of First Fruits and the Government which supported the Established Church. The Board of First Fruits, which went back to the early 18th century, only gave grants for the building of new churches, and not for the repair of old ones. It was replaced in 1833 by the Ecclesiastical Commissioners, who in turn lasted until the Disestablishment of the Church of Ireland in 1870. After Disestablishment, the Church was deprived of state backing and support, and had to fend for itself. That it survived and thrived, is a testimony to the clergy and people at the time and since.

There have been several different architects and builders over the years. The 17th century ones are not generally known now, with the exception of **William Parrott** who built St. Columb's Cathedral in Londonderry for £4,000. Its style is known as Planters' Gothic. In the 18th century, **the Earl Bishop, the Hon. Frederick Augustus Hervey** built or enlarged several churches in Revival Gothic style. Examples are Ballykelly and Banagher. **John Bowden** was a designer of churches in the early part of the 19th century. An example of his work is Faughanvale Parish Church at Eglinton. One of the most renowned architects of the 19th century was **Joseph Welland**, (1798-1860), a pupil of Bowden. In 1826, he became architect to the Tuam division of the Board of First Fruits. In 1839, he was appointed one of the four architects of the Ecclesiastical Commissioners. In 1843, he became their sole architect. Examples of his work are the churches at Redcastle and Gleneely, both of which are now closed, and Milford which has been demolished. Welland died in 1860, and was replaced by his son, **William Welland**, who joined with a **Mr. W. Gillespie** to serve the Commissioners. Until 1870, **Welland and Gillespie** had the monopoly on church design, and many of the churches in Derry and Raphoe owe their design to them. Welland and Gillespie's work can be seen at Mountcharles, Urney and Myroe. The architect **W.H. Lynn**, (1829-1915), of the firm of *Lanyon, Lynn & Lanyon*, was responsible for one of the finest large churches, All Saints, Clooney in Londonderry. **Sir Thomas Drew**, (1838-1910), appeared as a major architect in the second half of the 19th century. His greatest monument is St. Anne's Cathedral, Belfast. In Derry and Raphoe, as elsewhere, his main work was in church extensions, the building of chancels and aisles. His work can be seen at Raphoe Cathedral. He also rebuilt Ballynascreen Church at Draperstown, and improved Welland and Gillespie's church at Clanabogan, both of which are churches of the first rank for their beauty. Another of the lovliest churches is Christ Church, Castlerock, which was designed in 1868 for the Clothworkers' Company by **F.W. Porter. John Ferguson** and his son, **John Guy Ferguson**, were active in the Victorian period. An example of the former's work is Christ Church, Londonderry, 1830, which was re-modelled by Welland and Gillespie in 1862, and enlarged with the erection of the chancel and transepts by John Guy Ferguson.

There are sixty-seven churches in Derry Diocese, and fifty-four, including Inishowen, in Raphoe Diocese, as well as twelve closed churches in Donegal, making a grand total of one hundred and thirty-three. It is difficult to describe so many churches without becoming repetitive, as many of them are of a standard design. The design is usually a hall of three or four bays, with a tower and/or spire at the west end. In some cases, there is a chancel, and often, one or two transepts. However, several of the churches are strikingly different, such as the Church of the Good Shepherd at Sion Mills, which was designed by **W.F. Unsworth** who designed the Shakespeare Theatre at Stratford-upon-Avon, and St. Peter's in Derry by **A.T. Marshall**. Nevertheless, they all have character, and each one has something that sets it apart from all the others. It is a truly wonderful heritage which we have received, and which we must pass on.

## CLONLEIGH, LIFFORD, St. LUGADIUS

Clonleigh, *"the calves' meadow"*, includes the town of Lifford in east Donegal. The patron saint, Lugadius, was one of the twelve who accompanied St. Columba to Iona in 563.

*Clonleigh Church.*

In the 1622 survey, the old collegiate church, a mile or so from Lifford, was in ruins, but a new one was soon erected. This is the present church. The foundation was laid according to the provisions of the will of Sir Richard Hansard.

Clonleigh church is entered through two doors in the tower at the west end. The tower is three-storied, the upper two levels containing louvered windows. It is surmounted by stepped battlements and corner finials. The nave is flanked by a north aisle, which is separated from it by two arches. This was built in 1864 to accommodate members of the Donegal Militia from Lifford barracks. At the east end of the aisle is the baptistery, and beyond that is the passage to the vestry room on the left. The choir stalls are on either side of the chancel.

There are two small windows in the west wall, two windows of two lights and coloured insets above in the south wall, a window in the west wall of the aisle, and three windows of three lights in the north aisle wall. The east window is of coloured glass, and has three lights, and there is a window with two lights in the south sanctuary wall.

The wood panelling in the sanctuary is very fine. Part of it, as well as the oak door leading to the vestry is in memory of John Clarke of Inchenagh, 1913, and part of it, as well as the prayer desk and seat are in memory of Canon Arthur Hunter, Rector 1896-1909. The reredos, inscribed IHS, is in memory of John Cochrane. There is a brass lectern, and the wooden pulpit is to the left. On the marble steps to the chancel is a plaque in memory of Mary Isabella Knox, who died in 1914. Two chairs and a prayer desk are in the sanctuary. The font is in memory of William Knox who died in 1867. The large brass ewer on it commemorates Nathaniel Henry Hunter who died in 1887. The organ by Telford and Telford, has one manual and pedals, and was given in memory of Anna Elizabeth Edwards who died in 1869. The electric blower was installed through the generosity of Mrs Jane Mahaffy in 1955.

Clonleigh Church has many interesting monuments and memorials. On the north aisle

*The Chancel.*

wall, Lt.Col. Andrew Clarke, Knight of the Royal Hanoverian Guelfic Order, Governor of Western Australia, who died in 1847, is commemorated. Robert Little, Surgeon, Co.Donegal Infirmary, Lifford, who died in 1881 is commemorated, as is Col. Benjamin Humfrey of the Leicestershire

Regiment, who died in 1912, and his wife. There is a wooden plaque to Kathleen Dickie, who died in 1964, and to Willa Clarke, who died in 1970. On the east wall of the aisle, Francis Dabine, son of Lt.Col. D.M. Stewart, Indian Army, who died in 1862, is commemorated.

In the sanctuary, there is a monument to the Rev. William Knox, Rector of Clonleigh 1821-1860, and his first wife, Sarah, who died in 1819, and his second wife Louisa, who died in 1849. He

*Hansard Monument.*

replaced the old bell with a new one in 1859. There is a monument to Lt. Col. Benjamin Humfrey, who served in the Peninsular War, who died in 1865, and to his wife Mary. On the south sanctuary wall, Rev. William M.Edwards, Rector 1860-1872, who died in 1883, and his wife Anna, who died in 1869, are commemorated, as is Canon John McClintock, Rector 1872-1896.

The first monument on the south wall is the great monument to Sir Richard Hansard and his wife, Dame Anne, both of whom died in 1619. They came from Lincolnshire. The monument contains two large painted statues of them at prayer with a lectern between. Sir Richard Hansard was Governor of Lifford at the time of the Tyrone and Cahir O'Doherty rebellions just before the Plantation of Ulster in 1609. King James awarded him the town of Lifford. As has been noted, in his will, he left money for the building of Clonleigh Church, as well as for a school and schoolhouse.

Other memorials on the same wall commemorate Alexander Humfrey, Surgeon Major, 9th Regiment, who died in 1876, Doreen Cochrane, who died in 1935, John Keys Humfrey, Capt., Donegal Militia, who died in 1870; Barbara Ann Hunter, wife of Rev. A. J. Hunter, Rector 1896-1909, John Cochrane of Combermore, Lifford, who died in 1901, Hugh and Lucy Cochrane, whose daughter donated the heating system in 1960, Travers Barton, M.D., Surgeon at the Infirmary, and the Rev. A. J. Hunter. Eliza Clarke, who died in 1937, Andrew and Elizabeth Clarke and others of the family, 1839-1939, and Andrew Clarke who died in 1836, and his wife, Louisa who died in 1820, of Belmont, Lifford, are commemorated.

On the north wall is a brass plaque in memory of Margaret Neely, servant of Dr. and Mrs Little, Combermore House, Lifford, who died in 1907. To the left of this, a plaque records various benefactors, and it was dedicated at a service of re-hallowing on 10th December 2000. There is also a brass memorial to Archie Smyth and Mary Smyth. In the porch is a large brass memorial to William Gaston Boyd, 2nd Lt. Royal Inniskilling Fusiliers, who was killed in the Great War in 1916. The monument also commemorates those from the parish who fell. Finally, in the porch, there is a plaque acknowledging the donation of the electric lighting by Sarah Clarke in 1943.

Combermore House, Lifford, is now the home of the Simms Family. A famous son of the family was the Most Rev. George Otto Simms (1910-1991), Archbishop of Armagh and Primate of All Ireland, 1969-1980.

The Prior School, Lifford, was an important educational establishment associated with the parish of Clonleigh. It was provided for in the will of Miss Eleanor Prior, and was opened in 1879. The school was amalgamated with the Royal School, Raphoe in 1971, and that school is now the Royal and Prior Comprehensive School. The old Prior School buildings in Lifford have since then been used as an army base.

## CLONMANY, St. COLUMBKILLE

Clonmany, *"the meadow of Maine"*, is in the north of the Inishowen peninsula. St. Columba founded a church there in the sixth century.

The parish church was built in 1772 by the Earl Bishop of Derry. It was a simple two bay hall with a two storey tower at the west end. It was closed in 1927, and is now a ruin.

*Clonmany Church.*

## CONVOY, St. NINIAN

The perpetual curacy of Convoy, five kilometres south of Raphoe, was created when a deed establishing a new chapel was issued on 24th July 1773. The site was granted by Robert Montgomery of Convoy House in 1822. The present church, which is pleasantly situated on the village green, was built in 1824. It is a rectangular hall church, with a battlemented tower at the west end, and a sanctuary at the east end. The vestry room is to the right.

*Convoy Church.*

Entry is through the door to the porch in the south side of the tower. The interior entrance doors are in memory of members of the Watson family, 1967. There is a small baptistery with a hexagonal font to the right. The pulpit on the left of the nave is finely carved, and the lectern and a prayer desk are on the right. The altar and reredos are in memory of those who served and who died in the First and Second World Wars, 1914-1918 and 1939-1945. The War Memorial is on the east nave wall, to the left of the sanctuary.

There are three windows on the north wall, and three on the south wall. These are of opaque glass, and each has a stained glass coloured inset. Each one has a commemorative brass plaque, stating its donor and date of donation. The first window in the north wall is entitled "Born for us", and is in memory of Meta Wallace, 1973. Opposite, in the south wall is, "Baptised for us", in memory of William Watson, 1973. The middle window in the north wall is, "Suffering for us", donated by Convoy "Go Club" in 1973. Opposite is, "Crucified for us", in memory of William and Elizabeth McClure, 1970. The third window in the north wall is, "Risen for us", in memory of the Ashe Family, 1970, and opposite is, "Ascended for us", in memory of Mr and Mrs James Wilkie and Mr and Mrs T.Wilkie. There is a small window in the north sanctuary wall in memory of John and Bella Quinn. The east window is a fine stained glass light in memory of R.A.S. Boyton, Convoy House, 1968.

On the north wall is a brass plaque commemorating Eileen Barclay, from the Barclay family, who donated the carpeting in her memory. There is a plaque in the north sanctuary wall commemorating Samuel Oliver, in whose memory the Communion cloths were given by his wife, Greta and the family. The donation of the amplification system in memory of Jennie Kennedy, who died in 1983, is noted on a brass plaque on the south wall.

## CONWALL, LETTERKENNY

The name Conwall, from the ancient *Congbhail,* means, *"the habitation of the stranger".* Three kilometers to the west of Letterkenny, the principal town of the parish, is the site of the Abbey of Congbhail. St. Fiacra, who died c.625, was Abbot here. The abbey is mentioned in the Annals of the Four Masters, and it survived until as late as the 18th century.

*Conwall Church.*

Conwall Parish Church was reported to be in good repair in 1729, and to have been slated in 1733. This building was demolished in 1776, and the nave of the present church was built. The three storey tower, judging by a carving in the wall, was built in 1636, and was incorporated into the new building. The spire was added in 1832. A three-gabled south aisle was built between 1860 and 1865. The chancel was enlarged and improved in 1902. The vestry room and porch are to the right of the sanctuary.

The church is entered through the main door in the south side of the tower. The interior main doors, dating from 1960, are of Austrian oak. They were presented in memory of Cecil Harris who was killed accidentally in 1945. There is a gallery at the west end. The marble font in the baptistery, which dates from 1921, is in memory of Archdeacon William Fitzroy Garstin, Rector 1905 to 1916. The oak pulpit in the north-east corner of the nave, and prayer desks to the left and right of the sanctuary step, were given in memory of Dean Richard Baillie, Rector 1876 to 1903. The Choir stalls date from 1938. In the sanctuary, the altar is in memory of Charlotte Agnes Boyd who died in 1933, and the

*The Pulpit.*

oak panelling was erected in 1941 in memory of Hannah McIlroy. The carpet in the sanctuary commemorates Richard Harron who died in 1960. The brass communion rails were erected in 1902. The oak chairs in the chancel are in memory of Fannie A. Butler who died in 1924. The brass lectern to the right, below the sanctuary, was given by officers of the Donegal Artillery in memory of officers and men of the regiment who fell in the South African war of 1899 to 1902.

The organ is a two manual Telford and Telford instrument, with pedals. It was built in 1889, and was in the gallery until it was placed in its present position in the aisle in 1938.

*St. Fiacra Chapel.*

Following renovations in 1986, the south aisle was consecrated as a chapel with the dedication, St.Fiacra. The altar in it is in memory of Archdeacon Louis W. Crooks, Rector of Conwall, 1946 to 1980, and father of the author. There are plaques in the chapel which record the donation of the altar cross in memory of the Rev. S.B. Crooks and Mrs Violet Crooks, the parents of Archdeacon Crooks, and the candlesticks in memory of Robert and Matilda Watson. The altar frontal and cloth commemorate Joseph Patterson who died in 1979, and the carpet and curtain behind the altar commemorate James and Margaret Bonar. Brass plaques record these gifts. The altar rails came from Aughanunshin Church, and the sanctuary chairs commemorate Fannie Butler who died in 1924.

Conwall Church has some particularly fine stained glass windows. In the west wall, in the gallery, the two windows on either side are in memory of John and Sarah Wilkinson who died in 1962. Under the gallery, on the north wall, the first window has clear lattice glass, with two lights and Y tracery. There is a similar window opposite in the south wall. The middle window in the north wall is in memory of Dr. Fenwick Carre, who died in 1915. It depicts our Lord healing. The window by the pulpit is in memory of W. H. Boyd who died in 1913. It has two lights and depicts on the top left, King Hezekiah's prayer, and on the right, St.Peter at prayer. The east window was presented by Mrs Dougherty of Fahan in 1895 in memory of her brother, Canon Edward Dougherty, Rector of Fahan Lower, who died in 1890. It is thought that it was originally intended for Fahan Lower Church, Buncrana. It has three lights and geometric tracery. It contains patterned stained glass with elaborate floral designs, and the text, "Blessed are the pure in heart for they shall see God". The three windows in the south aisle contain three lights each, and a large

***Conwall Church, Nave and Chancel.***

circular window. The first of these has plain, coloured glass, and is behind the organ. The next window, one of two in the St.Fiacra Chapel, is the Great War memorial window. It depicts King David as Valour, Abraham and Isaac as Sacrifice, and Jonathan as Love. On it are inscribed the names of those from the parish who fell in the Great War of 1914-18. The circular window above depicts an angel with a sword. To the right, there is a brass tablet, on which are the names of those who returned after the war. The brass support for the poppy wreath on the window is in memory of Archdeacon Crooks. The third window commemorates Mrs Violet McAuley who died in 1959. It was erected in 1970. The circular window has an angel, and below, on the left is Joseph. The Blessed Virgin Mary is on the right, and the boy Jesus is in the centre.

There is a number of interesting monuments and memorial tablets in Conwall Church. The first one on the north wall at the west end is a brass plaque in the baptistery which records the presentation of a book case for hymn books in memory of Frederick McKinley. A monument commemorates Dr. William Maddock of Buncrana, who died in 1876. The next monument is a memorial to Henry Wray who died in 1652, to his son Henry who died in 1666, and his wife, Elizabeth who died in 1674. There are two brass tablets in memory of Archdeacon Henry St.George McClenaghan, Rector 1919-1938, and of his wife, Queenie who died in 1941. The other tablet on the north wall is in memory of Major Doyne who died in 1912, and of his wife who died in 1911.

Two distinguished families in the parish were the Stewarts of Rockhill and the Boyds of Ballymacool, Letterkenny. On the east wall, to the left of the sanctuary, the first monument is to John Vandeleur Stewart, J.P., D.L., 1802-1872, and Mary, 2nd daughter of the Marquis of Drogheda, and Helen, his wife, daughter of the 2nd Earl of Norbury, and their son, Major-General A.C.H. Stewart, J.P., D.L. Below it, there is a memorial to Dean Potter, Rector 1903-1905, and beside it is a memorial to Charlotte Agnes Boyd who died in 1933. On the east wall to the right of the sanctuary is a monument to Rear Admiral Hector Stewart, 1841-1922 and to Charles Stewart, K.B.E., 1851-1932, and his wife. Below is a memorial to Captain Gerald Charles Stewart and Second Lt. John Maurice Stewart, both of whom were killed in the Great War. This monument has three different kinds of marble, and is exceptionally fine. The main Boyd monument is at the south end of the east wall, and is in three sections. On it are commemorated, on the left, William Porter who died in 1883 and his wife May, eldest daughter of John Boyd of Ballymacool who died in 1886. John Robert Boyd, J.P., D.L., of Ballymacool, 1806-1891, and his wife Mary Louisa, daughter of the Rev. William Knox, Rector of Clonleigh, who died in 1878, are commemorated in the middle section. On the right, Patty, daughter of John Boyd who died in 1887, and her sister Frances Boyd of Kiltoy, Letterkenny who died in 1892, are commemorated. There is a small font close to the Boyd monument. Adjacent to this, a plaque records the donation of hymn books in memory of Capt. Horobin who died in 1958. There are also memorials to Canon Peter Cartwright, Rector of Conwall, 1980-1984, and to the Very Rev. Richard Aemilius Baillie, Rector of Conwall and Dean of Raphoe.

By the altar in the St. Fiacra Chapel is a brass plaque in memory of Archdeacon L.W.Crooks. On the west wall of the nave, a plaque records the installation of the heating system in 1953, and the donation of light shades in memory of Alexander Spratt who died in 1973. Plaques record the donation of Church Wardens' wands in memory of William Logue who died in 1976, and of his wife, and the tiling in the porch in memory of John Harris who died in 1963.

In the 19th century, Rectors of Conwall resided at Glendooen, five kilometres west of Letterkenny. Glendooen Rectory was built in 1814 during the incumbency of Dr. Stopford, F.T.C.D. Stopford Brooke, who translated from German, the Carol, "Still the Night", was born in Glendooen Rectory in 1832. In 1913, Lancelot Smyth presented his residence, "Murrac-a-Boo" to the parish as a Rectory. His wife Fanny was daughter of Major Doyne. The present rectory was built in 1998.

Glendooen School was opened in 1877. It closed some years ago. In 1878, the parochial hall on the Port Road in Letterkenny was built. It was used also as a school until 1976, when the joint Presbyterian/Church of Ireland Ballyraine National School was opened. The parochial hall was demolished in 1999. A fine new hall was built and opened adjacent to the church in 1998.

# Some Raphoe Diocesan Houses

### The Volt House, Raphoe

The Volt House in the Diamond in Raphoe was built in 1738 by Bishop Nicholas Forster as a home for Clergy Widows. It is administered by the Bishop, the Archdeacon of Raphoe and the Dean of Raphoe. Now no longer a residence, the building has been tastefully restored in keeping with its 18th century style, and is used by several community organisations. Bishop Forster, a philanthropist, also built and endowed schools, including the then new premises of the Royal School, Raphoe, the Diocesan Library, and hospitals.

### St. Ernan's, Donegal

John Hamilton, (1800-1884), a wealthy and philanthropic landlord, owned large estates at Brownhall in south Donegal. In 1824, Hamilton decided to build a small dwelling on St. Ernan's Island in Donegal Bay, and in due course, with the help of local tenantry, and with great difficulty, he built a causeway over to the island. Hamilton was a good landlord, and was liked and respected by all creeds and classes. He liked St. Ernan's so much, that he soon decided to build a much larger house there.

Over the years, this house was sold a number of times to different buyers, until it came into the possession of the Deane-Morgan family. In the early 1950s, they bequeathed St. Ernan's to the Church of Ireland. Thus, it became a holiday house for clergy families. It remained as such until closure in the mid-1970s. It is now a hotel.

### The Mevagh Centre, Carrigart

The Mevagh Centre at Carrigart was set up in 1982 when Captain, (later, the Rev.) David Griscome of the Church Army came to the parish. It caters for youth groups and conferences. It can be used as a centre for such organisations to engage in pony-trekking, golf, water sports and fishing, but its main purpose is to provide a place for spiritual development and renewal. The house, formerly the Rectory, belongs to the Leitrim estate, and must be used for church-based activities.

## CULDAFF, St. BUADAN
## CARROWBEG

CULDAFF, *"the black church"*, or *"the black field"*, or *"wood"*, is a village in the northern part of Inishowen. The area is rich in pre-historic and early Christian relics, including St. Buadan's Cross, and the remains of an old church. St.Congellus is said to have founded a monastery in the area around 690. The parish church is dedicated to St. Buadan, a missionary to Scotland. A very ancient bell which is said to have belonged to him, still exists.

Culdaff church is a small, rectangular building with a tower at the west end. The present church was built in 1747, and is thought to contain much of the original building. The tower was added in 1828. It has four storeys, and battlements and finials on top. There is a sundial on the outside south wall.

*Culdaff Church.*

The porch in the base of the tower has three entrances. Inside, there is a large gallery. The vestry room is to the left, outside the sanctuary. The pulpit is on the right, and the lectern in front of it is the gift of pupils of Foyle College, Londonderry, 1872, in memory of their Headmaster.

*Monument to George and Anne Young, Culdaff.*

There are two windows in the north wall, one of which is of lattice design, and the other, of stained glass, commemorates Letitia, widow of Robert George Young who died in 1914. Similarly, in the south wall, one window is of lattice design, and the other of stained glass, commemorates Robert George Young. The east window is diamond paned, and contains three lights.

On the north wall are monuments and tablets commemorating Private Alonzo Reid of the Canadian Forces, Rev. James L. McHenry, curate 1817, and Lt. George Young who was killed in the Great War. There is also a war memorial plaque. Also on the north wall, there is a beautiful, coloured tile monument to Capt. Robert Young, who was also killed in the Great War.

On the south wall is another coloured, tiled monument to George L.Young who died in 1926, and to his wife. There are also memorials to Robert Staveley Young and to the Rev. William Haslett, Rector 1923-1944. The Youngs of Culdaff are still a prominent land-owning family in the parish.

On the east wall, on each side of the sanctuary, are decoratively painted texts from the Gospels. There are some more of these on both sides of the entrance door in the west wall. The old gas and oil lamps are still in position, though not now in use.

A dwelling house at Carrowbeg near Culdaff, was used for some years as a place of worship. This was closed in 1986.

*Former church of Carrowbeg.*

## DESERTEGNEY

*Desertegney Church ruin.*

The parish of Desertegney, *"the desert or hermitage of Eagneach"*, is just north of Buncrana, on the east shore of Lough Swilly. It is said to have been founded by St. Columba. The church was built in 1779. It was a three bay hall with a tower. It was closed in 1972, and is now a forlorn ruin.

## DONAGH, CARNDONAGH

CARNDONAGH was one of the earliest Christian settlements in Donegal, and is supposed to have been founded by St. Patrick in 442 A.D. Near the present church is a lintel stone from a 12th century church. St. Patrick's Cross outside the church is an important relic, possibly dating from the 7th century. It has a carving of Christ on the east face. Beside it are two pillar stones, one with David the warrior and David the harpist, and the other with a bishop carrying a book, a crozier and a bell.

*Ancient Cross, Carndonagh.*

The present church was built in 1769. It is a plain, rectangular building, with a vestry room in the north-west corner. The bell in the bellcote over the west end of the nave, is thought to have come from the *Trinidad Valencera,* a ship which was wrecked in the Spanish Armada in 1588. The main entrance is at the west end. It contains an original 15th century doorway. There is a sundial in the south wall, dated 1835.

*Donagh Church.*

There are two windows, with two lights in each, on the north wall, and two similar windows in the south wall. The fine stained glass window in the sanctuary commemorates the Rev. Mungo Neville Thompson, Rector 1876 to 1893, and his wife, Charlotte, and was the gift of their surviving children. It depicts the Resurrection, and was installed in 1905.

*1835 Sundial, Carndonagh Church.*

The oak pulpit, to the right of the sanctuary, was carved by the Rev. P. C. Duncan, Rector 1911-1932, and it commemorates those who fell in the Great War, 1914-1918. The font is of Carrara marble.

On the north wall, monuments commemorate the Rev. George Marshall, Rector 1808 to 1851, and his wife and also, John Harvey of Trinity College, Cambridge, a barrister, who died in 1856. On the south wall, beside the pulpit, is a brass plaque commemorating those who fell in the Great War. There is a plaque in memory of Lt. James Kerr who died in the Great War, and a memorial to Capt. James Marshall, son of Rev. George Marshall who was killed in India in 1842.

## DONAGHMORE, CASTLEFINN, St. PATRICK

St. Patrick is supposed to have founded a church at Donaghmore, near what is now Castlefinn, ten kilometres south-west of Lifford in east Donegal about 450. The name, which is also sometimes spelt Donoughmore, means literally, *"the Great Sunday (Church)"*.

At the Plantation of Ulster, Sir John Kingsmill became one of the chief landowners around Castlefinn. In 1622, the church was reported as being, "much decayed, having neither cover nor good walls". The present church may be early 18th century. By 1768, it was in good repair. In 1837, it is described in Lewis as being a plain old edifice. Major renovations were carried out in 1864.

Donaghmore Church is a large, plain rectangular building with a spacious porch at the west end, over which is a bellcote, and a semicircular sanctuary at the east end. There is a large east window in the sanctuary, with three lights. To the left of this is the vestry room, and there is a small store room to the right.

On the north wall are two clear glass paned windows, with two lights, and Y tracery. There are four similar windows of two lights each on the south wall. The pulpit, prayer desk, altar and lectern are beautifully carved. The lectern is in memory of Thomas and Isabella, 1913, and the altar, credence table and panelling, dated 1918, commemorate the Rev. Fenwick Hamilton Verner, Rector 1906 to 1917 and his wife, Ada.

On the north wall are monuments to Mary I. Hegarty who died in 1935, and to Mary Hamilton Lighton, who died in 1826, the wife of Rev. Sir John Lighton. Below is a monument to the Rev. Sir John Lighton, Baronet, Rector 1816 until his death in 1827. The brothers Desmond Humphreys, D.S.O., and George Humphreys are commemorated. They were killed in the Great War. There is a Latin monument to the Rev. John Nicolson, Rector 1720 to his death in 1729. He was the son of William Nicolson, Bishop of Derry and later Archbishop of Cashel.

On the south wall is a Latin monument to Charles Hamilton, Magistrate, who died in 1770, and another to Sarah, wife of Robert Mansfield, who died in 1841. On the floor in the aisle, before the sanctuary, is a large flagstone with a coat of arms. Apart from the date 1696, most of the inscription is indecipherable.

***Donaghmore Church.***

## DONEGAL

Donegal, *"the fort of the strangers"*, is a mediaeval town. In the 12th century, the O'Donnells built a castle, and in 1474, a monastery was built by Hugh Roe, son of O'Donnell, Prince of Tirconnell for the Observantine Order of Franciscan friars. In 1612, Donegal was elevated to borough status. At the Plantation of Ulster, Captain Henry Brooke was granted land in the area. The Annals of the Four Masters were compiled in Donegal in 1631.

In 1722, Donegal became a vicarage, created out of the neighbouring parish of Drumholm. The congregation worshipped in a church which was

*Donegal Church.*

situated in the grounds of the old abbey. The present church was built in 1828, and was consecrated in 1831. In 1889, the chancel, a vestry room, and the organ chamber on the north side of the nave were added. The organ is a two manual Telford and Telford instrument with pedals.

At the west end is a tower which is surmounted by a spire. The clock was installed in 1910 in memory of David Crawford Pearson. Inside is a gallery, beneath which, to the left, is the baptistery. The font is in memory of Olive Andrews who died in 1958. The east window is of coloured glass. There is one small window in the south wall of the sanctuary, three windows with rectangular panes in the south wall, and two in the north wall.

The Holy Table was given in memory of A. W. Galbraith, W.Arnold and R.Kearney, who died in the Great War. On it are two brass book stands in memory of John Greer Fawcett who died in 1921, and Constable Thomas Satchwell, RIC, who was killed in an ambush in 1921. The pulpit on the left, and the reading desk in it, are in memory of the Rt.Rev. Robert Miller, Bishop of Cashel, and Rector of Donegal 1894-1900. It was erected in 1932. The brass lectern commemorates the Rev. Samuel Reed, Rector from 1866 until his death in 1893. The Prayer Desk is in memory of Alexander Thompson.

On the north wall is a monument which records that the Communion Table commemorates those who died in the Great War, and there is a monument in memory of Alfred Banks, a doctor who died in 1879 of typhus. He was the son-in-law of the Rev. S. Reed. On the south wall is a brass memorial to the Rev. William E.B. Chapman, Rector from 1900 until his death in 1916. The Very Rev. Stephen Cave, Dean of Raphoe, and Rector of Donegal from 1947 to 1972, is commemorated, as is Edwarda Williamina, daughter of the Rev. Samuel Reed, who died in 1882. There is also a memorial to those from the parish who fell in the second World War, 1939-1945.

The Parish Centre in the church grounds was built in 1996. Also of interest is the recent restoration of Donegal Castle beside the church.

*Donegal Church interior.*

## DRUMHOLM, BALLINTRA

DRUMHOLM PARISH is situated between Donegal and Ballyshannon, to the south of Laghey. One ancient name was Drumtomma, *"the ridge of Tomma"*. The village of Ballintra is in the parish. St. Ernan, who died about 640, was the abbot of a monastery in the area.

The present church was built in 1795, and remodelled in 1854. It is a large, impressive rectangular building, with a four storey tower. The entrance doors in the north side of the tower were presented by Thomas and Mary Craig, Mayor and Mayoress of Londonderry in 1979. There are two interior entrance doors to the nave which commemorate Thomas and Mary Craig.

Inside the church is a large gallery which runs round three sides of the nave. It is supported by

***Drumholm Church.***

four doric columns on each side. There is a central aisle and two side aisles. On both the south and north walls are three windows of three lights each. The east window is of opaque and coloured glass, and has three lights.

The baptistery is under the gallery, half way up the north side of the church. The font was presented by the Vicar of Drumholm, the Rev. John Kincaid in 1851. The vestry room is to the right of the sanctuary. The altar was presented in memory of Kathleen Corscadden who died in 1899 aged 17 years, and of her grandmother, Catherine Léger who died in 1908. The prayer book stand on it is in memory of Oliver McCausland and his wife, 1923. The sanctuary chairs were the gift of the Fyffe family. There is a prayer desk in memory of John and Mabel Harron, 1998, and the chair commemorates John Stronge. The pulpit is on the left, and the brass eagle lectern is in memory of William Finlay Russell, 1926. The one manual organ was restored by the Wells Kennedy Partnership of Lisburn in 1996.

In the porch is a brass memorial to Alexander Hamilton who was killed at the Battle of Jutland in 1916, during the Great War. Plaques in the porch also record the resurfacing of the entrance grounds in memory of Letitia Manoe who died in 1978, the donation of a ramp and handrails at the entrance in memory of the Warde family, the sanctuary kneelers and runners in memory of Kathleen Fawcett, the refurbishment of the gas lamps in memory of Andrew and Margaret Dinsmore, the presentation of the clock in the tower in memory of Capt. James Hamilton, the presentation of the public address system in memory of Robbie Edgar, and the donation of the carpet on the landing and stairs to the gallery in memory of Andrew and Bella Harron. In the porch, upstairs, outside the gallery are monuments to Andrew Hamilton who died in 1881, to Anna Hamilton who died in 1895, to Alexander Hamilton, J.P. who died in 1873, to Ellen Thompson who died in 1882 and Lt. Hamilton Thompson, Royal Inniskilling Fusiliers, and to Susan Beaufoy who died in 1859, to Abraham Hamilton and to Catherine Thompson. Surgeon William Thompson who died in 1840 is also commemorated. The memorial to those who fell and to those who served in the Great War is on the west nave wall. Over the door is a plaque which records the renovation and rehallowing of the church in 1996. On the other side of the entrance is another memorial to those who served in the Great War. On the east wall, a brass memorial commemorates the Rev. John Kincaid, rector of Drumholm from 1847 until his death in 1883.

The rectory of 1871 was replaced with a new house in 2000.

***Drumholm Church interior.***

## DUNFANAGHY, HOLY TRINITY

DUNFANAGHY, *"Finnchu's Fort"*, is beautifully situated on the north coast of Donegal. The parish was formed in 1872 out of Clondehorkey parish, and was originally called Clondehorkey West. In 1877, the name was changed to Dunfanaghy. The church was built in 1873, and was consecrated a year later on 2nd May 1874.

*Dunfanaghy Church.*

The church is entered by a small porch in the north-west corner. It is in the shape of an inverted L, with the sanctuary at the east end of the nave, separated by the altar rails, and a large transcept to the right. The vestry room and a porch are behind the east transcept wall. The window in the west wall is of three lights. There are two windows in the south nave wall, one in the west transcept wall, one of three lights in the south transcept wall, and another window of similar coloured and clear glass design, containing three lights in the north wall. Also in the north wall by the entrance, is a stained glass window depicting the Good Shepherd, in memory of Robert and Martha Alcorn, 1967. The east window over the sanctuary is particularly striking. It depicts the Ascending Christ with arms outstretched. It contains small depictions of the three crosses on Calvary, and a chalice and Host, and of our Lord's footprints. It is richly coloured. The pulpit is to the left of the sanctuary. The altar and reredos, undated, are in memory of Valentine Griffith. The small prie Dieu is in memory of Mrs Lily Merrick, and the accompanying chair commemorates Patricia Gamble. The prayer desk commemorates William and Enid Arnold. The right-side prayer desk and chairs commemorate Dean Pirrie Conerney, Rector 1905-1940. The brass lectern is in memory of Major V.S.Griffith, East Yorkshire Regiment, who died in 1917, and of his father, the Rev. V. P. Griffith, Rector of the neighbouring parish of Tullaghobegly, who preached at the opening of the church on 3rd May 1873. The church was not consecrated until the following year. The organ in the transcept came from Kilmoe Church in the Diocese of Cork, and was installed in 1992.

On the north wall, there is a monument to Edmund Murphy who died in 1897, and to his wife. There is a small memorial to Annie MacLean, 1980, and a memorial to five men of the parish who fell in the Great War, 1914-1918.

*Holy Trinity Church, Dunfanaghy, interior.*

The memorial plaques and monuments to the Stewart Family of Horn Head, Dunfanaghy, are in the transcept. The Stewarts came to Donegal in 1700 from Co. Offaly, when Charles Stewart bought the estate of Horn Head from John Forward and Captain William Sampson. The property remained in the family until it was sold in 1936. The Stewarts were descended from the Stewarts of Darnley in Scotland. The Rev. Charles Frederick Stewart, (1800-1868), was curate of Clondehorkey, 1823-1830, and Rector of Raymunterdoney 1831-1842. His daughter Emily married the Rev. John Brodie, first Rector of Dunfanaghy in 1883. On the east wall, to the right of the sanctuary are three brass plaques commemorating Eleanor Louisa Stewart who died in 1914, and Thomas Francis Stewart who died in 1916, Dr. Richard Stewart, M.C., youngest son of Charles Frederick Stewart, D.L. who died in 1957, and Charles Frederick Stewart, eldest son of C. F. Stewart who died in 1920. There is a monument to their father, Charles Frederick Stewart, D.L., who died in 1917, which was erected by his wife Georgina.

On the west wall of the transcept is a monument to their son, Commander Bertram Robert Stewart, R.D., R.N.R., who died in 1958, to his daughter, Anne Howard, who died in 1960, and to Lindesay Stewart, son of Captain Charles Frederick Stewart, who died in 1990. On the south wall of the nave is a monument to Elizabeth Frances Stewart, wife of Charles Frederick Stewart of Horn Head, parents of C. F. Stewart, D.L., and grandparents of the other Stewarts above mentioned, who died in 1881.

The Rectory, which is adjacent to the church, was designed by Sir Charles Lanyon, the distinguished 19th century architect. It was completed in 1880.

## DUNLEWEY

Dunlewey means, *"Lewe's Fort"*. Dunlewey Church was consecrated as a chapel of ease in Tullaghobegley Parish, Gortahork, on 1st September 1853. In 1872, the perpetual curacy was absorbed into neighbouring parishes. The church is a four bay hall with a tall tower at the west end which has prominent finials.

Dunlewey church was closed in 1955, and is now a ruin on the shores of Dunlewey Lough, at the foot of Mount Errigal.

The bell is now at Cashel Church near Creeslough, and on it is inscribed the date 11th October 1860, and the name of the Incumbent, Rev. J. H. Bor, who was Incumbent 1856-1872. James Henry Bor was the only man to hold the incumbency without any other parish.

***Dunlewey Church.***

## FAHAN UPPER, FAHAN, St. MURA
## FAHAN LOWER, BUNCRANA, CHRIST CHURCH

St. Mura founded a monastery and school at Fahan between Derry and Buncrana. Relics of the saint include a cross, St. Mura's bed, and a holy well. He died about forty years after Columba, c.640 A.D. Fahan can be translated, *"the little green plot"*. The parish was also anciently known as *Athanmura, "the little ford of Mura"*.

*Fahan Upper Church, Fahan.*

A church was built at the time of the Plantation. It is reported as having been in good repair in 1768. The parish was divided in 1794 into Fahan Upper and Lower.

The present Parish Church of Fahan Upper at Fahan was built in 1820, and the chancel was added in 1897. At the west end is the tower, through which one enters the building. It has three stories and is surmounted by prominent finials. A plaque in the porch records that the notice board is in memory of Allen Foster who died in 1970.

Inside the nave is a gallery, under which, in the south-west corner is the baptistery. To the left of the nave is the vestry room. The mosaic tiles on the sanctuary floor are in memory of the hymn writer, Mrs Cecil Frances Alexander, 1818-1895. Her husband, the Rev. William Alexander, later Primate, was Rector of Fahan from 1855 to 1860. The pulpit is on the left. The brass lectern is in memory of Conolly and Georgina Norman of Fahan House, 1898. There is a one manual organ with pedals, on which there is a plaque commemorating Canon William Atkinson Dickson, Rector from 1891 until his death in 1912.

On the south wall are three lattice windows, each of two lights. Two of the three windows in the north wall are of lattice design, and the middle one, of stained glass, depicts St. Elizabeth of Hungary. It is by Evie Hone, the celebrated Irish stained glass window designer, and it is in memory of Mary Dickson of Fahan Rectory and Fahan House, who died in 1941. There is a small window on each side of the sanctuary. The east window of three lights, depicts the text from St. John's Gospel, "I am the Resurrection and the Life", and it commemorates George Workman Dickson who died at sea in 1900.

On the north wall is a monument which replaces one from the old church, and which mentions the tomb of Major Richard Samson who died in 1652, and various descendants. There are monuments to the Maxwell family of Birdstown House, Fahan, on the north wall. Peter Benson Maxwell, J.P., who died in 1867 and his wife Emily and their sons, as well as Richard Ponsonby Maxwell, son of the Rev. Charleton Maxwell, Rector of Leckpatrick, Strabane, 1853-1872, are commemorated on a monument. There is a memorial to the Rev. Charleton Maxwell who died in 1895, and one to Robert Walter Maxwell, who died in 1879. The next monument commemorates Major Guy Vernon Goodliffe M.C., Royal Fusiliers, who died in 1963, and his wife Grace of Birdstown House. There are memorials to Lt. Col. Joseph James of Fahan House who died in 1850, to Mary Dickson, who was a nurse in France during the Great War, and who died in 1917, to Josiah Marshall, rector of Fahan Upper, 1761-1793, who died in 1794, and to Hugh W. E. Lane, a pilot in the R.A.F., who died in Egypt in 1941 during the second World War.

On the east wall, to the left of the chancel entrance, is the memorial to those who fell in the Great War. On the north chancel wall, Charles Norman who died in 1843, and his wife, Anna, are commemorated. On the south chancel wall is a monument to Agnes Elizabeth Jones, who was a nurse, and who worked with Florence Nightingale. She died in 1868. On the south wall are memorials to the Rev. William Hawkshaw, Rector 1823 to 1855, the year of his death, to Rear Admiral William Heath who died in 1815, and to Mary Annesley, Mistress of Fahan School, who died in 1900. The handrail on the gallery stairs is in memory of Edward and Kathleen Short, 1997.

*Fahan Lower Church, Buncrana.*

Fahan Lower Parish Church on Buncrana Main Street, was built in 1804, and enlarged in 1816. The chancel was built in 1902 in memory of Canon Edward Newland, Rector 1890 to 1900. The four-storey tower at the west end has small finials on top. The clock in it is in memory of Elizabeth Savage who died in 1909. Inside the church is a gallery, beneath which, to the left, is the font. The large transcept is entered through an arch to the left of the nave. This is closed off. To the right is a porch which houses the organ chamber. The vestry room is to the left of the nave, beyond the transcept.

*Detail of ceiling, Christchurch, Buncrana.*

The window in the north nave wall is of stained glass in memory of Ernest Alfred Pitts and his wife Elizabeth. It depicts a lady with a treasure chest and Jesus holding a lamb. The two windows in the south wall have two lights each. One of these is of stained glass, and depicts St. Brigid and St. Columba and other figures. It is in memory of John Cunningham and his wife Nora, and family. In the transcept, the west wall has three windows of two lights each and Y tracery. The north wall has a window of three lights, with fleur de lys patterns, and the east wall has one window with two lights. There is one window in each side wall of the sanctuary. The east window is a triple lancet with cusped tracery. It depicts the Ascension, and is in memory of Canon Ralph P. Meredith, Rector 1924-1944, who died in 1945. A brass plaque records this.

A brass plaque in the sanctuary records the erection of the chancel in memory of Canon Newland in 1902. The oak panelling in the sanctuary commemorates Margaret Gray Colquhoun who died in 1912, and the reredos is in memory of William Graham Murphy, Rector 1919-1923. A brass plaque notes this. A plaque in the sanctuary records the donation of the chancel carpet in memory of members of the McKinley family, and another one records the donation of the altar cross as the gift of the wife of Samuel McKinley in 1970. The brass lectern is the gift of Samuel Price Edwards, 1874, and the stone pulpit is in memory of Canon Edward George Dougherty, Rector 1873-1890. There is a two manual Conacher organ with pedals, which was installed in 1895.

On the north wall of the nave is a brass memorial from Desertegney Church to those who fell in the Great War, and a memorial to Canon Dougherty. On the south wall, Mary Colquhoun who died in 1873, is commemorated. Other memorials in the sanctuary apart from those already mentioned, commemorate Georgina Emily Knox, whose husband, the Rev. Thomas Knox, Rector 1900-1920, gave the site for Lower Fahan School in her memory, and Canon Gerald Dickson, Rector of

*Christchurch, Buncrana, the Chancel and Sanctuary.*

Fahan Upper, 1939-1965. In the sanctuary is a memorial to Mrs Ruth Mervyn who died in 1993, in whose memory the storm glazing was installed.

In the transcept, a monument commemorates Emily Doherty who died in 1907, and her husband Edward who died in 1918. Rear Admiral George Hart who died in 1812, and his wife who died in 1818 are commemorated on a fine monument which has statues of two figures under a sun. There is a brass memorial to members of the Dunsterville family in the 19th century, and a memorial to Christina Dalrymple Sabi.

The Rectory was built by Canon Dougherty for his own use, and was purchased by the parish in 1908. It was sold and replaced with a new rectory in 2001. The parochial hall was built in 1876.

## GARTAN, St. COLUMBA

THE STORY OF the life of St.Columba of Gartan is well known. He was born at Gartan, which means, *"little field"*, in 521. A cross erected by the Adair family in 1911 marks the site of his birth. Columba was educated at Temple Douglas nearby. He went to Iona in 563 to begin the conversion of Scotland. The Columban sites at Gartan include a holy well and the remains of an old abbey church which probably dates from the 12th century.

*Gartan Church.*

A new church was built in 1729. This was in turn replaced in 1819 by the present church in Churchhill village. To this was added in 1895, the tower, chancel, east window and south aisle, through the generosity of Mrs Cornelia Adair of Glenveagh Castle.

The church is entered through the door in the south side of the tower. In the north wall are two windows, each with two lights. Beyond is a small north transcept with one window. The south aisle is joined to the nave by three arches. In the south wall are three windows, each with three lights.

*St. Columba Window.*

There is a small window at each end of the aisle. All these windows have opaque, square-paned glass. The sanctuary is lit by a fine stained glass east window with three lights, depicting from left to right, the Baptism of St. Columba, Columba landing in Iona, and the Death of St. Columba. There is a vestry room to the left of the sanctuary.

*Cross marking St. Columba's birthplace, Gartan.*

The font is in the north-west corner of the nave. Beside it is the oar which was used by Mr. Billy Patterson in the curragh which sailed to Iona in 1963 to mark the 14th centenary of Columba's voyage. The wooden pulpit is on the left by the transept. The prayer desk and lectern are on the right. The old oil lamps are still in place.

On the north wall of the sanctuary, a monument commemorates the Rev. Canon Edward George Dougherty, Rector of Lower Fahan, 1873-1890. On the south wall of the sanctuary are memorials to the Rev. Henry Maturin, Rector of Gartan, 1831-1880, and to Archdeacon L. W. Crooks, Rector 1957-1980*. On the north wall of the nave are tablets commemorating Hannah Isobel Black, and Mrs Cornelia Adair, in whose memory electric lighting was installed. On the east wall, to the right of the sanctuary is a memorial to Edward Daniel Hewetson who died in 1906. In the aisle is a memorial to Mr Henry McIlhenny, the American multi-millionaire who lived in Glenveagh Castle, and who died in 1986.

**Archdeacon Crooks was father of the author.*

# Saint Columba

*"In the roll-call of God's sons, sounding sweet and solemn,*
*Name we mid his chosen ones, Ulster's own Saint Columb".*

THESE LINES FROM a hymn of Mrs Cecil Frances Alexander, call to mind one of the great figures of the early Celtic Church. The life story of St. Columba, or Columbcille, *the Dove of the Church,* is well known. He was born at Gartan, Co. Donegal of royal parentage in 521. He was educated at Temple Douglas near Kilmacrennan, and at the great monastery of Clonard in Co. Meath. He was duly ordained to the priesthood.

In the age of Saints and Scholars, Columba founded many monasteries. His greatest was at Derry, the Oak Grove, which he founded in 546. He also founded monasteries at Kells, Durrow and Swords. Many of these monasteries would have been small communities. The monastic buildings would have included a church, a dormitory, a refectory and a library and there would have been a small farm. Some Irish monasteries, including those mentioned, became great seats of learning, where manuscripts such as the Book of Kells were produced.

*Holy Well, Gartan.*

Columba was very keen on copying books. He borrowed a Latin Psalter from St. Finnian of Moville and copied it. Finnian demanded both the original book and Columba's copy, claiming it on the grounds that, "as to every cow belongs its calf, so to every book belongs its copy". Columba refused to give up his copy. He sought the help of Diarmit, King of Meath who ruled against him. Being an impetuous man, a wolf as well as a dove, Columba then gathered all his clan together, and with the help of the King of Connaught, he attacked Diarmit. In the ensuing battle near Sligo, 3,000 men were slain. Columba felt so remorseful about the consequences of his impetuosity, that he vowed to bring to Christ as many people as had lost their lives in the battle.

Columba resolved to leave Ireland for ever. He and his twelve companions sailed in a curragh from Derry in 563, and continued their journey until Ireland was out of sight over the horizon. They arrived in Iona, where a monastery was established. This became the base for the conversion of the Pictish people of Scotland. Columba's mission over the following years was a resounding success.

Columba did actually return to Ireland a number of times. He attended the Convention of Drumceatt near Limavady in 575. This was held to sort out a dispute about whether the Kingdom of Dalriada in Argyll should pay tax to the Irish King, and to determine the place and position of the poets and bards.

Columba's long life ended on 9th June 597. That evening he was copying Psalm 34, verse 10, "They who seek the Lord shall want no manner of thing that is good". He handed the work to his companion, Baithin to finish. He died at the altar of his chapel that night.

*St. Columba Window, St. Columb's Cathedral, Derry.*

In fulfilling his vow, Columba and his followers began the process which would lead to the eventual re-conversion of Europe after the fall of the Roman Empire.

## GLENALLA, St. COLUMBCILLE

Glenalla parish, which lies to the west of the Ramelton to Rathmullan road, was formed as a district curacy from Tullyaughnish parish about 1820. The name means, *"the glen of the swan"*. The present church was built about 1850, and the parish became a separate incumbency in 1870.

Glenalla church is entered by a small porch in the north wall. Inside, the nave is lit by two windows in the north wall, one of which has two lights, and by three windows in the south wall. These windows all have patterned coloured glass. There are two similar windows in the west wall, and a small rose window above. There is a window of two lights in the north chancel wall, and the east

*Glenalla Church.*

window has three lights of coloured glass. The vestry room is to the right.

The pulpit, which is of stone with wood panels, is on the left and the lectern is adjacent. The prayer desk and an organ of one manual are on the right side.

On the west wall is a monument to Thomas Barnard Hart, who built the church. His wife Elizabeth Anna Hart of Glen Alla House, who died in 1888, is commemorated by a plaque in the sanctuary. The Harts were an old Plantation family who owned extensive areas of land in Inishowen, Muff and Culmore and around Glenalla, and they owned Doe Castle near Carrigart.

On the north wall is a brass memorial to George Alcorn who was sexton, who died in 1959. Patricia Moore who died in 1931, and Flight Lt. Edward Chichester Hart of the Royal Air Force are commemorated. He was killed during the second World War in 1943.

Glenalla church is surmounted by a conical belfry which is supported by four pillars.

## GLENCOLUMBCILLE, St. COLUMBA

GLENCOLUMBCILLE PARISH is situated in the far south-west corner of Donegal. Columba founded a monastery in the area. The ruins of several ancient churches, and some ancient crosses are nearby.

*Glencolumbcille Church.*

The present church was built in 1828, and was extensively renovated in 1963. On the tower, over the entrance door is the inscription, "A.D.1913 This tower was erected by Henry Musgrave, the surviving member of the Musgrave Family, owners of the Glencolumbkille estate since 1867." The tower is of three storeys, and it is surmounted by stepped battlements and a short pyramid. The nave is lit by four lattice windows on the south side and three on the north side. It is supported externally by five buttresses on each side. The vestry room is to the left of the chancel. The east window is of stained glass and depicts the text, "I was hungry and ye gave me meat", from St. Matthew Chapter 25, verse 35. It is in memory of John R. Musgrave who died in 1895.

There is a small baptistery. The wooden font cover commemorates Elizabeth and William James Maxwell, 1963. There is a wooden eagle lectern. The pulpit is on the right, and the prayer desk adjacent was given by the Rev. Alexander Munro, Rector 1912-1918. One of the chairs in the sanctuary

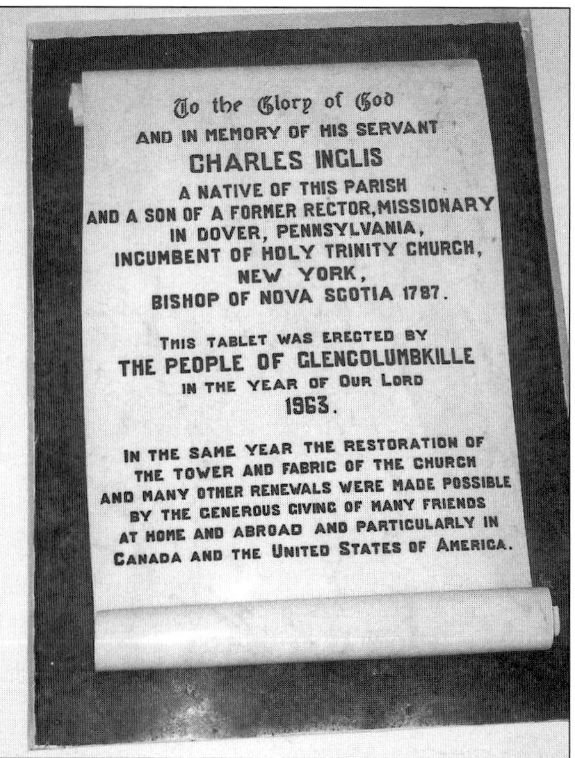


*Inglis Memorial, Glencolumbkille.*

# Charles Inglis, 1734-1816, First Bishop of Nova Scotia

CHARLES INGLIS was born in 1734, the son of the Rev. Archibald Inglis, Rector of Glencolumbcille in Co. Donegal. His brother Richard was Rector of the neighbouring parish of Kilcar. The Inglis family had Scottish ancestry, and they were forced to flee to Donegal during the reign of King James II.

Inglis went to America in 1754, where he taught at the Free School in Lancaster, Pennsylvania. He was ordained in London in 1758, and took up duty as a missionary with the Society for the Propagation of the Gospel in what was known as the Dover Mission near Philadelphia. In 1765, he was appointed curate of the prestigious parish of Holy Trinity, New York. He became Rector there in 1777.

The American Wars of Independence were to be a difficult time for Inglis, as he was a staunch royalist, indefatigably opposed to the loss of the American colonies. Independence however was achieved, and this resulted in the end of the link with the Church of England and the Crown. At the time Inglis was acquainted with Samuel Seabury who was consecrated in 1784 as the first Bishop of Connecticut. Seabury could not be consecrated in England, as no American bishop could take the oath of allegiance to George III, which was required, so he was consecrated in Aberdeen in the Scottish Episcopal Church.

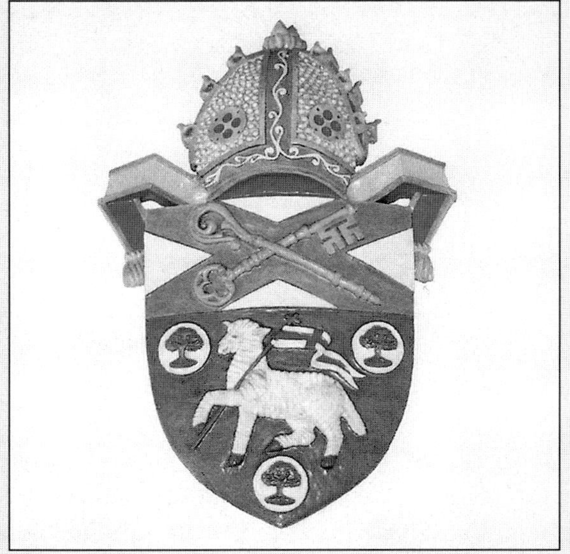

*Crest of the Diocese of Nova Scotia, Glencolmcille Church.*

Inglis' days in America were numbered following Independence, so in 1783, he left New York for England. In 1787, he was appointed the first Bishop of Nova Scotia in Canada. He was consecrated at Lambeth Palace in London on 12th August 1787, and thus became the first Bishop of a diocese in a British colony.

At that time, the Diocese of Nova Scotia was enormous, covering Ontario as well. It has since been divided into many new dioceses. Inglis was a conscientious pastoral bishop. He travelled throughout his vast diocese and built many new churches. He insisted on public worship being conducted properly and decently. In Nova Scotia during his episcopate, he founded a society for the promotion of agriculture. He also founded the University of King's College, and the King's School at Windsor, Ontario. He recruited many more clergy so that missionary as well as parochial work could be advanced. His son John became the third Bishop of Nova Scotia in 1823.

Dr. Charles Inglis died in 1816. He truly was a great son of the Diocese of Raphoe. His work was crucial in the early development of the Church in Canada. His memorial in his native Glencolumbcille Church was erected in 1963.

*Charles Inglis of Glencolumbkille, first Anglican Bishop in Canada.*

was presented in 1901 by Mrs. M. E. Thompson, whose husband, Rev. David Thompson, was Rector 1875-1910, and the other was presented by Samuel Craig, Dublin, in 1882.

The church has a very fine Telford and Telford chamber organ. It was built in 1874, and was brought to Glencolumbcille in 1916. It was restored to its original condition in 2000.

On the north wall is a memorial to Col. James Hamilton Powell, Chairman of the Land Board, and High Sheriff of the District of Bathurst in the Province of Upper Canada, who died in 1831. On the south wall is a brass plaque commemorating Norman Blain who died in 1986. There is a brass memorial to Samuel Musgrave, J.P. of Lisburn who died in 1893, and a plaque commemorating David Buchanan who died in 1993. A monument commemorates William Walker Rutherford who died in 1880, and a brass plaque commemorates Major William Rutherford who died in 1896.

On the left side of the east wall, Canon David Thompson is commemorated. On the other side is a monument to a famous son of the parish, Bishop Charles Inglis who was consecrated as the first Bishop of Nova Scotia in Canada in 1787. He was bishop of the diocese until 1816, and was the first Bishop of a diocese in a British colony. He had an illustrious career which included the incumbency of Holy Trinity Church, New York. Bishop Inglis' father, the Rev. Archibald Inglis, was rector of Glencolumbcille 1715-1743. The crest of the Diocese of Nova Scotia is over the west door. The Inglis monument was erected in 1963, in the same year as substantial restoration work was carried out to the tower and fabric of the church.

## GLENEELY, ALL SAINTS

GLENEELY VILLAGE is in the north of the Inishowen peninsula. The church nearby, which is by Joseph Welland, is supposed to have been built at the instigation of Miss Catherine Ball of Grousehall. It was consecrated on 27th March 1856. It is a simple, rectangular church with a belfry. A chancel was to have been built, but never was - the arch can be seen outside behind. Gleneely church was closed in 1990.

*Gleneely Church.*

## GLENTIES

GLENTIES PARISH CHURCH, Glenties, in south-west Donegal, was built about 1860. At the west end is an impressive two storey battlemented tower. The door is in the south wall. Inside the nave, the baptistery, with the font just outside, is to the left. There are four windows of plain, square glass on each side. The east window is of coloured and patterned glass. The Ten Commandments are painted on the east wall of the sanctuary. The vestry room is to the right of the chancel.

The altar is in memory of John Hanlon and his wife, Ann. The prayer desk was given by T. H. Mearn, and the brass lectern commemorates the Very Rev. Michael Bell Cox who was appointed Dean of Raphoe in the year of his death, 1897. He was Rector of Glenties, 1856-1897, and Archdeacon

*Glenties Church.*

of Raphoe, 1880-1897. There is also a monument to him which at present lies in the porch. On the north wall, a brass plaque records the donation of the heating system in memory of Charles Duncan, 1965.

Glenties village has won the national Tidy Towns competition on several occasions.

## GWEEDORE, BUNBEG, St. PATRICK
## CARRICKFINN, St. ANDREW'S CHAPEL OF EASE

The parish of Gweedore, *"Dore's inlet"*, is in the north-west corner of Donegal. It was originally a district curacy in the parish of Tullaghobegley. It became a parish in 1872 when it was detached from Tullaghobegley. Carrickfinn was detached from Templecrone Parish, Dungloe that year, and added to Gweedore. Templecrone and Gweedore were united in 1923 during the incumbency of Rev., later Canon James Williams.

*Gweedore Church, Bunbeg.*

The parish church of St. Patrick at Bunbeg was built in 1844 as a dual purpose church and school. It was consecrated for use specifically as a church in 1914, when the tower was added. The church is a simple hall building. On each side are four small windows, each with two lights, and there is one window in the east wall in memory of Lord George Augusta Hill, builder of the church, who died in 1879. The cross on the altar commemorates the Very Rev. John Watson, Rector of Gweedore, 1945 to 1976, the year of his death. The vestry room is to the left of the sanctuary. The pulpit on the right, was a gift from Derg Parish Church, Castlederg in 1979. The prayer desk on the left was presented by Senator and Mrs W. A. Sheldon in 1979.

*Gweedore Church interior.*

The first of three brass memorials on the north wall commemorates Hugh and Florrie Boyd. The church gates were given in their memory in 1999. The second commemorates Dean John Watson. The

*Iona Curragh Monument, Gweedore Church.*

church was restored in his memory in 1979, during the incumbency of his successor, the Rev. Iain Knox. The third commemorates Mrs Nan Boyd who died in 1968. The organ was presented by her husband, Jack, and the family. On the south wall is

*Carrickfinn Church.*

a brass plaque in memory of Louis Alcorn, Sexton, who died in 1992, and there is a marble monument to William Alcorn who died in 1990. There is also a model of the curragh which was built by Jim Boyd in 1963, which made the voyage to Iona in 1963 in the fourteenth centenary year of Columba's journey. In the sanctuary, there is a memorial to Lord George Hill.

The hall adjacent to the church was built in 1914, and was used as a school until the mid-1920s.

St. Andrew's chapel of ease on Carrickfinn, now joined to the mainland by causeway, was built in 1857. It was originally a watchtower, and was converted into a church around 1870. It was consecrated and given the dedication St.Andrew in 1977. It is a small, rectangular building with two porches, one to the left of the sanctuary in the north wall, and the other, half way along the south wall. Each has a door in memory of John R. Boyd who died in 1998. The south porch has a bellcote. The bell was erected in 1978.

The lectern is in memory of Canon James Williams who was Rector from 1923 to 1945. He had been Rector of Templecrone since 1914. The pulpit is on the left side of the sanctuary. The pews were crafted by William Boyd from pine logs.

There are two clear glass windows of two lights on each side. There is one window of two lights in the east wall.

# The Protestant Orphan Societies

IN THE MIDDLE of the 19th century, the Church of Ireland established societies in most of the counties to care for orphans in the days when social welfare was not available. These societies continue to function and benefit needy children.

**The Tyrone Protestant Orphan Society** was established on 26th October 1843, "to provide maintenance and religious and secular education for children who are eligible under the rules and in need of assistance in their advancement of life".

**The Donegal Protestant Orphan Society** was formed at a meeting of ten clergy of Raphoe Diocese at the Gweedore Hotel on 10th September 1857. They were concerned at the desolate condition of orphaned children whom they wanted to help to a better standard of life and education. In this, they were inspired by the Dublin Protestant Orphan Society which had been founded some thirty years earlier. The Society continues the same work today.

**The Londonderry Protestant Orphan Society** was founded in 1866 for the same good purpose. It is supported in some instances by the **Lord Enniskillen Memorial Orphan Fund.**

There are some other funds available to assist needy children. Amongst these there is the **Poston Trust.** Robert Poston who died in 1925 came from the Parish of Cumber Lower. He came into possession of glebe land in that parish and tried to set up an orphanage there. This was not a success, so it was duly sold, the proceeds providing funds for the Poston Trust to assist the Orphan Societies in educating children in their care. Poston built the Poston wing at the City and County Hospital in Londonderry.

The **Mary Abercorn Trust** assists orphan girls who are in the care of the Londonderry P.O.S. **The Alexander Fund** assists Londonderry P.O.S. children with further education. Over the years, many thousands of poor families and their children in need have been helped by these charities.

## INCH

INCH, WHICH MEANS *"an island"*, is an island in Lough Swilly, which was joined to the mainland by a causeway in 1850. It is just below Fahan, near Buncrana.

Inch church was one of five chapels of ease in the parish of Templemore, Derry Cathedral in 1693. The church which was built in 1766, was a simple hall building. It was closed in 1965, and is now a ruin.

*Inch Church ruin* .

## INNISKEEL, PORTNOO

INNISKEEL, *"the island of Coel"*, is a parish in south-west Donegal, which contains the village of Portnoo. St. Conall Coel was abbot of a monastery on an island in the bay in the middle of the sixth century. Ancient and mediaeval ruins can still be seen on the island. By 1622, it was considered desirable to build a new church on the shore. In 1729, it was reported that there was a church and a chapel.

*Coel's Island, Portnoo.*

The present church was built and consecrated on 8th June 1828. The entrance is through the door in the south wall of the tower, opposite which is a window. There are three clear glass windows in both side walls of the nave. The east window has coloured, patterned and diamond paned glass. The vestry room is to the right of the sanctuary.

The font is to the right of the entrance. There is fine wood panelling round the sanctuary. The communion rails and altar are in memory of Eileen Boyle and her sons, Gerald and Anthony, 1955.

*Inniskeel Church.*

*Inniskeel Church interior.*

There is a prayer desk on each side of the sanctuary, and a chair in memory of Patrick Billingsley, 1978. Outside the sanctuary, the pulpit is to the left, and a brass lectern is on the right.

On the north wall is a brass memorial to Captain Anthony Trevor Boyle of the Royal Inniskilling Fusiliers who died in North Africa in 1943, during the second World War, and on the south side, his brother, Captain Edward Fitz-Gerald Boyle of the same regiment, who died in 1952, is commemorated.

Part of the parish of Inniskeel was detached in 1820 to form the parish of Ardara.

## INVER, St. JOHN THE EVANGELIST

Inver, *"a river mouth"*, is a parish about half way between Donegal and Killybegs. St. Natalis was abbot of a monastery in the area in the middle of the 6th century. In the 1729 survey, the church was reported to be in good repair.

The present church in Inver was built in 1807. The chancel was added during renovations by Welland and Gillespie in 1861. It is entered through the porch at the base of the three storey, louvered tower. The tower has corner finials and is surmounted by a spire. The clock in the tower was built by the Rev. Frederick Carre, Rector of Inver, 1869 to 1904. He also built the clock in Raphoe Cathedral. There are two rooms, one on each side of the porch. The entrance door in the west end of the tower is in memory of Sarah, James and Andrew Britton, 1977. The door into the vestry room to the right of the porch, and the door opposite are both in memory of James Wilson who died in 1983, and his wife. A plaque in the porch records the kerbing in the avenue in memory of Matthew Wilson, 1977.

*Inver Church.*

Inside is a spacious, two-aisled nave. There are three windows of two lights and Y tracery on both side walls. The east window is of three lights, the middle section of which depicts St. John the Evangelist, in memory of Bobby Wilson, 1991.

The font is in memory of Donald Sinclair who died in 1879. The prayer desk on the right is of wood on a stone base. The pulpit is on the left, and in the centre, a brass eagle lectern commemorates William Sinclair, D.L., who died in 1896. A plaque in the chancel records the erection of the chancel, the roof and new windows, and the donation of the pulpit and prayer desk by Jemma Stewart in memory of the family at Holly Hall, Co. Tyrone. The two sanctuary chairs commemorate those who served in the Great War. Behind the Holy Table is a flower shelf in memory of Andrew and Margaret Scott, 1991. The electric organ is of two manuals with pedals, in memory of George Hanlon who died in 1990. A table at the front of the nave commemorates George and Isabella Henderson, 1997, on which is a cut glass bowl in memory of Susan Graham, 1996, and at the entrance, there is a table in memory of Andy Armstrong, 1977.

In the chancel are plaques commemorating Wesley Pearson, and Canon Alexander R. S. Munro, Rector of Inver, 1918 to 1957. On the east wall, a plaque records the installation of electric lighting in memory of Louisa Henderson, 1968, and another commemorates the Rev. Alexander Montgomery, Rector 1802-1803. On the east wall to the right of the chancel is a monument which commemorates Jusaun Conyngham, daughter of Lt. General Conyngham, and the Rt. Hon. Mary, Lady Shelborn. She was born on 14th September 1607, and died on 24th July 1706. On the other side of the east wall to the left of the chancel is a memorial to the Rev. Henry Carre, Rector of Inver, 1848 to 1869. He was father of his successor, the Rev. Frederick Carre. On the south wall, a monument commemorates Sir Henry Montgomery, M.P. for Donegal, who died in 1830. He was a Lieutenant Colonel in the Yeomanry Corps. Adjacent, a monument was erected by Isaac Colhoun to record an endowment donated by Catherine Babington who died in 1847. There are memorials to those who fell and who served in the Great War, and to Robert McConnell who died in 1926.

## KILBARRON, BALLYSHANNON, St. ANNE

KILBARRON PARISH CHURCH is one of the most beautiful and impressive churches in the Diocese of Raphoe. It is situated on a hill overlooking the town of Ballyshannon, and can be seen for miles around. St. Barron was bishop in the area, of a church which was founded by St. Columba. Also in the area was the ancient Abbey of Assaroe.

The church was reported to be in good repair in 1729. However, a new church was built in 1795. This was rebuilt in 1841 during the incumbency of the Rev. George N. Tredennick, Rector 1829-1872. A stone above the outside of the east window records this, and one below states that the builder was Thomas Keague, 1841.

The church is entered through the massive, four storey tower at the west end. In the porch is a memorial to those who fell in the Great War. A plaque states that the clock in the tower is the gift of Henry Stubbs, D.L., and Alfred Stubbs, 1903. The clock was electrified in 1977 in memory of R. Laird. A peal of six bells was presented in 1884. The present peal of eight bells was presented by Henry Stubbs in 1901. Plaques in the porch note the donation of the public address system in memory of Margaret and James Boyd, the tiling in the porch in memory of Canon James Kermode, Rector 1949-1962, and the donation of the south door in memory of Emily and Bertie Laird.

*Kilbarron Church.*

The vestry room is to the left of the porch. A gallery runs round three sides of the church. The enormous capacity of the church is a reminder that it was built partly to accommodate soldiers from nearby Finner Army Camp. A door in the west wall was presented by the Griffith family in 1977, and the vestry door was presented in memory of Minno Vance in 1990. There is a central aisle and two side aisles in the nave. The interior of the church is two-storied, so there are five windows in each storey in both the south and north walls. All of these except two, are of two lights with clear glass. One of these is downstairs on the south wall, and depicts on the left side, the bringing of children to Jesus, and on the right side, the baptism of Jesus. It is in memory of Mary Chinnery Britton who died in 1886. Appropriately, there is a font in a small niche adjacent. There is a corresponding niche in the north wall opposite. The other stained glass window is in the gallery, and depicts on the left, St. Peter, and on the right, St. John. It is in memory of Robert Lyon Moore D.L. of Molenan House, Londonderry, who died in 1902. The east window is of three lights, and depicts the Resurrection, the Ascension and the Sermon on the Mount. A brass plaque nearby records that it was presented by Alfred Stubbs in 1900.

The baptistery is outside the chancel, on the south side of the nave, beneath the gallery. It is the gift of the Patton family in memory of George Patton and Isobel Clarke, 1971. The font is dated 1850. The kneelers in the baptistery commemorate Mrs Lewers, 1971. There is wood panelling round the sanctuary. The altar is in memory of Robert Hannah, 1932. There is a porch to the right of the sanctuary. The stone pulpit in the chancel commemorates Canon S. G. Cochrane, Curate of Kilbarron, 1862, and Rector, 1872-1898. The brass lectern is in memory of Annie Thompson who died in 1884, and there is a marble prayer desk and chair. The organ of two manuals and pedals, is on the left side of the chancel.

There are numerous monuments in the church, some of which are particularly fine. On the west wall downstairs is a memorial to Joseph Irwin Walsh, M.D. who died in 1886, and another which commemorates William Martin of the Royal Irish Constabulary who was murdered in 1889, and Thomas Crawford, a surgeon in the Donegal Regiment of Militia, who died in 1842, is commemorated. On the north wall downstairs, a plaque records the renovation and re-hallowing of the church in 1994. There is a memorial there to Mary O'Neill who died in 1860. On the south wall, downstairs are memorials to Elizabeth Major who died in 1802, to Charles O'Neill of Rockville who served in the Peninsular War, and who died in

*The Sanctuary.*

1852, to John Allingham who died in 1841, to 2nd Lt. Alan Ramage and Pte. Thomas Lapsley who died in the second World War, and to those who fell in the Great War.

In the gallery, on the west wall is a monument to Thomas Atkinson, D.L., who died in 1921, and to his wife, and one commemorating Capt. Thomas Atkinson, D.L., who died in 1949, and his family. On the north gallery wall is a monument to Major Robert Lyon Moore, D.L., who died in 1953, and to Johnston Teevan who died in 1872. On the south gallery wall, the monuments commemorate Thomas John Atkinson, J.P. who died in 1881 and his wife, their daughter Mabel who died in 1911, and Lydia, wife of the Rev. George Tredennick who died in 1866, who was the daughter of William Magee, Archbishop of Dublin. The Rev. Walter Rikey who died at sea in 1865 is commemorated along with his widow, Sarah Emily who died in 1883.

On the east wall are six fine monuments. These commemorate Thomas Stubbs who died in 1872, Elizabeth Chinnery who died in 1887, Henry Stubbs, donor of the clock and bells, who died in 1921, Anna and Emily Troubridge, the Rev. Charles Stubbs, and Alfred Stubbs who died in 1930. The Rev. Charles Stubbs was Rector of Camus-juxta-Bann near Coleraine from 1884 until his death in 1905. He was the son of Thomas Troubridge and Elizabeth (née Chinnery) Stubbs. An ancestor, Archdeacon Philip Stubbs was one of the founders of the Society for the Propagation of the Gospel at the beginning of the 18th century.

The poet William Allingham (1824-1889), was brought up in the parish of Kilbarron.

## KILCAR

KILCAR, *"the church of Carthagh"*, is a small parish in the south-west of Donegal, between Killybegs and Glencolumbkille. St. Carthagh is thought to have presided over a monastery in the area about 540 A.D.

The present church was built in 1828. It was a plain building with two bays and a tower. It was closed in 1960 and is now a ruin.

*Kilcar Church ruin.*

## KILLAGHTEE, DUNKINEELY, St.PETER

KILLAGHTEE PARISH, with Dunkineely village, is between Donegal and Killybegs. Nearby are the ruins of an ancient church. The present church was erected in 1826. It has a three storey tower with unusual crenellations. The entrance door was presented by John and Eileen Given, and the west window commemorates M. W. Robinson, 1993.

Inside is a gallery. There are two small windows in the west wall, and two windows of clear glass in the north wall. There is one similar window in the south wall, and the other, of stained glass, depicts Jesus, the True Vine. It is in memory of Georgina and Sophia Hawkins. There are three windows of coloured glass in the east wall.

*Kilaghtee Church.*

There are two aisles in the nave. The baptistery and font are in the north-west corner, adjacent to the pulpit, which is in the chancel. The pulpit, which is finely carved, is in memory of Samuel and Elizabeth Cassidy. Opposite, is the prayer desk, which was presented by John O'Donnell in memory of his parents, 1904. The chairs in the sanctuary are in memory of Francis and Elizabeth Rogers, 1891. Behind the Holy Table, which is surrounded by fine panelling, is the vestry room. A plaque states that the Communion rails and Holy Table are in memory of William O'Donnell, M.D., 1936, and that the east window was given by Killaghtee branch of the Girls' Friendly Society in 1935.

The memorial to those who fell in the Great War is on the north wall. On the south wall is a monument to Bessy, wife of the Rev. Joseph Welsh, Rector of Kilaghtee, 1831-1859, the year of his death. He himself is commemorated in the lower part of the monument. There is a memorial to the Rev. Matthew T. Moriarty, Rector, 1875 to 1888, and to his wife Sarah, who died in 1894. Ellen Williams who died in 1931, and her daughter and granddaughter are commemorated, as is Helen Sinclair who died in infancy in 1925. A memorial commemorates William O'Donnell, M.D., who died in 1935, and another commemorates Capt. Percy McClenaghan, M.C. of the Punjab Regiment, who died in 1930. He was the son of Archdeacon McClenaghan who was rector 1894-1919, before going to Conwall. Mrs McClenaghan who died in 1941, is also commemorated.

The old parish school building is now in use as a parish hall, and there is a new school nearby.

## KILLEA

THE PARISH OF Killea gets its name from *Cill Fhéich,* or Fiach's Church. Who St. Fiach was, or when he lived, are not now known. In 1693, Killea Church was one of five chapels of ease in the Parish of Templemore, centred around Derry Cathedral. The present church in Carrigans, eight kilometres south-west of Londonderry, was built in 1765, during the incumbency of the Rev. William Law, Rector from 1753 to 1793. His initials, W.L. are over the inside porch door of the church. There is a bellcote over the west nave wall above the porch.

*Killea Church.*

Inside, the baptistery is in the north-west corner of the nave. The sanctuary was erected in 1899. There is fine oak panelling all round it, and the marble steps were donated by William Montgomery in 1956. The altar is in memory of Henrietta Forster, wife of the Rev. William Forster, Rector from 1872 to 1894. Mrs Forster died in 1911. The communion rails and chairs in the sanctuary were given in memory of those who fell in the Great War, 1914-1918. The prayer desk in the sanctuary commemorates Thomas Bradley who died in 1988. The pulpit was given in memory of Colonel William McClintock, who died in 1912, and of his wife who died in 1875. The prayer desk is in memory of the

Rev. Cuthbert Thompson who was Rector from 1905 to 1922. He died in 1926. The brass lectern was given in memory of Henrietta Forster. The electronic organ commemorates Maxwell Lyon Moore of Molenan House who died in 1994.

The nave is lit by three round-headed windows on both the north and south sides. Each has two lights and tracery, and clear, square paned glass. The east window is a triple lancet, and it depicts the Ascension of our Lord. It commemorates Robert McClintock of Dunmore House, Carrigans, who died in 1899.

There are some fine monuments in Killea Church, some of which commemorate the McClintocks of Dunmore. On the north wall is a cross-shaped marble memorial to Lilian Edith Smyth who died aged two years in 1868, and on the south wall is a memorial to Frederick Edwards Peoples who died in 1990. On the south wall, a brass plaque records the destruction by fire in 1971 of Carrigans Memorial Hall. On the north wall of the sanctuary is a monument to Margaret, wife of Robert McClintock of Dunmore who died in 1893. Below, a brass plaque commemorates her daughter, Letitia who died in 1917, and on the south sanctuary wall opposite, her husband Robert who died in 1859, is commemorated on a monument. He was father of Robert in whose memory the east window was erected. In the vestry room, to the right of the nave, a brass plaque commemorates James McCready who died tragically in 1990. The tiling in the vestry was given in his memory.

The McClintock family of Dunmore House, Carrigans came to the area at the end of the 16th century. They acquired Dunmore when William McClintock married Elizabeth Harvey of Dunmore in 1685. The present house dates from 1709. Their grandson, Robert McClintock, was High Sheriff of Tyrone in 1759, and of Donegal in 1764. His grandson Robert, in turn, was High Sheriff of Donegal in 1835.

In 1938, there occurred a triple shooting tragedy at Dunmore. Robert McClintock's brother, Lt. Col. William McClintock had a grandson, Lt. William George McClintock, who was engaged to be married to Miss Margaret Helen Macworth of Sidmouth, Devonshire. His mother did not approve of the engagement, because Robert had been crippled in a fall from a horse. The wedding was planned for Monday 26th September 1938, but on the previous Saturday, Mrs McClintock shot her son dead, and then, shot herself. Miss Macworth was so grief-stricken, that she took the gun and shot herself. The triple funeral took place at Carrigans Church on 26th September 1938, on the day on which the wedding would have been celebrated. The McClintocks left Dunmore in 1940. Dunmore has been the residence of Sir John and Lady McFarland since 1958.

## KILLYBEGS, St. JOHN

KILLYBEGS, *"the little churches"*, is on the south coast of Donegal, and claims to be the biggest fishing port in Ireland. A charter was granted to the town by James I, and Killybegs had two members in the Irish Parliament up to the Union in 1801. The original church, which was dedicated to St. Catherine, dates from the time of the Plantation in 1609, and was reported to be in good repair in 1729.

The present church was consecrated on 6th June 1828 and is dedicated to St.John. The chancel was added in 1860. The porch at the west end is surmounted by a tower and spire. There are two blind windows in the west wall and two windows of clear glass and Y tracery in the north wall of the nave. In the south wall is one similar window, and another of stained glass depicting the Ascension, in memory of Arthur Brooke and his sister. There are

*St.John's Church, Killybegs.*

*The Sanctuary.*

two windows in the chancel. In the apsidal sanctuary, there are five windows. Each contains stained glass, depicting various Biblical themes and stories. The central window was erected in memory of Elizabeth Augusta Brooke who died in 1895. The other four windows were erected in memory of Arthur Brooke, J.P., who died in 1909. The wooden ceiling of the chancel is in the shape of the inverted prow of a ship.

Half way up the left side of the nave is the Baptistery. The font in it came from St. Catherine's old church, and is dated 1717. Opposite is a similar area containing the harmonium. The vestry room is to the left of the nave. The pulpit is on the left, and the brass eagle lectern commemorates Grace Frances Brooke who died in 1895. The prayer desk is to the right.

On the north wall is a brass memorial to those who fell in the Great War. Another monument records the presentation of the glebe house by the parishioners and the Right Rev. Edward Stopford, Bishop of Meath, and Rector of Killybegs, 1809 to 1821. He died in 1850. The monument also records the birth of his son Edward who became Archdeacon of Meath. A small brass plaque records the donation of the lighting in memory of William, Robert and Henry Watson, 1971.

A monument on the south wall commemorates William, son of the Rev. John G.Ball, who died in a railway accident in 1871, and Mildred Ball who died in 1865. There is a memorial to J. Howard Deazeley, Rector of Killybegs, 1905-1921, who died in 1924, and a monument on the south chancel wall commemorates Henry Lodge, M.D., Assistant Surgeon, 2nd Battalion, 2nd Queen's Royal Regiment who died in 1864.

## KILLYGARVAN, RATHMULLAN, St. COLUMB

KILLYGARVAN, *"the wood of the rough field"*, is a parish half way up the west coast of Lough Swilly. The church is in Rathmullan, where there are the remains of an ancient priory. At the survey in 1622, the church was considered to be in such bad repair, that it would be better to worship in the old priory. By 1729, the church which had been consecrated in 1706, was in good repair. Another church was built in 1814.

The present church dates from 1887, when the chancel, organ chamber and vestry were added to the building of 1814. At the west end is a tower, with a window on either side, and the entrance to the porch in the west end. Inside is a gallery, under which, to the left is the baptistery.

In the north wall, at the west end, are two small square windows, one below the other. There is also a large window with three lights, commemorating Thomas Batt of Rathmullan House who died in 1857. It contains the Batt family crests. In the south wall are three windows, each with two lights. The first two are of clear lattice glass. The third window depicts Jesus with Martha, her sister, Mary, and Lazarus, and is in memory of Letitia, daughter of the

*Killygarvan Church.*

Rev. and Mrs C.Gayer. There is an opaque glass window in the south sanctuary wall. The east window, dated 1883, is in memory of Elizabeth Otway, daughter of Thomas Batt, who died in 1878. The four lights depict Jesus walking on the water, the miraculous draught of fishes, the woman caught in adultery, and the raising of Lazarus.

The prayer desk was presented by David Kelly in memory of his sons. The lectern is nicely carved. The pulpit is in memory of the Rev. Henry Stewart Cochrane, Rector of Killygarvan, 1835-1880. The organ and the altar, which is dated 1936, are in memory of the Rev. William Battersby Lloyd, Rector 1883-1907.

Three important families left their mark on the parish in the 18th and 19th centuries, and their monuments are in the church. One of these was the Knox family of Prehen, Londonderry, descendants of Andrew Knox, Bishop of Raphoe 1611-1633. On the north wall are a roll of honour and a monument to those who fell in the Great War. Next is the monument to Andrew Knox of Prehen, M.P. for Donegal who died in 1774, and his daughter Mariana who died in 1761. In the south wall, Dominick, son of Andrew Knox, who died in 1851, is commemorated.

In 1832, the Batt family of Purdysburn, Belfast arrived in Rathmullan. They had come up from Co.Wexford in the 18th century. They were bankers, founders of the Belfast Bank. Thomas Batt bought the Knox properties around Rathmullan, and rebuilt Rathmullan House, now a hotel. The east window, as has been said, commemorates his daughter.

The Montgomery family was prominent in military life in the 19th and early 20th centuries. Their residence was Fort Royal, also now a hotel. On the east wall of the nave, to the right of the sanctuary, and adjacent to them on the south wall, are several brass plaques to the family. On one, General George Samuel Montgomery who died in 1898, and his wife, Letitia, who died in 1894, are commemorated. His son, Major T. R. A. G. Montgomery who died in 1922, is commemorated on another brass plaque, and another son, Col. C. A. S. Montgomery is also commemorated. Brigadier Harold Matthews, C.B.E. who died in 1947, and his wife Sybil, daughter of J. H. Jellett are commemorated on two plaques. J. H. Jellett was in the Royal Artillery. He died at Fort Royal in 1938, and is commemorated, as is his daughter, Salisbury Mabel who died in 1950. There are two brasses to Brigadier General Arthur B. Stopford, Royal Artillery, who died in 1902, and his wife Evelyn who died at Fort Royal in 1949. In the south wall is a monument to Gardiner Trouter who took part in the Crimean War, and who died at Sevastopol in 1851.

In the north wall of the sanctuary is a monument dated 1887 to Henry S.Irwin, who died in 1823 aged eight years, and in the east wall of the nave, a brass memorial commemorates the Rev. Andrew Noblett, Rector of Killygarvan, 1924-1937, who died in 1948.

## KILLYMARD

KILLYMARD, *"the church of the poets"*, is just to the west of Donegal Town. In the 1622 survey, the ancient church was in ruins. By 1729, the church was in good repair. The present church was built in 1829-30, and was renovated and partly rebuilt in 1891, when the chancel and vestry were added. In the porch, a carved stone from the original church is preserved. The ruins of this church are nearby.

There is a bellcote over the west end of the church above the entrance porch. Inside is a large gallery. There are three windows of coloured glass on each side of the nave, each of which has two lights and Y tracery. The vestry is to the left.

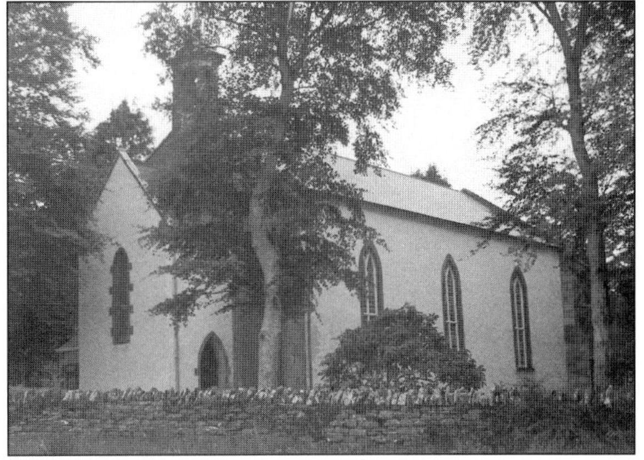

*Killymard Church.*

The east window is a triple lancet with coloured glass.

The altar is in memory of George and Isabella Stewart, 1958. One of the two chairs in the sanctuary is in memory of Mary Leitch who died in 1903. The font in the chancel commemorates John William Barber who was killed in action in the South African war in 1901. The pulpit is on the left, and the prayer desk is to the right. The fine brass lectern is in memory of the Rev. William Hughes, Rector of Killymard from 1853 to 1879. A brass plaque gives the information that the organ was given in memory of Mrs Jean Wilson who died in 1993.

On the north wall are two monuments. The first commemorates George Crommer of the Royal Irish Constabulary who died in 1922, and the second commemorates Samuel George Stewart, M.C. and bar, F.T.C.D., Major in the Royal Field Artillery who was killed in action in 1918, just before the end of the Great War. On the south wall is the memorial to those who gave their lives in the Great War, and there is a memorial to 2nd Lt. Percy Wray who was killed in action in 1917.

In the porch is a plaque which notes that the improvements to the church grounds were carried out in memory of David and Elizabeth Ellis, 1991.

## KILMACRENNAN, St. FINIAN AND St. MARK

KILMACRENNAN, *"the church of the son of Nennain"* is a village some eleven kilometres north-west of Letterkenny. Columba spent his childhood here, and was educated at Temple Douglas nearby. He is said to have founded a monastery in the locality.

Kilmacrennan old church was built after 1622. In the 1729 survey, the church was in good repair.

*Kilmacrennan Church.*

*Pulpit showing carvings of figures from the Reformation.*

This was demolished in 1845, and was replaced with the present church which was completed in 1846. It is a hall church with a porch near the west end of the south side. To the west of that, almost on the south-west corner is a square tower which is surmounted by a small conical spire. The vestry room is opposite on the north wall. The baptistery occupies the whole length of the west wall, and it was arranged in its present form in 1979. It was at that time that the church was given its present dedication. The sanctuary was refurbished in 1939.

There are three diamond paned clear windows on both the north and south walls and a diamond paned window of two lights in the west wall, and a large similar window of three lights in the east wall, which is decorated with fleur de lys and other patterns in colour. There is one small window in each side of the sanctuary. Thus, the whole building is spacious, airy and brightly lit.

The pulpit, which is on the right side of the nave, came from a Congregational chapel in Galway via a Jesuit church there! It is finely carved with figures from the Reformation. The prayer desk was made and presented by Canon James Gerald Harvey, Rector, 1921-1957.

On the north wall is a monument to the Rev. William Allman, Rector 1873-1895. There is also a memorial to Hugh Kennedy and his parents, in whose memory the amplification system was installed. On the south wall is a brass plaque to George Allman, son of Rev. W. Allman, who died in 1911, as well as a memorial to Alex Baxter who died in 1999, and to Jeannie Baxter who died in 1992. The chancel lights and other gifts were presented in their memory.

The former Robertson school adjacent to the church, is now in use as a parish hall.

## KILTEEVOGUE, St. JOHN

KILTEEVOGUE PARISH is seven kilometres to the west of Ballybofey on the Glenties road. It was formed as a perpetual curacy out of Stranorlar in 1773. The church was consecrated on 16th July 1879. It is a large hall church with a two storey tower in the south-west corner. The tower is surmounted by an octagonal spire. At its base is the entrance porch. The vestry room is to the right of the sanctuary.

There are five clear glass windows in the north wall, and four in the south wall. The stained glass window in the west wall is a triple lancet. It depicts the Beatitudes from St. Matthew Ch.5, and is in memory of Sir William Style, Baronet, who died in 1904. The east window which is also a triple lancet, commemorates the Hon. Lady Style who laid the foundation stone of the church on 13th November 1877. She died in 1883.

The pulpit was erected in 1919 in gratitude for victory in the Great War, and in memory of Captain William Kee, M.C., 1st Battalion, the Royal Dublin Fusiliers, and of Pte. James Witter, 11th Battalion, West Australian Imperial Force. The brass lectern is in memory of Robert Warren Meade who died in 1893, and the prayer desk commemorates Samuel Donaldson, M.R.C.S., who died in 1939. The flagon was presented by the Confirmation candidates on the occasion of the first Confirmation in the church by Bishop William Alexander on 8th July 1881.

*Kilteevogue Church.*

On the north wall, a brass plaque commemorates Arthur S. Donaldson, Secretary and Treasurer of the parish, 1949-1974, and there is a brass plaque in memory of Canon J.E.Henderson, Rector 1985-1993.

The Donaldson Memorial Hall adjacent to the church dates from 1901.

## LAGHEY

Laghey, *"a muddy place"*, is a small village between Donegal and Ballyshannon. The parish originated as a perpetual curacy which was formed out of Drumholm parish. The church was built in 1834, and its design has some unusual features. The west

*Laghey Church.*

front has gabled buttresses, each side being capped by a pinnacle. Over the centre is a belfry, topped by a pinnacle. This was erected in 1837 and was restored in 1911. The porch was built in 1971 in memory of Charles A. Brooks. The porch door commemorates the Rev. Joseph G. Sheldon, Rector, 1924-1954, and the west entrance door is in memory of Alexander McClay. The window in the porch is in memory of Robert Wray who died in 1958, and of his wife Sarah who died in 1966, and it depicts the Good Samaritan.

The baptistery in the south-west corner of the nave contains a font in memory of William and Martha Harron. The baptismal bowl is in memory of John and Margaret McCleery. There is a transcept on the north side of the two bay nave, and the vestry room is to the south side of the chancel. The doors into it are in memory of Addie and Florrie Bustard. The railings on the chancel steps are in memory of Edith Kee who died in 1995, and of Robert Kee who died in 1979.

The Holy Table was presented in 2001 by the Deane family, and the pulpit commemorates James Johnston. The reading desk and seat commemorate Evelyn Scott. The brass eagle lectern is in memory of Charles Rutherford who died in 1906. It did not originally belong to the church. The two manual Compton organ is along the north wall. The choir stalls commemorate Hannah Browne, and Canon S. J. Warner, Rector of Laghey, 1964 to 1979, and one marks Gertrude Scott's service to the choir. Chairs, along with a number of pews, were given in 2001 in memory of parishioners.

There are two windows in the west wall. The one on the right depicts *Ecce Agnus Dei,* Behold the Lamb of God, and is in memory of Charles Johnston who died in 1975. The window on the left side depicts the theme, "I am the Vine", and it was presented in 2001 in memory of Thomas and Annie Graham and of their son, James. The window in the north wall depicts the Good Shepherd, and commemorates James Johnston and his wife and family. It was presented by Sir James Kilfedder, M.P. in 1993. There are two stained glass windows in the south wall. One depicts the text, "Suffer the little Children", and was presented by the Mothers' Union in 1995, and the other depicts "the Sower went forth sowing", and commemorates Milton McGrath, 1995. There are two windows in the transcept. One of these has lattice glass, and the other, which is in the west wall, includes the head of St. Patrick from a window at Notre Dame Church in Glasgow, dated 1923. It was installed in 2001 to commemorate Hannah Browne who died in 2000. The east window has opaque and coloured patterned glass and a Bible, and it commemorates Francis and Elizabeth Brooks, 1925. Window ledges in the church commemorate Florence Browne.

Plaques in the porch record the installation of the amplification system in memory of Thomas and Annabella Scott, the electrification and restoration of the bells in memory of Sheila Hamilton, the donation of the west door in memory of Alexander McClay, and the electrical installations in memory of Sir James Kilfedder. On the north wall is a memorial to Robert Kilfedder who died in 1964, and to his wife Elizabeth who died in 1968 and to their grandson who died in 1993. There is also a monument to Jane, Countess of Ross. On the south wall is a memorial to 2nd Lt. Newton Collins, Royal Inniskilling Fusiliers who was killed in action in

1916 in the Great War. There is a wooden memorial to those who fell in the Great War, and to those who served in both World Wars. A plaque on the sanctuary wall notes that the kneelers were the gift of Laghey Church Lads' Brigade, 1993.

Major renovations to the church were carried out in 2001, when many of the memorials and gifts mentioned above were donated. Laghey parish has a fine hall which was built in 1988.

## LECK

THE PARISH OF Leck, the name of which means, *"a great stone"*, is four kilometres to the east of Letterkenny. In the eighteenth century, the church was in good order. This building was replaced in 1839 with a new building which was built by the Ecclesiastical Commissioners. It was a simple rectangular three bay hall.

Leck and Aughanunshin parishes were amalgamated in 1872, and both were amalgamated with Conwall in 1900 to form Conwall Union. The church was closed in 1972.

*Leck Church.*

## LETTERMACAWARD

LETTERMACAWARD, *"the hillside of the son of the poet"*, is a parish on the west coast of Donegal, to the south of Dungloe. The remains of the ancient church are adjacent to the present church which was built about 1788-1791. There were extensive renovations in 1904.

The church is entered through a porch at the west end. The door commemorates Alexander and Ellen Brown and their son, Thomas. There is another door opposite, and a window in the west wall. Inside are three windows in the south wall of the nave, and two of two lights each in the north wall. The east window has three lights. Each window has a mixture of square and diamond paned coloured glass.

The vestry room is to the left of the sanctuary, in which there is good wood panelling. The font is to the left of the entrance, the pulpit and lectern are to the left outside the sanctuary, and the prayer desk is on the right. There are also two small brass lecterns which were presented in memory of the Rev. Andrew Graham, Rector of Lettermacaward from 1905 until his death in 1923.

*Lettermacaward Church.*

## LOUGH ESKE, CHRIST CHURCH

The parish of Lough Eske, as its name suggests, is beautifully situated around the shores of Lough Eske, just to the north of Donegal Town, with wonderful views of the Bluestack Mountains behind the lake. The church, which was built in 1846, was originally a chapel of ease in Killymard parish, but it became a parish in its own right at the Disestablishment of the Church of Ireland in 1870. The chancel and vestry room were added during extensive renovations in 1905.

There is a tower at the west end of the church, at the base of which is the entrance porch. A plaque in the porch records that the window in it was presented in memory of James and Margaret Ellen Crommer in 1993. The tower is capped by an unusual four-gabled structure which is Scandinavian in style. Each side has a louvered window. Inside the church is a large gallery with a window in the rear wall entrance. On each side wall of the nave are two windows with clear square glass panes and Y tracery. The vestry room is to the left of the sanctuary. The east window has coloured square glass panes, and is in memory of Lt. Col. Alexander Thomas Wallace of the Royal Horse Artillery who died in 1866.

The font is in memory of A. R. Wallace who died in 1912. The wooden lectern commemorates Private Francis Hammond and Corporal Harry Millar who fell in the Great War. On the pulpit is a plaque with the words, "A thank-offering to God for his great mercy, 1901-1902". On the Holy Table, a crystal vase commemorates Allen and Elizabeth Ramsay, 1996.

On the south wall, a plaque commemorates Thomas Brooke, D.L. of Lough Eske Castle who died in 1886, and his wife Susan Maria who died in 1883.

*Lough Eske Church.*

It was largely due to his efforts that Christ Church, Lough Eske was built. The Brooke family came to the area at the end of the 16th century, and in time, became the principal landowners in the district. Lough Eske Castle dates originally from 1621, but is mainly 19th century. It is now a ruin, but it is hoped that it will be re-developed in the future.

Sir Thomas Brooke, an ancestor of Thomas Brooke above, built Ardnamona House in 1792. In time, it passed into the possession of the Wallace family, who played a leading role in the affairs of the parish over the years. It was Sir Arthur Wallace who was instrumental in the 1905 renovations, which included the provision of the east window.

The origins of the Royal School Raphoe were in what is now the parish of Lough Eske, for in 1618, King James I set up a school near Donegal, which was later transferred to Raphoe. There were also other Royal Schools at Armagh, Enniskillen (Portora), Cavan and Dungannon.

## MEENGLASS, THE CHURCH OF THE ASCENSION

Meenglass parish is situated in the hills to the south-east of Ballybofey, and runs up towards the border in the direction of Castlederg. The large old church was built as a chapel of ease on the estates of Lord Lifford.

The old church at Meenglass was severely damaged by "Hurricane Debbie" which struck Donegal on 16th September 1961. The church, which was very much too big for its small congregation, was demolished and replaced with

*Meenglass Church.*

the small and attractive little church which stands on the site today. It was consecrated on Sunday 27th May 1962, and given the dedication, the Church of the Ascension.

Meenglass church has a porch at the west end, which also contains the vestry room. There is a small window in each room and a bellcote over the east wall. There are three round-headed lattice windows in each side wall of the nave. The chancel is separated from the nave by a semi-circular communion rail. This replaces a brass rail which came from Christ Church, Blackrock, Dublin, now closed. On the east wall above the altar is a depiction in copper of the Last Supper. The small wooden lectern replaces a brass eagle lectern which was stolen.

James Hewitt, (1709-1789), first Viscount Lifford, was appointed Lord Chancellor of Ireland in 1768. He had a successful legal career. In 1768, he was created Baron Lifford in the Irish peerage, and was advanced to a viscountcy in 1781. He died in 1789 and is buried in Christ Church Cathedral, Dublin. His descendants survived until relatively recent times in the area. In the vestry room is a monument which came from the old church, in memory of James, 4th Viscount Lifford, who died in 1887. It was erected by his widow, Lydia Lucy Lifford. The estates have all been sold.

The parish has been amalgamated with Stranorlar since 1886.

## MEVAGH, CARRIGART, HOLY TRINITY

Mevagh, *"the plain of the birch tree"*, is beautifully situated on the north coast of Donegal, with the villages of Carrigart and Downings at its centre.

*Mevagh Church.*

In the 1622 survey, the old church was in ruins. A church was built in 1675, and in 1729, it was reported that it was in good repair. The present church, which is impressively situated in Carrigart, was built about 1895, and was consecrated by Primate Alexander on 17th August 1896. It is a rectangular, sandstone building with an aisle along the north side. There is a massive tower to the north-west, with a round stair turret to the rear. It is connected to the nave of the church by a small passage. Both the aisle and the tower and the clock in the tower were given by James Hay of Philadelphia in 1902. A brass plaque in the porch beneath the tower commemorates this generosity. There is a small porch in the south-west wall. The baptistery is in the south-west corner. The font is inscribed with the date 1681, and the cover is in memory of the Rev. W.Murphy, Rector, 1874-1893. The aisle is separated from the nave by five arches. The vestry room is to the left of the sanctuary.

*Font, 1681, and old chair.*

There is a single light window and a window of two lights in the west wall. In the aisle wall are four windows, the middle two being of two lights. There are four windows in the south wall. All of these windows but one in the south wall, are of square-paned coloured glass. The other window in the south wall depicts the Risen Lord, and is in memory of Rebecca Wilson who died in 1914. There are four coloured glass windows in the south sanctuary wall. The east window has three lights, and depicts from left to right, the Tablets of the Law, Christ the Light of the World, and the Prophet Elijah. It was erected by James Hay of Philadelphia in 1898 in memory of members of his family.

The pulpit, to the left of the nave, is of Caen stone, and was the gift of Charles Hay. The brass lectern is in memory of William Connor Magee, Archbishop of York in 1891, and of his father, the Rev. John Magee, Rector of Mevagh, 1820-1825. He in turn was a son of William Magee, Archbishop of Dublin. The lectern is dated 1892. There is a two manual Conacher organ with pedals. There are two very old carved chairs at the back of the church.

The estates of the land-owning family, the Earls of Leitrim, are in the parish. The land originally belonged to Lord Boyne who inherited it through marriage. The first Lord Boyne in the late 17th century was succeeded by a grandson, the second Lord Boyne. He sold the estates, and in 1743, they were bought by Nathaniel Clements, father of the first Earl of Leitrim. The third Earl was murdered in the land wars in 1878, accused of being a bad landlord. The fourth Earl, who succeeded him, built a number of houses in Carrigart. He died in 1892. He in turn was succeeded by the fifth Earl who died in 1952. The title died with him, though descendants still live on the estate.

On the south wall of the church is a brass plaque commemorating Charles Clements, fifth Earl of Leitrim who died in 1952, and his wife, Anne Mary Chaloner who died in 1984, which was erected by their nephew, the Hon. Hedley V. Strutt. In the porch is a second brass plaque in memory of James Simms who died in 1926, and of his wife who died in 1899, and of her brother James Hay who died in 1915.

Mevagh parish Select Vestry is responsible for the running of the Mevagh Centre in Carrigart. This was set up in 1982 to provide facilities, mainly for youth groups and conferences, and is based in the old Rectory. It has been a tremendous success.

*Mevagh Church interior.*

## MILFORD, St. COLUMBA

St. Columba's church in Milford village, situated at the southern end of Mulroy Bay, was consecrated on 7th August 1860. The ancient parish in the area was Tullyfern, which also seems to have included parts of Kilmacrennan and Tullyaughnish. Tullyfern was absorbed into Tullyaughnish about 1660.

Milford church was a plain, five bay hall building with a sanctuary, a vestry room to the right of it, and a porch in the south-west corner. There was a large bellcote over the west end. The east window was a triple lancet. The building was struck by lightning and severely damaged on 7th October 1982. It was subsequently closed, and the building was demolished. All that remains today is the porch.

*Milford Church, now demolished.*

## MONELLAN, KILLYGORDON, St.ANNE

St. Anne's Church, Monellan, was built in 1833 in Dromore townland, Crossroads, Killygordon, near Ballybofey. It was a chapel of ease in the parish of Donaghmore. It became a parish in 1872, and except for a short period in the 1960s, it has always been joined to its parent church at Donaghmore.

Monellan church is a rectangular hall church with a tower at the west end. Inside, the baptistery is on the left, and a similar area is separated from the nave opposite. The vestry room is to the right of the chancel. Behind is the east window, which has three lights and clear diamond panes.

The windows are interesting. There are three on the north wall, and three on the south wall, each of two lights. The first on the north wall marks the fifty years of service of Mr. George Kee, Sexton, 1989. The second commemorates James Bates, who died in 1989, and the third was donated in 1989 by the parishioners. The first window in the south wall was also donated by the parishioners in 1979, the second is the gift of Thomas Pearson in memory of his wife and son, 1979, and the third is the gift of the Slevin family in memory of their parents, undated.

The pulpit, lectern and prayer desk are all nicely carved. The prayer desk is in memory of the Rev. James Stewart Green, Rector of Donaghmore, and curate-in-charge of Monellan, 1884-1906. The organ, dated 1978, commemorates Jennie Taylor, Organist 1930 to 1954.

*Monellan Church.*

On the north wall a brass plaque commemorates Elizabeth Young of Mount Hall, who died in 1933, and there is a memorial to Thomas Proctor who died in 1971. On the south wall is the memorial to those from the parish of Donoughmore and Monellan who fell and who served in the Great War. On the east wall, to the left of the sanctuary is a monument to the Rev. Robert Delap, Curate of Monellan from 1830 until his death in 1885.

## MOUNTCHARLES

Mountcharles parish, seven kilometres west of Donegal on the Killybegs road, was originally a district curacy which was formed out of the neighbouring parish of Inver. The church was built in 1860. It is entered through a porch in the south-west corner. The exterior door is in memory of Oliver and Cassie Wilson and their son and daughter. In the west wall are two windows, with a small circular window above. There are three windows of two lights in the north wall, and two of two lights in the south wall. The east window is of three lights. All the windows are of clear diamond pane glass.

The font is adjacent to the entrance door. The Holy Table commemorates those who fell in the Great War, including the Marquis of Conyngham.

*Mountcharles Church.*

The pulpit is in memory of James Reed, J.P., 1890, and the prayer desk was presented by John Arthur Pomeroy and Louisa, his wife, 1913. The old oil lamps have been preserved.

On the north wall is a monument to the Rev. Benjamin Darcus, who was the first priest in charge of the newly formed curacy, from 1860 until his death in 1867. On the south wall is a brass plaque commemorating Robert Russell who died in 1880. In the porch, a monument commemorates those who served in the Great War, and there is a plaque in memory of those who served in the second World War.

Henry Conyngham, first Marquis Conyngham was born in 1766. In 1789, he was created Viscount Conyngham of Mountcharles in the Irish Peerage. For his military services, he was created Viscount Mountcharles and Earl Conyngham in 1797. He had great influence in the Court of King George IV, and thus, he was created Lord Minster of Minster Abbey in the Peerage of the United Kingdom in 1821. He was also lieutenant of Windsor Castle. The Conynghams always lived with the King, whether at Brighton, or at Windsor Castle. Henry Conyngham was made a general in the army in 1830. He died in 1832, whereupon a son succeeded him as the second Marquis. The Conyngham influence waned after the death of George IV. The family owned land in the Mountcharles area until relatively recent times.

## MOVILLE UPPER, REDCASTLE, St. FINIAN
## MOVILLE LOWER, GREENCASTLE, St. FINIAN
## MOVILLE LOWER, MOVILLE, St. COLUMB'S CHAPEL OF EASE

St. Patrick is supposed to have founded an abbey at Moville, which means, *"the plain of the ancient tree"*. A church was built as a private chapel for the Carey family in 1741. This in due course, became a chapel of ease, and eventually, the parish church.

The original parish of Moville was divided into Upper and Lower Moville in 1781. Upper Moville Church is in Redcastle, a few kilometres to the south of Moville. The church was built, and consecrated on 18th August 1853. It has a three bay nave, with a large porch to the west, and a bellcote. Over this in the west wall, there is a sexfoil window. The transepts are lit by paired lancets with sexfoils above, and the east window is a triple lancet. Redcastle Church was closed in 1990. The ruins of an older church are in the graveyard.

The parish church of St. Finian at Greencastle was built in 1782. It is a rectangular building with a

*Moville Upper ruins, Redcastle.*

louvered and battlemented tower at the west end, and a sanctuary with a vestry room adjacent to it to the east. Inside, is a gallery. On the north wall are three plain windows, each with three lights, and each has three small circular lights overhead. In the south wall, there is one plain window. There is one plain window on each side of the west wall below the gallery. The sanctuary is lit by three stained glass windows.

*Moville Upper Church, Redcastle.*

The hexagonal stone font to the right of the entrance, is in memory of CMMcC and ARMcC, who are not otherwise identified. The pulpit is in memory of the Rev. Thomas McClellan, Rector of Macosquin near Coleraine, who died in 1896. The reredos behind the altar is inscribed Holy, Holy, Holy, and on each side are, on the left, the Apostles' Creed, and on the right, the Lord's Prayer.

There are eight memorial monuments or brass plaques on the south wall. The first, from the left is

*Moville Lower Church, Greencastle.*

to William McClellan who died in 1858, and to his wife. There is one to W.A.Brown, who died in 1859, and to his wife. A brass plaque commemorates the Rev. Richard Smyth Benson, Rector 1923 to 1944, and his wife, and another commemorates Lt. Col. Walter Crosbie, D.S.O. Catherine, wife of Rev. Richard Hamilton, Rector of Culdaff and Cloncha 1823 - 1847 is commemorated on a monument. She died in 1842. Mr.Hamilton was one of thirty-nine children! Next, a plaque commemorates the three men from the parish who died in the Great War. Also, William and Adelaide Press and the family, 1933, and Mrs Hugh Corbett, who died in 1859, and her family, are commemorated.

As the town of Moville grew larger than its neighbour, Greencastle, a new church was built there. It was consecrated on 16th April 1858 as a chapel of ease in the parish of Lower Moville. It is a rectangular building with a sanctuary extending to the east, to the left of which is the vestry room. On the south side, near the west end is the entrance porch, which is topped by a short octagonal tower and spire.

On the west wall are two clear windows with a circular light above. On the north wall are four plain windows, each with two lights. On the south wall are three stained glass windows, each with two lights. The first of these depicts the Good Shepherd, and is in memory of Thomas Wetherall and Mary Sproule, 1887. The middle window depicts Mary and Martha with Jesus, and the window by the pulpit depicts Moses and Miriam. In the south wall of the sanctuary, a window depicts the Good Shepherd in memory of Charles Seymour, D.D., Rector of Moville Lower, 1852-1862, and Dean of

*Moville Lower Chapel of Ease, Moville.*

Derry, 1872-1882. There are three stained glass windows in the east wall.

The pulpit also commemorates Dean Seymour. The brass lectern is in memory of Laura Jane Forster who died in 1966, and a brass plaque states that it came from St. Michael's Church, Norwich, and was given in 1976 by Ellen de Vere Walker. The prayer desk was given in memory of Canon Peter Cartwright, Rector, 1966-1980. There is a hexagonal stone font. The pipe organ is on the south side of the nave.

On the north wall are memorials to Bertie Kane who was killed in 1940, to Lt. James Montgomery of the Indian Army who died in 1843, and to Charlotte Morrison who died in 1940. There are monuments to Annie Hyland who died in 1839, to Capt. J.E.Hillman who died in 1877, to Richard Anderson who died in 1891, and to Pechell Irvine who died in 1884, and his family.

The memorials and monuments to the Montgomery family are on the south wall. Samuel Montgomery was a Derry merchant, and Sheriff of the city in 1774. He built New Park, the family residence in 1776. He also bought the site of Moville in 1768 and leased it. There is a monument to his son, the Rev. Samuel Montgomery, Rector of Lower Moville, 1812-1830. The next monument is to Maud, wife of Bishop Montgomery, who was daughter of Dean Farrar, Dean of Canterbury. She died in 1949. A brass plaque commemorates Katherine May Montgomery who died in 1932, and another, Charlotte Montgomery who died in 1889, and May Montgomery. Another brass plaque commemorates Col. James Montgomery, Knight of the Order of St. John of Jerusalem, who was a brother of Bishop Montgomery. He died in 1940. Rev. Samuel Montgomery and his brother, Sir

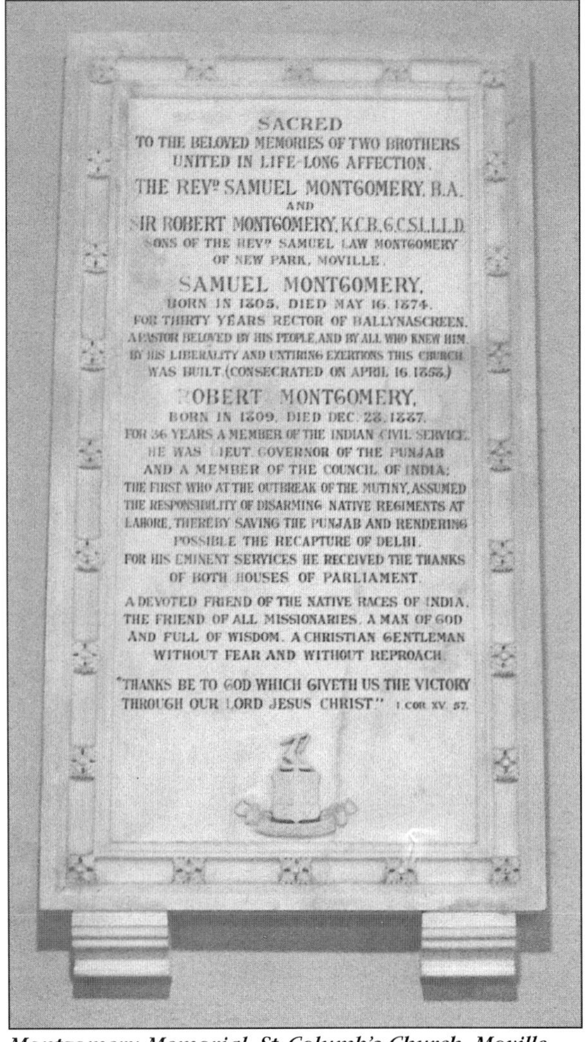


*Montgomery Memorial, St. Columb's Church, Moville.*

Robert Montgomery of the Indian Civil Service, sons of the Rev. Samuel Montgomery, are commemorated on a monument. There is a monument to the Rt. Rev. Henry Hutchinson Montgomery, Bishop of Tasmania, 1889-1901, and Secretary of the Society for the Propagation of the Gospel, 1901-1919. Bishop Montgomery was father of Field Marshal Montgomery of Alamein, a distinguished soldier in the Second World War.

The other memorials on the south wall commemorate Jane Baskerville who died in 1922, Col. Hugh Chetham Lyle, Royal Artillery who died in 1897, and Gilbert Thomas Baskerville, Royal Navy who died in 1914.

## Episcopal Highwayman, Bishop Philip Twysden

Philip Twysden was consecrated Bishop of Raphoe in 1747 in St. Michan's Church, Dublin. He and his brother of Twysden Hall in Kent, inherited a fortune. However, somewhat of a prodigal son of his father, Philip squandered his share of the inheritance and went into a far country, Ireland. It is believed, though, that he never actually visited Raphoe Diocese.

In 1752, Philip returned to Twysden Hall, bankrupt to visit his brother, possibly in the hope of re-couping some of his share of the money. A doctor who was staying there was somewhat mysteriously told, "look to your pistols", which he found unloaded. He loaded them and set off for London. On the way, a masked man approached the coach and demanded money. The doctor threatened to shoot, but the highwayman ignored the threat. The doctor fired, killing the highwayman, who fell down dead. When the mask was removed, it was none other than Philip Twysden, Bishop of Raphoe!

## RAYMOCHY

The parish of Raymochy, *"the Fort of Mothaigh"*, is just north of Letterkenny on the east shore of Lough Swilly. It contains the village of Manorcunningham, which as its name suggests, was the area planted after 1609 by the Cunningham family. Nearby are the remains of Balleighan Abbey which was founded for the Franciscans in the 15th century by the O'Donnell clan.

The present church was built in 1792. It was rebuilt and rededicated on 28th August 1910, with the addition of a chancel and vestry. There is a crenellated and louvered tower at the west end. The stained glass window in the porch is in memory of the Rev. William Archer Butler, Rector of Raymochy from 1842 until his death of famine fever in 1848.

Archer Butler was born in 1812. He possessed one of the most brilliant minds of his day, and was a great thinker, preacher, philosopher and writer. There is also a monument to him in Raphoe Cathedral.

*Raymochy Church.*

The nave of Raymochy church is lit by six lattice windows, three on each side. The vestry room is to the left of the chancel. The east window has three lights, and depicts the Transfiguration of our Lord. It was presented in memory of John Mills who died in

1906, by his son, John, of Maffra, Australia. A brass plaque in the sanctuary notes this gift.

The pulpit is in memory of those who fell in the Great War. The wooden eagle lectern commemorates the Rev. James William Irwin, Curate of Raymochy, 1848-1868, then Rector from 1868 until his death in 1877. The lectern was given by his children in 1905. The prayer desk is in memory of John Beers who died in 1888, and was presented by his son at the time of the restoration in 1910.

As well as the plaque in the sanctuary, already mentioned, there is a brass memorial in the porch in memory of Andrew Lindsay, whose family gave the heating system.

## RAYMUNTERDONEY, FALCARRAGH, St. PAUL

RAYMUNTERDONEY, *"the fort of the family of Doney,"* is a parish on the north-west coast of Donegal. The church is situated just to the east of Falcarragh. The ruins of the ancient church and a cross are still to be seen nearby. In the 1622 survey, the church, like most others in the Diocese, was in ruins. It was in good repair, however, by 1729.

The present church was built in 1805. The north aisle was added in 1821. Consecration, and dedication to St.Paul were delayed until 22nd May 1828. The church is entered through a small porch. The baptistery is at the east end of the aisle, beyond which is the vestry room. There is a store room at the other end of the aisle. The sanctuary is lit by a coloured glass window of three lights with smaller pieces above. The middle section depicts the Good Shepherd, and the window is in memory of Alexander Stewart, 1864.

There are two lattice windows with small insets, of coloured glass in the aisle, and a small window in the store room part of the aisle. Of the three windows in the south nave wall, two are similar to the aisle windows. The middle window in the south wall depicts *"Talitha Cumi"*, the raising of the synagogue ruler's daughter by Jesus, St. Mark 5:41, and is in memory of Constance Olphert, 1864.

The altar is in memory of Nannie McCulloch, and it came from the Abbey Church in Bangor and is dated 1918. It has a carved Agnus Dei on the front. The cross is in memory of Adam and Margaret Moffitt, 1994. The pulpit is on the left side of the sanctuary, and the sanctuary chairs commemorate Margaret Sayers who died in 1983. The brass eagle lectern is in memory of Adam Olphert who died in 1904. There are two enormous candelabra, and the old oil lamps have been retained.

***Raymunterdoney Church.***

The Olphert family in the parish was of Dutch extraction. There is a monument on the south wall to Wybrants Olphert of Ballyconnell House, and to Marianne Constance, his wife, which was erected by their son, Sir John Olphert, C.V.O. There is also a framed war memorial. The monument on the east wall in the sanctuary commemorates Wybrants Olphert, D.L. of Ballyconnell who died in 1892.

## ROSSNOWLAGH

ROSSNOWLAGH, *"the apple wood"*, is a parish and village on the south coast of Donegal, to the west of the Donegal to Ballyshannon road. The parish was created originally as a perpetual curacy out of its neighbour, Drumholm, in 1831. The church was consecrated on 21st September that year, and dedicated to St. John.

*Rossnowlagh Church.*

The church is entered through a small porch at the west end, over which is a bellcote. There are two windows, each of two lights in the side walls, as well as a window with two lights above the porch. There are three windows of two lights in each side wall of the nave. The east window, which has three lights, is of stained glass and depicts the Risen Lord at the empty tomb. It commemorates Francis Jennings, his wife and three of his daughters, and is dated 1951.

The sanctuary is separated from the nave by three-sided communion rails, set into which, on the right side, is a prayer desk. The vestry room is to the right of the sanctuary. The Holy Table is in memory of Robert Hannah, and is dated 1932. Outside, and to the left, is the pulpit, before which stands the font. The lectern on the right side of the nave commemorates Robert Gray. There is a one-manual organ by Evans and Barr of Belfast in the south-east side of the nave.

A plaque records the dedication of the lighting and heating systems in 1955 in memory of William and Hannah Smyth. Another plaque records the dedication of the entrance gates in 1963 in memory of the Thompson family. Another plaque on the west wall records the re-hallowing of the church after extensive renovations in 1995.

## STRANORLAR

THE NAME STRANORLAR means *"the holm of the floor"*, or, flat ground which is often submerged by a river. In the 1622 survey, "the parish church is decayed, and is repairing at the Parishioners charges." In 1729, the church was too small for the congregation, so it was enlarged in 1733. The north and south transepts and the chancel were erected in 1863. The clergy of Stranorlar were perpetual curates until 1829.

*1677 Bell.*

*Stranorlar Church.*

At the west end of the church is a tower with a door in two sides. Externally, the tower is of two storeys. Internally, there are three levels, the middle one of which contains the bell-ringer's gallery, and the upper part, a total of nine bells. The original bell, which is placed in the porch, is inscribed, "Henricus Paris me fecit 1677". It was replaced in 1922 with a bell which commemorates those who fell in the Great War. In 1999, a peal of eight more bells was installed. These were brought from Holy Trinity Church, Castlerea, Co. Roscommon, and were cast in 1899.

*The Chancel.*

Before renovations in 1964, there was a gallery at the west end of the nave, beneath which, to the right, was the baptistery. In that year, the gallery, which had been erected in 1825, was closed, and the space below became an inner porch, with robing rooms to the right and left. A diamond stained-glass window over the inside entrance door depicts the Feeding of the 5,000. Beneath it, a plaque records its donation by the Lawson Family in memory of Marjorie Lawson in 1964.

The nave is lit by three windows of two lights each on each side. They all contain plain, lattice glass. There is a window of two lights in the east wall of both transepts, and a similar window in the west wall of the south transept. There is a window of three lights in the north wall of the north transept of which the centre window is taller, and a similar window opposite in the south transept. In 2001, new stained glass depicting various Christian symbols, was installed in the quatrefoil tracery in each window to commemorate various parishioners. In the north wall of the nave, the first inset was donated by Percy Kee, the second commemorates George and Blanche Magee, and the third is in memory of Leonard and Rena McGuckin. In the south nave wall, the first window is in memory of the Stewart Family, the second was donated by the Raitt Family, and the third commemorates Dr. Frederick Kee. The inset in the window in the west wall of the south transept commemorates the Rev. Bertie Clarke. In the south wall window, Samuel and Sadie Given are commemorated, and the inset in the east wall window was donated by Mr and Mrs Whitby and Myrtle McClay. In the north transept, the east window quatrefoil commemorates the Deasley Family, and that in the north window is in memory of David and Sheena Armstrong. There is a porch door in the west wall of the north transept.

*Window with quartrefoil.*

The east window is of fine coloured glass, and is in memory of Edmund Hayes, Bart., who died in 1860. The vestry room is to the left of the sanctuary.

The baptistery is situated at the crossing of the nave and north transcept. The font is in memory of Mary Forbes and her husband Henry. In the sanctuary, the credence table commemorates Alice Wyatt who died in 1950, and the sanctuary chairs commemorate George McGuckin who died in 1947. A small Prie Dieu which came from Drogheda commemorates the Porter family there, 1953.The panelling round the sanctuary is in memory of Edmund Frances Hayes, 5th Baronet, who died in 1912. The sanctuary carpet and alterations to the Communion rails are in memory of the Rev. Joseph Dunlop, Rector of Stranorlar, 1937-1957. The fine stone pulpit, which is to the right of the chancel entrance, is in memory of Mellicent Johnston who died in 1903. The brass lectern commemorates Sir Samuel Hayes, 4th Baronet, 1901, and the stone prayer desk commemorates Henry Bloomfield Trench who died in 1900, and Henry William Bloomfield Trench, Oxfordshire Light Infantry who died in 1898. The two manual pipe organ was built by Bishop & Co., London. A brass plaque on it commemorates Kathleen Crawford, Organist from 1923 until her death in 1926, and another plaque states that the electric blower is in memory of the Forbes family.

On the north wall is a memorial to George McGuckin who was Secretary of the Select Vestry for 26 years. On the south wall is a monument to Emily, wife of Sir Edmund Hayes, Baronet, M.P., daughter of Lt.Gen., The Hon. Sir H. Packenham, K.C.B. Emily died in 1883. The Hayes family were distinguished landowners around Stranorlar in the 19th century. Further along, a plaque commemorates those who fell in the Great War, and those who returned. There is a memorial to Squadron Leader E. H. C. Kee, D.F.C., who was killed in 1942 on active service, and another to Herbert Augustus Johnston, 2nd Lt., Royal Flying Corps, who was killed in France in 1916. These three monuments comprise the War Memorial.

In the north transcept is a memorial to Elizabeth Ann Johnston who died in 1883, and to John Style Johnston of Rockfield House, Stranorlar, who died in 1917. Near the baptistery, a plaque commemorates Muriel Gunning Jones, in whose memory there were improvements to the chancel and porch, along with a heating system, 1965. On the east wall, to the left of the chancel is a memorial to Canon Robert Wright, Rector of Stranorlar from 1909 until his death in 1928. In the south transcept, a monument commemorates Joseph Barclay of Strabane who died in 1818.

The present parish Robertson School dates from 1965, and a fine new hall was built to replace the old hall in 1991.

A famous son of the parish was Isaac Butt, (1813-1879), son of the Rev. Robert Butt, Perpetual Curate, Stranorlar, 1814-1829. Isaac Butt was the founder and first leader of the Home Rule Party in 1871.

## TAUGHBOYNE, St. BAITHIN
## CRAIGADOOISH, St. COLUMBA'S CHAPEL OF EASE

About 560 A.D., St. Baithin, a cousin of St. Columba, founded a monastery near St. Johnston in the Laggan Valley of east Donegal. This monastery was known as *Tigh Baithin,* the House of Baithin, hence the name Taughboyne. Baithin accompanied Columba to Iona in 563, and was his successor as Abbot of Iona. He died on 9th June 600.

The Laggan Valley derives its name from the Irish *lug,* or *lag,* a hollow place. The land is very fertile. The area was planted by Scottish Presbyterian settlers from 1609. Their presence was resented by the Established Church, and their ministers spent considerable periods of time in Lifford Gaol for refusing to conform.

*Taughboyne Church.*

At the Royal Visitation in 1622, Taughboyne Church was discovered to be in ruins. A new church was started in St. Johnston, but was soon abandoned, as the church population was centered around the old church. What had been built can still be seen. The old church, which is situated half way between Newtowncunningham and St. Johnston, was restored and was ready for use in 1627. Over the door is the Latin inscription, *"Thomas Bruce aedificavit restoramus 1627"*. At the door, set into the wall, are some curious carved figures of beasts, which are thought to date from the 15th century.

*15th Century beasts, Taughboyne Church.*

Taughboyne Church is a rectangular five-bay hall. At the west end is a porch with a bellcote overhead. Inside the porch is the vestry room which is lit by a large window. There are four identical windows on each side of the nave. Each has two lights, and Y tracery, and clear lattice glass. The sanctuary is lit by a fine stained glass window which has three lights and tracery. It illustrates the 23rd Psalm, "The Lord is my Shepherd". It was presented in 1949 in memory of William John and Susan Crawford Baird.

The altar commemorates John Peoples who died in 1936, and the panelling round the sanctuary was erected in memory of Thomas Woods Peoples and his wife Maude in 1956. The prayer desk in the sanctuary commemorates Ena Turner who died in 1990. The pulpit on the left side of the chancel and the prayer desk on the right commemorate Hannah, wife of the Very Rev. Edward Bowen, Dean of Raphoe, who was Rector of Taughboyne in succession to his father from 1868 to 1886. Mrs Bowen died in 1884. The lectern, which is situated

*The interior of the church looking east.*

at the chancel step, commemorates John McNeely, 1890. The carpeting in the sanctuary commemorates the Very Rev. Edward Moore, Dean of Raphoe, and Rector of Taughboyne from 1972 until his death in 1983. A plaque records this gift from the parishioners. There is a two manual electronic organ adjacent to the prayer desk.

On the north nave wall are monuments to Andrew Colhoun who died in 1865, and to the Ven. John Molloy, Archdeacon of Raphoe, and Rector of Taughboyne from 1886 until his death in 1915. On the south wall are monuments commemorating the Rev. Edward Bowen, Rector of Taughboyne from 1819 until his death 48 years later in 1867, and his wife, Jane, who died in 1864. There is also a memorial to those who fell in the Great War. The memorial to those who served in the Great War is in the porch.

Taughboyne School was opened in 1826, and closed in 1919. The building is now used as a hall. There is a teacher's residence which was built in 1907, and a sexton's house. The Rectory was built in 1882. The original Rectory, Bogay House at Newtowncunningham, was built about 1700.

Taughboyne Parish originally had two chapels of ease. All Saints Chapel to the north served the parishioners of Newtowncunningham. This became a parish in 1870. At the south end of the parish, Craigadooish school, which had been built about 1834, was also being used as a place of worship. There still exists correspondence from Bishop William Bissett to the Rector, the Rev. Edward Bowen, concerning the erection of this building. In a letter, dated 31st October 1829, Bishop Bissett informs the Rector, the Rev. Edward Bowen, that he had obtained a grant of £600 from the Board of First

Fruits for the erection of a chapel of ease at Craigadooish. The building which was erected at this time, was used as a school in which worship also took place. In 1869, a new school building was erected, and the older building of 1834 was altered so as to be used exclusively for worship.

*Craigadooish Chapel of Ease.*

Craigadooish Chapel of Ease, half way between St. Johnston and Raphoe, is a rectangular building with a five-sided apse. Adjacent to it is the sexton's house. There is a small entrance porch in the south-west corner. The bell above was obtained in 1966 from the coastal light vessel, H.M.S. *Kittiwake*. It dates from 1898. Inside, there are three single-light windows in the north wall. In the south wall, the first two windows have one light The third and fourth windows are together. There are five windows in the sanctuary. Each window has clear lattice panes.

The font is at the west end of the church. The prayer desk on the left side of the chancel, and the pulpit on the right, which date from 1896, commemorate Mrs Hannah Bowen. The prayer desk chair commemorates John and Margaret Hepburn, 1982. The brass lectern on the right is in memory of John Hill who died in 1895. In the sanctuary, there is a prayer desk on the right, and two chairs. The chair on the left commemorates Sarah McConnell who died in 1980. The organ was presented in memory of James Pearson who died in 1967. The vestry room is to the left of the chancel.

A plaque on the south wall records renovations to Craigadooish Chapel of Ease in the 160th anniversary year of the erection of the building. At the service of re-hallowing on 30th January 1994, the church was given the dedication, St. Columba.

Craigadooish School, which opened in 1869, was closed in 1969. It has been renovated and extended recently for use as a hall.

## TEMPLECRONE, DUNGLOE, St. CRONE

THE PARISH OF Templecrone is centered in the village of Dungloe on the west coast of Donegal. St. Crone lived in the 7th century, and the original church at Maghery, nearby, dates from that period. In the survey of 1622, "the church was ruined and fitting to be repaired in the ancient place; parish small". Another church was built in 1760 at a cost of £400.

The present church was built in 1844 and was consecrated on 15th August that year. It is a rectangular building with a spacious porch at the west end, and inside is a large gallery. The chancel was added in 1860. On either side are vestry rooms. There is a window of three lights in the east wall, one window in the north choir wall, and three in the south wall. Each has lattice diamond panes.

The baptistery inside the entrance has a stone hexagonal font. The pulpit is beautifully carved, and the lectern is in memory of Canon James Williams, Rector 1914-1945. The cross and

*Templecrone Church.*

candlesticks on the altar, and other furnishings were the gift of Thomas Hanlon of Toronto, Canada, a native of the parish.

There are three monuments on the north wall. The first is to Francis Forster of Roshine Lodge,

Burtonport, who died in 1858, and the second commemorates Dr. William Smyth, Roshine Lodge, who died in 1901 aged 42 years, of typhus fever which he contracted from his patients on Arranmore Island. The third monument commemorates the Rev. Thomas Stewart, Rector of Templecrone from 1781, who died in 1803. His wife and daughter are also commemorated.

On the south wall, a brass plaque commemorates Everina Maxwell who died in 1966. A brass plaque commemorates the Rev. Dr. Richard Kelly, Rector 1993 to 1998, who died in 1998, and another commemorates Violet Hanlon who died in 1993, and her husband who died in 1973, and their daughter.

Dungloe church is picturesquely situated on the quayside at Dungloe, overlooking Arranmore Island.

## TULLAGHOBEGLEY, KILLULT, St. ANNE

TULLAGHOBEGLEY PARISH is in north-west Donegal, and includes Tory Island. The name means, *"O'Begley's Hill"*. Tully O'Begley founded a monastery in the district. There is an ancient round tower, abbey ruin and two crosses on Tory Island. One of these is the famous Tau Cross, shaped like the Greek letter "tau", T. The renowned landscape and portrait painter, Dr. Derek Hill, (1916-2000), did some of his best work on Tory Island.

The old church was replaced with a new one in 1792. A church was built at Killult, just to the west of Falcarragh, and was consecrated in 1820. This, the present church, was rebuilt in 1840. There is a tower at the west end, with a window in one side, and two doors. It has four small finials on top. Inside, the nave is lit by three square paned windows on each side, and the vestry room is to the left. The east window is of three lights, and has plain, lattice glass.

The pulpit is on the left. The two chairs in the sanctuary are in memory of the Rev. William Stewart Griffith, Curate of Tullaghobegley, 1870-1876, and Rector from 1886 until his death in 1911. The font stands in the centre of the nave near the entrance, and there remains a large old stove in the middle of the church with a chimney which goes up through the roof. There are four huge circular candelabra over the nave.

*Tullaghobegley Church.*

The Tau Cross and candlesticks are in memory of Anne Warren, daughter of Canon F.N. Warren, Rector 1988-1997, and Mrs Warren, who died in a tragic car accident in 1990.

On the south wall, a monument commemorates the Rev. Stewart Griffith, in whose memory the two altar prayer book stands were given.

## TULLYAUGHNISH, RAMELTON, St.PAUL

THE PARISH OF Tullyaughnish, *"the hill of the horse island"*, is situated on the west shore of Lough Swilly, with the town of Ramelton at its centre. The survey of 1622 observed that the original church was on Aughnish Island in Lough Swilly. It was moved to Ramelton to which Sir William Stewart had come in the Plantation of Ulster, and had built a castle and a village. His descendants still live in Ramelton today. There was also in the parish, a Franciscan friary at Killydonnell which had been founded by the O'Donnell clan in the 16th century. The neighbouring ancient parish of Tullyfern near Kilmacrennan, was joined to Tullyaughnish about 1660.

## Diocesan Magazines

One means of communication throughout the Church over the years has been Diocesan Magazines. **South Raphoe Diocesan Magazine** first appeared in November 1925. It contained notes from the parishes in the south of Raphoe, along with other items of interest. It soon extended to cover the whole Diocese of Raphoe as the remaining parishes began to contribute to it. For a number of years, the **Church of Ireland Monthly Magazine** was included with it. This gave people information about the wider Church of Ireland and about events further afield.

**Mid-Ulster Magazine** has been going for many years. It covers several parishes in Derry Diocese, as well as some in Clogher and some in Armagh.

**Diocesan News** first appeared about 1983. It subsequently became **Derry and Raphoe Times,** and eventually, from 1993, the **Derry and Raphoe Vision Magazine.**

The Inishowen parishes used to have their own magazine, which continued to be produced for several years after the parishes of Inishowen were transferred from Derry Diocese to Raphoe Diocese in 1978.

*Tullyaughnish Church.*

The present church of St. Paul, Ramelton, dates from 1825. It cost £1,101, of which the rector, the Rev. Cornelius Ussher contributed £900. It is a large, almost square building with a tower at the west end and a sanctuary at the east end. The tower has louvers in the upper storey, and battlements at the top, with prominent corner finials. The nave walls are supported by buttresses, the easternmost of which are capped by finials. Inside, there is a large gallery, underneath which, to the left of the entrance, is the baptistery. This was erected in 1967 in memory of Forrest Mitchel. The sanctuary is approached up steps, through the choir, and the vestry room is to the left.

In the east wall is a magnificent window of three lights. It was installed in 1975, and depicts the Creation. Inscribed in it are the words from the canticle *Benedicite,* "All ye works of the Lord Praise Him". The window is by Patrick Pollen, and commemorates Major Robert Wood Grove of Castlegrove, Ramelton, who died in 1969. In the north wall are six opaque square paned windows. There are five similar windows in the south wall, and of the six there, the fifth is of stained glass, and commemorates Hamilton Verschoyle, Bishop of Kilmore, Elphin and Ardagh who died in 1870, and his wife who died in 1883. The window in the south wall of the sanctuary is in memory of James Grove who died in 1891.

*East Window, St. Paul's Church, Ramelton.*

The altar is in memory of Charles Lord who died in 1917, and the prayer desk commemorates John M. C. Grove and his wife Lucy and their daughter. It was presented by Eileen Grove in 1955. The lectern is in memory of Alex Mitchell who died in 1886, and the pulpit is on the right side of the nave. The organ, by Conacher, has two manuals and pedals, and was installed in 1900. It was restored in 1999.

On the west wall, a plaque acknowledges the gift by the Jacob family of vestry furniture, bookshelves, the sound system and pulpit area refurbishment. On the north wall are memorials to Edith Annie Gibbon who died in 1880 aged six years, to Ann Mitchell who died in 1895, and to Alma M. Mitchell who died in 1978. On the south wall, a monument commemorates Lt. Adrian Stewart of the Gloucestershire Regiment who died in the Great War, 1914. Another monument commemorates Lt. Col. Dan Webber of the West Yorkshire Regiment who died in 1993. There is a memorial to those who fell in the Great War, and a memorial to Lt. A. G. Hamon of the Royal Navy who was killed on HMS Eagle in 1958, and to his daughter who died in 1956.

On the north wall of the chancel is a memorial to two brothers, the Rev. John T. Browne from Ramelton, who was rector of Haigh, Lancashire, who died in 1862, and William Browne who died in 1880. Opposite, a plaque states that the east window is the gift of Eileen Grove in memory of her husband, Major Grove who died in 1969. Also in the south sanctuary wall is a monument to Samuel Sproule who was secretary to the Grand Jury of County Donegal, who died in 1866.

The old rectory, a fine house in spacious grounds, was built about 1875. This was replaced with the present rectory in 1995. The parochial hall was the Robertson school. It was renovated in 1999.

# Index of Names

## C

## T



## U



## V



## W



## Y

# Index of Places

## C



## D

## P



## Q



## R



## S



## T



## U



## V

## W



## Y

# General Index

## K



## L



## M



## N



## O



## P



## Q



## R



## S



## T



## U



## V



## W



## Y